Minorities, Scarcity and Conflict

This volume places scarcity as a defining aspect of minorities' experience and as a tool to comprehend ongoing and unresolved societal friction and global environmental challenges, strategies for survival and reproduction of the status quo, and aspirational desires for social mobility. The book is an experimental collective intellectual project departing from conventional approaches to scarcity solely as a resource-based economic or demographic concept. Boldly, the book looks at the ways in which disadvantaged social groups navigate their lives through scarcity, and how these circumstances are endured, interpreted, accepted or challenged.

In a thought-provoking turn, the book makes a novel contribution to minority studies by engaging with scarcity not only concerning resources but also emotion, memory and affect. In analysing scarcity as a multidimensional analytical framework and interrogating it from manifold angles, the book unpacks uncharted ramifications of debates around scarcity and opens new lines of enquiry.

The collection will be a valuable resource for academics, researchers and policymakers working in the areas of law, political anthropology and sociology.

Antonio Montañés Jiménez is a Margarita Salas postdoctoral fellow affiliated with the School of Anthropology and Museum Ethnography at the University of Oxford, UK, and ISOR (Research in Sociology of Religion) at the Universidad Autónoma de Barcelona, Spain. He previously held an Economic and Social Research Council postdoctoral fellowship at the University of St Andrews, UK.

Camila Ferreira Marinelli holds a PhD in social anthropology from the University of St Andrews, UK, and is Co-Coordinator of the MSCA Staff Exchanges Project (2024–2027) funded by Horizon Europe.

Stavroula Pipyrou is a senior lecturer in social anthropology and Founding Director of the Centre for Minorities Research at the University of St Andrews, UK.

Routledge Advances in Minority Studies

Series Editors Stavroula Pipyrou is

a Senior Lecturer in Social Anthropology at the University of St Andrews, UK, and Founding Director of the cross-disciplinary Centre for Minorities Research (CMR). She has published widely on minority politics, governance, and civil society in Italy and Greece.

Kyriaki Topidi is

Head of the Research Cluster on Culture and Diversity and a Senior Researcher at the European Centre for Minority Issues, Germany. Her research interests focus on diversity management, minority protection rights and mechanisms, with a special interest in religion, and human rights law. She has published extensively on these and related areas.

Routledge Advances in Minority Studies (RAMS) provides a platform for outstanding state-of-the-art research on interdisciplinary and intersectional understandings of minorities, globally. Monographs and edited volumes in the series advance scholarly and practitioner insights from Anthropology, Law, Politics, Sociology, History and beyond. The series foregrounds pluralism and diversity of both authors and subjects of study, with a particular focus on emerging fields and marginalized voices.

Under the editorial supervision of Dr Stavroula Pipyrou and Dr Kyriaki Topidi, the series will be a primary source for students, scholars and practitioners in minority studies while presenting authors with a valuable means to reach a wide and growing readership.

Titles in the series:

European Minorities in Times of Crisis
Negotiating Identities
Edited by Ruairidh Tarvet

Islamophobia in European Cities
Solidarities, Responses and Dilemmas for Young Balkan Muslims
Francesco Trupia

Minorities, Scarcity and Conflict
Edited by Antonio Montañés Jiménez, Camila Ferreira Marinelli, and Stavroula Pipyrou

For more information about this series, please visit: https://www.routledge.com/Routledge-Advances-in-Minority-Studies/book-series/RAIMSv

Minorities, Scarcity and Conflict

Edited by Antonio Montañés Jiménez,
Camila Ferreira Marinelli, and
Stavroula Pipyrou

Routledge
Taylor & Francis Group
LONDON AND NEW YORK

First published 2026
by Routledge
4 Park Square, Milton Park, Abingdon, Oxon OX14 4RN

and by Routledge
605 Third Avenue, New York, NY 10158

Routledge is an imprint of the Taylor & Francis Group, an informa business

British Library Cataloguing-in-Publication Data
A catalogue record for this book is available from the British Library

Library of Congress Cataloging-in-Publication Data
Names: Jimenez, Antonio Montañés editor | Marinelli, Camila Ferreira editor | Pipyrou, Stavroula editor
Title: Minorities, scarcity, and conflict / edited by Antonio Montañés Jimenez, Camila Ferreira Marinelli, and Stavroula Pipyrou.
Description: Abingdon, Oxon [UK] ; New York, NY : Routledge, 2025. | Series: Routledge advances in minority studies | Includes bibliographical references and index.
Identifiers: LCCN 2025006239 | ISBN 9781032636399 hardback | ISBN 9781032661773 paperback | ISBN 9781032661780 ebook
Subjects: LCSH: MInorities—Legal status, laws, etc. | Scarcity | Conflict of laws
Classification: LCC K3242 .M567 2025 | DDC 342.08/7—dc23/eng/20250306
LC record available at https://lccn.loc.gov/2025006239

ISBN: 978-1-032-63639-9 (hbk)
ISBN: 978-1-032-66177-3 (pbk)
ISBN: 978-1-032-66178-0 (ebk)

DOI: 10.4324/9781032661780

Typeset in Galliard
by Apex CoVantage, LLC

Contents

List of contributors *vii*
Acknowledgements *xii*

Introduction 1
ANTONIO MONTAÑÉS JIMÉNEZ, CAMILA FERREIRA MARINELLI, AND STAVROULA PIPYROU

1 **Unlearning scarcity within ethno-cultural minority groups: between perceptions and reality** 21
KYRIAKI TOPIDI

2 **Understanding scarcity in "the land of abundance": mexican migrants in Tulsa, Oklahoma (USA)** 36
ANA P. GUTIÉRREZ GARZA

3 **"The story of my father": life narratives and memories of scarcity of a Spanish Gitano family** 55
ANTONIO MONTAÑÉS JIMÉNEZ WITH GORY CARMONA

4 **The rise of fabricated majoritarianism: how nationalism based on 'othering' in democracies at times of scarcity is exacerbating existential threats to minorities** 74
JOSHUA CASTELLINO

5 **Beyond the Western idea of scarcity. Contributions to a relational theory of law from indigenous cosmovisions** 90
SILVIA BAGNI

6 **Vulnerabilities, minoritizing processes and concerted solutions for rural scarcities. Learning lessons and tackling marginalisation in Northern Italy** 107
ROBERTA MEDDA-WINDISCHER AND FEDERICA MAINO

7 **Emotional scarcity and well-being among international students at times of crisis in South Africa during the COVID-19 pandemic** 126
FAITH MKWANANZI, PATIENCE MUKWAMBO, MATOME WINTER SESHOKA, AND NOMZINGISI NOTENGA

8 **A people without a land: scarcity, biopolitics, and Romani people in the Middle East** 147
ARPAN ROY

9 **Epistemic violence from silencing to "scarcity of empathy": the experience of Indigenous scholars in Brazil** 158
CAMILA FERREIRA MARINELLI

10 **"A society only as wealthy as its most deprived"** 175
RITA IZSÁK-NDIAYE

Index *183*

Contributors

Silvia Bagni
University of Bologna
Italy
Associate Professor of comparative public law in the Department of Political and Social Sciences at the University of Bologna, Italy. Her research interests include Latin American constitutionalism and ecological law. She is a member of the UN Harmony with Nature Programme.

Gregorio 'Gory' Carmona
Spain
Gitano artist born and raised in Madrid. He collaborates as an interlocutor and co-author in Antonio Montañés Jiménez's research project on Romani Pentecostalism.

Joshua Castellino
Executive Dean, College of Arts, Law & Social Sciences, Brunel University London, UK. Joshua was Executive Director of Minority Rights Group International, UK (2018–2025) and holds visiting professorial positions at the College of Europe (Poland), Oxford University (UK) and the Irish Centre for Human Rights, Galway (Republic of Ireland). He serves on governing boards of civil society organisations pro bono in Germany, Sweden, Netherlands and the UK and is currently Chair of Privacy International. Born and brought up in Mumbai, he worked as a journalist for Indian Express Group in the 1990s before winning a Chevening Scholarship and completing his PhD in international law in 1998. He has published eight books and over 100 articles on international law and human rights over 25 years in academia, including the *Minority Rights Series* published by Oxford University Press. He engages with questions of minority and Indigenous peoples' rights at inter-governmental, parliamentary, apex courts, bar associations, civil society organisations and universities in over 50 countries. He participated in the European Union China Diplomatic & Expert Dialogue on Human Rights (2002–2006) and was appointed Chair by the United Nations Office of the High Commissioner for Human Rights of the 8th Forum on Minority Issues (2015),

an inter-governmental dialogue with civil society under the auspices of the United Nations Human Rights Council.

Camila Ferreira Marinelli
University of St Andrews
United Kingdom She holds a PhD in Social Anthropology from the University of St Andrews and is the Scientific Coordinator of the HORIZON-MSCA Staff Exchanges project EDGES: Entangling Indigenous Knowledge in Universities (2024–2028) funded by the European Union.

Ana P. Gutiérrez Garza
University of St Andrews
United Kingdom
Senior Lecturer in Social Anthropology, Director of the Gender Institute and the Centre for Amerindian, Latin American and Caribbean Studies at the University of St. Andrews. Her research focuses on care, gender, sexualised labour, migration and social inequality.

Rita Izsák-Ndiaye
United Nations Development Programme
United States of America
Human rights expert who started working on the protection of the rights of minorities and vulnerable groups after her own experiences of prejudices and discrimination due to her Roma origin. She has worked in several countries, including Somalia and Bosnia and Herzegovina, and was a consultant of the UN Office of the High Commissioner for Human Rights, the International Labour Organization, the Office of the UN Secretary-General's Envoy on Youth, and several international non-governmental organisations. She was chief of staff in the Hungarian Ministry of Public Administration and Justice (2010–2011) and president/CEO of the Tom Lantos Institute (2011–2012). She is a former UN Special Rapporteur on minority issues (2011–2017), a former member and rapporteur of the UN Committee on the Elimination of Racial Discrimination (2018–2022), and the former OSCE Personal Representative on Children and Security (2021–2022). Between 2022 and 2024, she was a senior advisor on Anti-Racism in UNDP. She is a Hungarian/Senegalese citizen and is based in Dakar, Senegal.

Federica Maino
Eurac Research Institute for Minority Rights
Italy
Researcher at the Eurac Institute for Regional Development since 2009. She holds a master's degree in environmental engineering (University of Trento), a post master's degree in urban management and city design (University of Wales) and a specialisation in conflict management. Her main research interests include different topics related to local development, granting particular attention to stakeholders' involvement, community's empowerment

and conflict prevention and transformation to foster well-balanced relationships between human activities and the environment. She is author of scientific publications and since 2012 she teaches in various athenaeums and institutes of formation.

Roberta Medda-Windischer
Eurac Research Institute for Minority Rights
Italy

Senior Researcher and Group Leader for Equality and Diversity in Integrated Societies at Eurac Research Institute for Minority Rights (Bolzano/Bozen, Italy), she is an international lawyer specialised in minority issues, human rights, diversity management and minority protection. She worked as legal officer for various international organisations, including the European Court of Human Rights (CoE/ECHR, Strasbourg), the UN High Commissioner for Refugees (UNHCR, BiH), the Organisation for Security and Co-operation in Europe (OSCE/ODIHR, Albania), and the UN Centre for Human Rights (OHCHR, Geneva). At Eurac Research, her research focuses on the protection of minorities in international law and on new minorities stemming from migration, on which she has authored and edited monographs and multi-authored volumes and published numerous articles and chapters in edited volumes in Italy and abroad.

Faith Mkwananzi
University of the Free State
South Africa

Associate Professor at the Centre for Development Support at the University of the Free State in South Africa. Her interdisciplinary work, grounded in collaborative stakeholder partnerships, focuses on [higher] education and global development in sub-Saharan Africa, cutting across migration, gender and youth studies. She also researches education in conflict settings and the internationalisation of higher education, with a focus on cross-border mobility, knowledge production and digital internationalisation.

Antonio Montañés Jiménez
University of Oxford
United Kingdom

Margarita Salas postdoctoral fellow affiliated with the School of Anthropology and Museum Ethnography at the University of Oxford (UK) and ISOR, Universidad Autónoma de Barcelona. He is also a Ruth Lee Kennedy/Fulbright postdoctoral researcher at the University of Miami. His research interest includes the anthropology of Christianity, sociology of religion and Romani studies.

Patience Mukwambo
University of Glasgow
United Kingdom

Lecturer at the University of Glasgow's School of Education. She is interested in how universities foster human development and create more just, inclusive and sustainable societies. Her areas of interest include the conceptions and operationalisation of quality in teaching and learning, internationalisation and students' experiences concerning access and participation in higher education. Patience focuses on the experiences of marginalised groups, such as girls, students from low-income backgrounds and migrants (both documented and undocumented) across different higher education contexts.

Nomzingisi Notenga
The University of the Free State
South Africa

She holds a master's degree in development studies from the University of Free State. She was previously a research intern for the Higher Education & Human Development Research Group. Her master's dissertation explores viable and innovative approaches to sustainable development in South African rural areas. She maintains an interest in participatory development, conflict management and the use of development communication as a facilitative tool in development initiatives.

Stavroula Pipyrou
University of St Andrews
United Kingdom

Senior Lecturer in Social Anthropology at the University of St Andrews, Founding Director of the interdisciplinary Centre for Minorities Research and editor of the interdisciplinary book series *Routledge Advances in Minority Studies.* She works on minority politics, displacement, humanitarianism, governance and the Cold War. She is the author of 'The Grecanici of Southern Italy: Governance, Violence, and Minority Politics' (University of Pennsylvania Press, 2016) and 'Lurking Cold War: Life Through Historical Communion' (Berghahn 2025).

Arpan Roy
Leibniz-Zentrum Moderner Orient
Germany

Marie Skłodowska-Curie Postdoctoral Fellow at Leibniz-Zentrum Moderner Orient in Berlin. He holds a PhD from the Department of Anthropology at Johns Hopkins University. He is the author of *Relative Strangers: Romani Kinship and Palestinian Difference* (University of Toronto Press, 2024) and the co-editor of *Naseej: Life-Weavings of Palestine* (Pluto Press, 2025).

Kyriaki Topidi
Centre for Minority Issues
Germany

Senior Researcher and Head of Cluster on Culture and Diversity at the European Centre for Minority Issues (ECMI). Her research interests focus on diversity governance and minority protection rights and mechanisms. She has lectured extensively and researched in Public International Law,

European Law, Human and Minority Rights as well as Comparative Law. Prior to joining the ECMI, she has occupied research and teaching positions in various academic institutions. She has been a guest researcher and lecturer in numerous research institutes and faculties across the globe. She is also the author and editor of several volumes and articles. Since 2023, she co-edits the *Routledge Advances on Minority Studies* book series. Her latest co-edited volume focuses on the intersection of minorities with social movements (*Minority Rights and Social Change: Norms, Actors and Strategies,* Routledge, 2024). At the ECMI, she is currently researching on minority identity and digital governance, preparing a monograph on *Intersectional Discrimination in Platform Governance* (BRILL, forthcoming).

Matome Winter Seshoka
University of Limpopo
South Africa
Lecturer in the Department of Education Studies at the University of Limpopo, South Africa. He holds a Doctor of Philosophy in Education from the University of South Africa, specialising in Curriculum Studies. His research interests include Curriculum Development, Curriculum Implementation, Curriculum Support, Teacher Professional Development, Assessment and e-learning.

Acknowledgements

This edited collection is based on a 2022 seminar series delivered at the Centre for Minorities Research (CMR) at the University of St Andrews, Scotland. CMR supports academic dialogue and real-time action on one of the most urgent global challenges of our time: achieving meaningful, intersectional engagement with vulnerable populations.

Titled 'Minorities in Times of Scarcity and Conflict', the seminar series brought together an outstanding group of scholars from various disciplines who hold dear issues of minorities and social vulnerability. In each session we pushed our thinking about the concept of scarcity. The contributors here tell different stories about the ways in which scarcity goes beyond material resources. As editors, we are deeply grateful to our colleagues who trusted us and responded to a lengthy process lasting from their seminar presentations to publishing the edited volume. We are cognizant that time is important in all collaborative projects!

We are grateful to all CMR seminar attendees and a global audience whose voices were fundamental in shaping and pushing our conceptual thinking further. Open to non-exclusive academic communities, the seminar enriched our interventions and acted as a framework for real-time feedback. Antonio Montañés Jiménez expresses his gratitude to the Economic and Social Research Council (ESRC) for the Postdoctoral Fellowship (Ref: ES/W006308/1), which supported his postdoctoral research in the Department of Social Anthropology and the CMR at the University of St. Andrews. This support was instrumental in making this book possible.

We would like to thank Alison Kirk, Routledge Senior Editor, and *Routledge Advances in Minority Studies* series editors Stavroula Pipyrou and Kyriaki Topidi for assistance and guidance in the publication process. Finally, we are grateful to each other for constant encouragement, motivation and intellectual stimulation.

Antonio, Camila, Stavroula

Introduction

Antonio Montañés Jiménez, Camila Ferreira Marinelli, and Stavroula Pipyrou

Minorities, Scarcity and Conflict places scarcity as a defining aspect of minorities' experience and as a tool to comprehend ongoing and unresolved societal friction and global environmental challenges, as well as strategies for survival and reproduction of the status quo and aspirational desires for social mobility. The book is an experimental collective intellectual project departing from conventional approaches to scarcity solely as a resource-based economic or demographic concept. Boldly, the book looks at the ways in which disadvantaged social groups navigate their lives through scarcity, how these circumstances are endured, interpreted, accepted, or challenged. In contrast to other approaches to scarcity, here we refrain from engaging with the study of political violence. Instead, we investigate more subtle and invisible dimensions of structural inequality and potential conflict permeating the social life of minorities by showing how minority groups face discrimination in numerous areas of social life, including housing, employment, environmental health, and education.

In a thought-provoking turn, *Minorities, Scarcity and Conflict* makes a novel contribution to minority studies by engaging with scarcity not only concerning resources but also emotion, memory, and affect. In analysing scarcity as a multidimensional analytical framework and interrogating it from manifold angles, the book unpacks uncharted ramifications of debates around scarcity and opens new lines of enquiry. This is indeed a more challenging endeavour, bringing fresh insights to the study of minorities in a global setting. More specifically, we look at notions of scarcity that capture the interplay between material provision and human needs. Scarcity thus intimately relates to living standards and discussions about what is adequate or ethical concerning material provision.

Across academic disciplines, scholarly literature has identified various types of scarcity. For economists, relative scarcity describes a situation where something is limited in supply compared to demand, whereas absolute scarcity refers to something being limited, regardless of demand. However, critical scholars have argued that scarcity can also be "lived/experienced" and "socially produced". Experienced scarcity can be triggered by objective biophysical shortage of food, water, fodder, and so forth in a given socio-historical context,

DOI: 10.4324/9781032661780-1

or "constructed" scarcity and manufactured through socio-political processes to suit the interests of powerful players (Mehta, 2005; see also Ross, 1996). Often, individual perception of scarcity and how people explain or understand their experiences of scarcity are as crucial as the condition of scarcity itself. From a sociological point of view, scarcity points to the intrinsic interdependence between communities, their environment, and the social organisations and distribution systems that are in place to meet material needs or demands. Scarcity is usually defined negatively as a source of fear, alarm, and concern. However, it may be argued that scarcity certainly is a ubiquitous and existential feature of the human condition (Huff and Mehta, 2019, p. 27; Hellberg, 2020; Jairath, 2010; Scoones et al., 2014).

Minorities, Scarcity and Conflict follows in the footsteps of collections that have turned attention to academic debates around scarcity whilst we offer a more complex approach to minorities studies. In *The Limits to Scarcity: Contesting the Politics of Allocation*, sociologist Lyla Mehta (2010) compiled essays challenging dominant Malthusian understandings of scarcity as a natural biophysical limitation and byproduct of lack of resources across three domains: water, food, and energy. The book primarily engages economic theory and stands against "the scarcity postulate": that is to say, "that needs, wants, and desires are unlimited, and the means to achieve these are scarce and limited unpins modern economics need not be universal" (Mehta 2010, p. 2). For Mehta, scarcity "is not merely a natural phenomenon that can be isolated from planning models, allocation politics, policy choices, market forces and local power, social and gender dynamics" (2010, p. 2). While recognising the existence of absolute scarcity across history and the potential biophysical limits and shortages of some natural resources, Mehta and collaborators shift the focus to the politics of allocations around the production and distribution of existing resources. They emphasised scarcity as a human-produced outcome by suggesting that "more often than not, the problem lies in how we see scarcity and the ways in which it is socially generated" (Mehta 2010, p. 3). Moreover, Mehta and others criticise how the "scare" of scarcity has become a political strategy for powerful groups to impose their ideas and self-interest in policy and public discourses and challenge perspectives on scarcity championing technology, more efficient institutional arrangement, and/or the market as solutions providers. Instead, Mehta and others argue that more democratic politics of knowledge and concerted solutions should be favoured, incorporating local understandings of scarcity into policy.

More recently, *Scarcity in the Modern World: History, politics, society and Sustainability, 1800–2075* (2019) shows how the meaning of scarcity has evolved in history and provides insights regarding how the interplay between political, economic, social, and natural forces has shaped the construction of debates around scarcity. The book takes a multidisciplinary standpoint by examining different critical understandings of scarcity across disciplines and time. Meeting the needs of the people on the planet in an increasingly resource-stressed environment, Albritton Jonsson and others appreciate, is a complex problem which cannot be addressed by a single discipline but requires a concerted effort to think about its political and social as well as technical and economic dimensions (Jonsson et al., 2019, p. 1). Also, this book focuses on "different responses on different scales and by different entities—states and governments, individual industries, and households—to circumstances of 'scarcity'" (Jonsson et al., 2019, p. 5) and examines strategies for coping, managing, and innovating by those actors. In a critical vein, the authors in this book question scientific "projections of scarcity" by investigating how projections powerfully shape public perceptions of scarcity and favour existing political and social hierarchies.

Our concerns in this book build on previous resonances of scarcity to illuminate aspects of majority-minorities interactions. For instance, we take further the interrelationship of social, political, and religious belief alongside violence. Regina Schwartz (1997) has argued that the scarcity inherent in biblical narratives—one God, one group, one people—spawned violence for humanity by fostering boundaries, competition, and exclusion. Building upon a similar impetus to redirect studies on scarcity to transit underexplored avenues for research, the current book takes two primary theoretical directions. First, scarcity is proposed as a contemporary all-pervasive socio-economic and material context informing subjectivities and shaping aspirations, capabilities, and forms of life for some social minorities. Most contributors situate scarcity as an inescapable global social background that defines core financial, ideological, and narrative dimensions of minorities' experience and their position vis-à-vis the State, majorities, and political factions. Then, shifting from material to immaterial perspectives, the book also explores emotional, socio-psychological, and representational scarcity structures and elaborates on their expressive dimensions. In analysing scarcity as a multidimensional analytical framework, as emotion, memory, and affect, and interrogating it from manifold angles, the book unpacks uncharted ramifications of debates around scarcity and opens new lines of enquiry.

Approaches to scarcity: a brief overview

Clearly a material concern, tackling scarcity effectively and creating technology and social organisations to that end is a survival need for social groups inhabiting environments from which humans utilise resources to exist, grow, and flourish. In that sense, scarcity can be understood as a generative condition driving people together to create social institutions. Yet, questions of scarcity are closely connected to the exercise of power, since "social institutions securing access to food and fresh water have been historically fundamental to statecraft, and famine, drought and other environmental disturbances have threatened the legitimacy of elites in political history" (Jonsson et al., 2019, p. 15). Critical scholars such as Bataille (1991), Achterhuis (1993), and Xenos (1989) have eloquently revealed how concerns about scarcity are situated historically and defined ideologically. As a matter of fact, distress about scarcity in the contemporary Western world finds its genesis in modern thinking and philosophy along with scientific revolutions, ambitions of controlling and conquering nature, and capitalism's ever-expanding project of hyperaccumulation and the creation of never-ending consumption needs.

Anxieties about social instability and scarcity heightened following the Industrial Revolution, along with a new corpus of scientific knowledge and debates about "what scarcity is, how it is produced and in which ways it can be prevented or taken advantage of" (Huff and Mehta, 2019). The notion of scarcity was fundamental in shaping modern Western political economy theories and how foundational classic economics understood the social. The modern debate about scarcity usually takes as its departure point the economic thought of T. R. Malthus (Jonsson et al., 2019, p. 3), who by the end of the eighteenth century famously examined how the existence of (un)limited resources determines the system of production, economic organisation, and sociological patterns of reproduction and life cycles. For Malthus (1798), against the fixed limitedness of natural resources, uncontrolled sexual reproduction produces scarcity through overcrowding and increasing demands only for the demographic equilibrium to be reinstated by periods of food shortage and disease. Assumptions about the imbalance between resources and demand are indeed still key in underpinning repressive policies regarding population control (Hartmann, 2010). From an opposing view, influential classical economist David Ricardo (1817) optimistically suggested that society responds to scarcity through price signals and technological advancement, leading to a substitution of scarce resources or improving the efficiency of production methods.

Scarcity became an incredibly influential notion in the economic thinking of the twentieth century, so much so that in the 1930s, Lionel Robbins defined economics as "the allocation of scarce resources between competing ends" (Robbins, 1932, p. 16). Scarcity is particularly relevant to economic theories of value. In fact, the mainstream notion of scarcity within contemporary economics originates in the marginalist revolution of the 1870s that was responsible for laying the foundations of orthodox economics as it is today (Luks, 2010, p. 99). According to neoclassical economists, the value of something is determined by how consumers perceive its scarcity. Likewise, scarcity—the amount of a good considered necessary or optimal—is shaped by desire. For neoclassic economists, emphasis to determine value is not placed on how useful (i.e. water for survival) something is, but how much people desire something, that is to say, on consumers' preferences.[1] In tandem with

1 The principle of scarcity is an economic assumption about how the dynamics of low supply and demand work. Accordingly, the price of a good with low supply and high demand rises to meet the expected demand. Following this principle, luxury brands create artificial scarcity for a given product or good to make it exclusive, raising prices and demand.

consumers' preferences, a good's availability (or scarcity) shall determine its value and final price.[2]

In economy and development studies, the idea of scarcity regained traction along with debates about growth, capitalism, technology, and population control following the publication of the influential report *The Limits to Growth* (Meadows et al., 1972) commissioned by the Club of Rome in the early 1970s. The report gloomily predicted that Earth's resources may not be able to support present economic and population growth rates much beyond the year 2100, even with advanced technology. Moreover, since the 1970s, scarcity debates around "planetary boundaries" and the Anthropocene, potential limits to growth and the future survival of humankind intersect with growing apprehension regarding environmental stress, capitalism-unfilled fantasies of abundance, and scarcity of natural resources (Huff and Mehta, 2019).

Along with resurfacing debates about scarcity and limits, some critical approaches have taken a constructivist turn, placing scarcity as key to understanding international politics and the production of global inequalities. Amartya Sen's work on human development and the underlying mechanisms of poverty and famine offers an excellent point of departure for understanding this school of thought. Sen draws upon the tragedy of the 1974 Bangladeshi famine and other historical examples to show how political elites blatantly create conditions of scarcity. During this period of severe starvation, high mortality, flooding, and rapid population growth, Bangladesh was not devoid of food but increased its food exports. Therefore, according to Sen, the lack of equitable distribution of resources and the prioritisation of market value led to famine, not scarcity itself (Sen, 1981). In a similar vein, and focusing on the evolution of the Kutch society in the drylands of south Gujarat in India, Mehta (2005) argues that the social acceptance of scarcity as being determined by nature is created and constructed by the social practices and ideologies of the social elite, and the solutions adopted to mitigate this perceived or real scarcity tends further to reproduce the existing relations of domination and subjugation, be it between classes, genders, or castes. In sub-Saharan Africa, critical constructivist perspectives on scarcity strike a chord with what is known as the "global resource grab", the large-scale acquisition of land and other resources by governments, agribusiness companies, and financiers, often in overseas territories (Scoones et al., 2014, p. 3). As an intrinsic part of this grab, systematic extractions of resources (e.g. minerals, hydrocarbons) orchestrated by powerful multinational companies and self-serving national elite actors from the Global South to the rich Global North impoverish local economies to meet the high consumption from Western and other wealthy nations.

2 Social psychologists and behavioural scientists have also used the notion of scarcity to shed light on how individuals experiencing persistent conditions of scarcity can prevent them from making "rational" decisions. For instance, Shafir and Mullainathan (2013) contend that poverty affects people's mindsets. Living with too little imposes huge psychic costs, reducing mental bandwidth and distorting decision-making negatively.

In the 1990s, literature on scarcity took a turn, as scholars placed emphasis on violent conflicts and threats to security in a global scenario potentially defined by scarcity. Even today, water supply shortages and general environmental degradation are perceived as fuel for potential social friction (Anand, 2010; Barbier, 2015). In Hobbes (1651), the state of nature is scarce and thus, rational men struggle and wage war over limited resources to satisfy their needs. Following a Hobbesian line of thought, Kahl (2006) examined the communist insurgency in the Philippines and ethnic land clashes in Kenya by contending that demographic and environmental stress leads to civil strife and violence in political settings defined by state failure and/or state exploitation. Similarly, Homer-Dixon (1999) argued that capitalism-based rapid growth in the global economy spurs ever-increasing demands for natural resources. Consequently, environmental scarcities will likely lead to insurrections, ethnic clashes, urban unrest, and other forms of civil violence, especially in the developing world (Homer-Dixon, 1999). Sustainability goals and forms of decision-making furthering democracy and inclusion of local communities are often proposed as a promising concerted solution to tackle the problem of scarcity and prevent conflict (Richter, 2014; Santos Pereira et al., 2009; Scoones et al., 2014).

In anthropology, scarcity can relate to economic resources, morality, and emotions. Taking the discipline back to its roots, Bronislaw Malinowski's (1922) analysis of the Kula Ring could be understood through the lens of desirable artefacts with increased social and economic value dependent on their scarcity. In mainstream economic anthropology, meanwhile, the social and economic "lives" of scarce objects has been a theoretical line of enquiry throughout the history of the discipline (e.g. Appadurai, 1986; Townsend et al., 2021). Recently, resource insecurity has become a line of enquiry beyond the more classic studies of food and water to incorporate the anthropology of energy and climate change (Wutich and Brewis 2014; Weszkalnys, 2015).

Based on research in Mexico, in 1965 George Foster put forward the argument that "peasant societies" believe there is only a certain amount of "good" to go around. This particularly related to land, money, and consumables, which were in short supply: people either possessed them or had to do without. In a Greek setting, Juliet du Boulay and Rory Williams (1987) extended the limited good framework beyond commodities to include intangibles such as morality, fortune, and divine intervention, all of which people sought while knowing they were in limited supply. Turning to the anthropological literature on trauma, emotional scarcity is often identifiable when discussing aspects of silenced stories, victimisation, and belatedness (e.g. Fassin and Rechtman, 2007; Pipyrou, 2020; Kidron, 2021). Emotional scarcity is thus linked to pseudo-Freudian studies of the psychosocial and the pathologisation of social insecurities.

Some recent approaches[3] understand scarcity not as lack of natural resources but the availability and access to specific socially produced resources, such as job opportunities, State aid, or common good such as education, healthcare, or social security. After the 2008 global financial-economic crisis, States and international financial institutions (World Bank, International Monetary Fund, European Central Bank) embraced austerity and limited government expenditure. Scarcity captured the national imagination of countries hit by the crisis and restrictive financial measure, such as Greece (Knight, 2015), Spain, or Portugal, and fear of lack of resources was reintroduced as a key ideological feature of neoliberal thinking and policies in a time of crisis (Knight and Stewart, 2016). Ross (1996), for instance, distinguishes between socially generated scarcity (insufficient necessities for some people and not others) and absolute scarcity (insufficient resources, no matter how equitably distributed) and argues that despite resources being available, and abundant, neoliberalism keeps encouraging a pro-scarcity climate reinforcing austerity measure against people experiencing poverty. Edsall (2012) analysed the link between conservative notions of scarcity and the re-emergence of austerity politics in the United States following the great 2008 financial crash. It predicted that fiscal pressures would reshape American politics into a zero-sum battle of who gets what and how much is taken from whom and that issues regarding

3 Scoones et al. (2014) suggest that the dominant framing of scarcity can be divided into three dimensions. Absolute scarcity is the primary framing for ecological economists, resource ecologists, and demographers, who understand scarcity as physical, real, and inescapable and identify the problem of scarcity as one of finitude and limits. Relative scarcity—such as neoclassical and agricultural economists proponents understand scarcity—is relative to demand but, and this is the critical point here, "physical limits can be mitigated through economic comparative advantage, science, technology and innovation" (Scoones et al. 2014: 9). The problem for those who understand scarcity as relative, thus, is "underproduction due to suboptimal allocation of resources" (Scoones et al. 2014, p. 9). Finally, scarcity can also be understood as a political construct. According to Scoones et al., political economists, sociologists, and political ecologists frequently understand scarcity relationally, as something that "can be manufactured, both politically and discursively" (Scoones et al. 2014, p. 9). The problem of scarcity here, thus, is one of "access, inequality and historical relations of power" (Scoones et al. 2014, p. 9). In a similar way, Huff and Mehta (2019) suggest a classification predicated on three standpoints: (1) the "systems, boundaries and thresholds" position, (2) the "technological and managerial fix" position and (3) the "structural-distributional" position. The systems, boundaries and thresholds position frames scarcity in terms of absolute biogeophysical limits to Earth System functioning (2019, p. 29) and is concerned about the negative impact of human activities on ecosystems. The technological and managerial fix position advocates the idea that further investment in technological, market-driven, and managerial solutions shall allow global society "to mitigate, and also adapt to, resource crises, across sectors of society and scales from local to global, without compromising goals of environmental sustainability and inclusive economic growth into the future" (Huff and Mehta 2019, p. 31). The structural-distributional position argues that "environmental degradation and resource scarcity are not, in fact, 'natural' but result from inequitable institutional arrangements that result in gross inequalities in access to resources" (Huff and Mehta 2019, p. 33).

immigration, cuts in long-term unemployment benefits, and failure to impose higher taxes on the wealthy would pervade the future of American politics.

Finally, advances in automated manufacturing technologies, robotics, space travel, nanotechnology, and, more generally, rapid productivity increases have captured the imagination of some futurists, technology enthusiasts, economic theorists, and science-fiction writers (e.g. *Star-Trek*) to speculate about the possibility of Humanity entering a post-scarcity society, one in which "technologies of abundance" enable the creation and distribution of unlimited energy, resources, and goods at very cheaply cost or even freely.

Minorities today: a general and distressing overview

Definitions and discussions about minorities across the social sciences usually depart from numerical approaches where demographic size is the defining factor. The concept of minority is usually traced to the 1648 Westphalia Treaty, when Western states claimed ultimate authority over subjects within their territory. However, the term minority was only truly globally widespread during the nineteenth and twentieth centuries. Debates over the status of Jewish subjects within European empires and nation-states, attempts from Imperial powers to legitimise military interventions in the Ottoman Empire to "protect" Christians, and the progress of mobilising social technologies of identification and enumeration to aggregate populations around new forms of difference and distinction coalesced to give momentum and spread the concept (Bar Sadeh and Houwink ten Cate, 2021). The interwar period in the twentieth century was central to the global establishment of minority as a category "of quasi-judicial regulation at both national and international levels, as well as across a wide array of geographies and languages" (Bar Sadeh and Houwink ten Cate, 2021, p. 320). As claimed by Bar Sadeh and Houwink ten Cate, "the Peace Treaties of 1919 that ended World War I and the imposition of cultural national minority rights during the Paris Peace Conference forecasted the internationalisation of 'minority' as a legal category" (2021, p. 320).

A growing number of recently published books dedicated to minorities (Bíró and Newman, 2022; Eichler and Topidi, 2022; Marushiakova and Popov, 2021; Orgad and Koopmans, 2020; Newman, 2022; Shahabuddin, 2021, among others) indicate an increasing interest in minority issues globally. And yet, despite the term's popularity in academic, legal, and political discourse, we lack a global consensually agreed and recognised definition of what a minority is under international law. Inspired by the provisions of article 27 of the International Covenant on Civil and Political Rights concerning the rights of persons belonging to ethnic, religious and linguistic minorities, the 1992 United Nations Minorities Declaration urged States to promote and guarantee the protection of the rights of persons belonging to national or ethnic, religious and linguistic minorities and as such to contribute to the political and social stability of States in which they live. According to the United Nations, then, the term "minorities" refers to members of the four categories set out in the Declaration on the Rights of Persons Belonging to National or Ethnic, Religious and Linguistic Minorities: national, ethnic, religious, and linguistic (UN and Equal Rights Trust, 2023, p. 127).

Some scholars have criticised the term *minority* because of its resonances with colonial politics of high governance and administration (see Roy, Chapter 8). Additionally, critics argue that the category of minority itself may lead to substantive definitions and fixing essentialist assumptions of who minorities are. New terminological developments, such as the introduction of the term "global majority" (Campbell-Stephens, 2021), challenge the normativity of a white majority or Eurocentric perspective and remind us that people of indigenous, African, Asian, or Latin American descent make up the majority of the world population. Proponents insist that thinking and engaging with decolonial language and moving from a minority to majority orientation encourage groups, leaders, and individuals to move from a place of subordination to one of agency (Campbell-Stephens, 2021). Indeed, social critics contend that the idea of minority often corresponds with national politics of recognition in which a State holds the power to bestow or deny rights, and this framework may create patterns of dependence and demobilise radical and revolutionary movements by integrating and containing minorities' claims within liberal State politics and policies.

Some members of groups usually defined as minorities reject being labelled as such. The word *minority* can foster representations and self-images of certain people as victims, frail or in need of being defended. However, it can also promote the politicisation of collective identities and inter-group relationships otherwise overlooked. Since the 1990s, calls by advocates and human rights experts to adopt comprehensive anti-discrimination laws to protect minorities have significantly grown (Collins and Türk, 2023). In parallel, most States appear actively involved in adopting and advancing such legal apparatus before the public. States' recognition of the need to eliminate all forms of discrimination—and their commitment to doing so—manifest in fact in both the opening words of the Universal Declaration of Human Rights and in the call of the 2030 Agenda for Sustainable Development and its Sustainable Development Goals to leave no one behind (Collins and Türk, 2023). Those who argue in favour of maintaining the term, nevertheless, underscore that the concept of minority brings to the fore power structures, provides legal grounding, and facilitates the establishment of a legal apparatus to protect and extend the rights of marginalised and vulnerable groups (Kugelmann, 2007; Macklem, 2008). Be that as it may, most scholars advocate utilising processual definitions of minority and encourage reflections and critical awareness for potential Western or other ideological bias in our definitions and usages of the term.

Minority studies witness robust and visible minority achievements in global and local governance of minority rights, in particular in the field of indigenous rights, the rights of Peoples of African Descent and, more moderately, the Roma. However, global cultural and political sensibilities seem to be at odds with international legal developments and discourses attempting to protect minority rights (Topidi and Relaño Pastor, 2024).

The first quarter of the twenty-first century stands as a turbulent and conflictual global period for minorities. The 11 September 2001 attacks in the United States, the 2004 Madrid train bombings in Spain, and the July 2005 London bombings in the UK ushered in a new era of hate crimes, racism, and xenophobia, for instance against Muslims in Western countries. The global financial crash of 2008 and the subsequent implementation of austerity policies and massive cuts in public services by the political establishment was met by a worldwide wave of anti-austerity movements, street protests, and grassroots campaigns in the West. Dissatisfaction with authoritarianism and economic inequalities exacerbated by the 2008 Great Recession also sparked anti-government protests, uprisings, and armed rebellions in the Arab world. Against this backdrop, progressive populist frameworks, which presented "the people" as a morally good force and contrasted them against a corrupt and self-serving "elite", disseminated widely. Neoliberal ideologies and the democratic legitimacy of the political and economic status quo were contested, and radical political movements such as Occupy Wall Street, the Spanish Indignados, The Arab Spring, and the Greek anti-austerity movement shaped the political conversations about welfare, financial markets' social accountability, and political corruption. However, recent significant social and political developments, such as the rise of far right-wing populist leaders in North and South America, such as Trump or Bolsonaro, the Syrian refugee crisis of 2015, Brexit, or the escalation of nationalism and far-right extremism in Eastern Europe, have shifted the target and content of populist narratives (Pipyrou and Sorge, 2021).

In today's social and political landscape, we witness a rapid transformation of collective sensibilities that break with long-standing norms and values of civic life and engender political and ideological polarisation. The historical weakening of Western liberal democratic governance is eroding respect and protections for human rights in general and minority rights in particular. In tandem with growing concerns regarding catastrophic natural disasters, anthropogenic climate change and lack of resources (e.g. food, water, energy, oil), global regimes of capitalist accumulations deepen social inequalities and further dispossess vulnerable populations (See Castellino, Chapter 4). The long-wave impact of sustained austerity policies under neoliberal ideological hegemony and the subsequent growing popular sympathies toward far-right discourses, as well as continuous wars over resources and refugee crises, favour the harbouring of hatred against minorities.

Under neoliberal policies and the right-wing populist threat, minorities face enormous challenges and become the subject of deep-seated resentment. In a zero-sum game, perceptions of scarcity prominently shape inter-group relationships. Real or imagined perceptions of scarcity ignite social tension, sometimes leading to radical views of Otherness, pitting community against community. Scarcity and resource competition can foster distrust and antipathy and promote discriminatory resource allocations between groups. In government and civil society, the prominence of scarcity-driven presumptions leads majorities to devalue social minorities' deservingness and justify withholding resources from them. Migrants and other racial, cultural, and religious minorities are frequently perceived and narrated as threatening nations' social cohesion and Western countries' values, security, and economic well-being. Repeatedly, minorities are linked to crime, cultural decline, poverty, and insecurity. Paradoxically, even though state aid directed to support minorities was usually the first to fall victim to austerity politics, minorities are often perceived as illegitimate recipients of costly public benefits.

Right-wing-leaning populist rhetoric thrives on political turmoil and economic crisis and masks itself as challenging the status quo while endorsing neoliberal policies. It also entwines the resurgence of chauvinistic desires and nostalgic narratives of an idealised golden past, enforcing colonial and imperial social hierarchies (Bissel, 2005). As opposed to contesting financial and political elites' ideologies and practices, emerging right-wing populist narratives redirect the anger of the politically disaffected and economically disenfranchised towards vulnerable groups. Additionally, right-wing populism enhances hate speech—on the internet, in bars and pubs, and in homes—to the extent it is becoming increasingly accepted. Worryingly, right-wing populism also drives fake news and online-driven propaganda, which are growing into mainstream forms of political communication and ideological manipulation. In the current political scenario, social and traditional media amplifies racist populist statements against minorities, aiming to capitalise on growing political discontent and economic working-class struggles. US President Donald Trump's repeated inflammatory statements—which have included wrongful allegations of Haitians eating pets; characterisations of Mexican migrants as criminals, drug smugglers, rapists, and "bad *hombres*"; and accusations to immigrants coming to the United States of escaping from prisons and insane asylums—are among the more distinct instances of using normalised anti-minorities rhetoric for political gains.

The COVID-19 pandemic added new layers of complexity to this emerging political scenario hostile to minorities. The Chinese communities outside China were the first minority groups to be scapegoated and stigmatised. China was identified as the geographical region where the pandemic originated, and the concept "Chinese virus" gained traction in popular conversations and right-wing discourses. Subsequently, in Europe and North America, Latino, Roma, and Black communities were often accused of propagating COVID-19 and portrayed as groups of people unable to comply with lockdown restrictions, a set of assumptions built upon previously deep-seated conceptualisations of these groups as undesirable (Montañes Jiménez and Gómez Ávila, 2024; Gay y Blasco and Fotta, 2023).

Minorities are also an intrinsic part of several contemporary geopolitical processes, such as the rise of non-Western global powers, changes in international orders, and subsequent wars over territories. After decades of persecution, Tatars, Buryats, Tuvans, and other minorities are being called up to the front lines as cannon fodder in the ongoing Russian aggression against

Ukraine, whereas widespread rhetoric over the protection of Donbas "Russians" in Eastern Ukraine instrumentalise minority issues to justify war.

Volume organisation

Minorities, Scarcity and Conflict brings together a mix of scholars across anthropology, law, education, political Science, and minorities rights. Methodologically speaking, the book combines a diverse range of ethnographic, qualitative, critical theory, and collaborative approaches to knowledge production. Economists, political demographers, and experts in sustainable development—scholars who have dominated the field of scarcity in the past—are saliently absent in the line-up of this book. This was indeed a deliberate choice. We do appreciate those disciplines' significant contributions to the progression of the studies related to scarcity; however, this book intends to navigate underexplored avenues for research outside of conventional approaches to the subject.

The book examines the contemporary social context of minorities involving six countries: Israel/Palestine, the United States, South Africa, Italy, Brazil, and Spain, in five geographical regions. All these research sites are pervaded by racial, religious, ethnic, and colonial hierarchies. Some are also historical and contemporary notorious examples of violence against minorities. Within this geographical context, *Minorities, Scarcity and Conflict* includes case studies involving a number of minorities or minoritised groups: Romani communities in Palestine and Spain, undocumented Mexican immigrant women in the United States, international students in South Africa, rural communities in Italy, indigenous academics in Brazil, and briefly the Ogoni in the Western Niger Delta region of southern Nigeria. While two groups investigated in this volume (international students and rural communities) fall outside traditional definitions of minority groups, they are included here because authors make compelling arguments to demonstrate that these groups face exclusion akin to minorities and that scarcity lenses can become fruitful frameworks for exposing power and interdependence relations between dominant and minority groups.

In addition, the book includes a conceptual chapter that examines the intersection of scarcity and minority studies—which also devotes attention to acute human, legal, and environmental conflicts between multinational oil companies and indigenous peoples in southeast Nigeria. Two thematic chapters focus on major political and ecological developments affecting minorities in capitalism-driven societies: one deals with the failures of the nation-state democratic system to protect minorities and prevent latent xenophobia from altering political landscapes in increasingly polarising and fragmenting societies and the second with the human impact on Earth's geology and ecosystems, mainly anthropogenic climate change and the exclusion of non-Western knowledge systems and cosmologies held by native minorities based on living in harmony and non-exploitative terms with Earth and Nature.

The authors explore multiple manifestations of scarcity through the prism of their respective areas of expertise while remaining attentive to power dynamics and contextual singularities. Every chapter engages creatively with the concept of scarcity involving a minority or minoritised[4] group in a different geographical region. Depending on the ethnographic/historical/legal context, the term *scarcity* differs in meaning and represents a range of distinct relations for each author. Admittedly, the authors show different degrees of engagement with the concept. Some utilise scarcity as their central focus, while others use it tangentially or as a secondary theme. However, they all embrace scarcity as a productive notion or framework with the potential to advance research agendas in the study of minorities. The diversity in case studies and interpretation of scarcity not only adds to the interdisciplinary appeal of the book but also strengthens our main claim on scarcity being a socio-political reality extending across geographical contexts and a broad range of domains.

In Chapter 1, "Unlearning Scarcity Within Ethno-Cultural Minority Groups: Between Perceptions and Reality", Kyriaki Topidi explores the conceptual nuances of scarcity and the different ways minorities may be affected by scarcity conditions. Drawing on an extensive literature analysis, Topidi focuses on conflict scenarios by highlighting the interconnectedness of scarcity, resource grabs, psychological strains, and stereotyping of minorities. Both perceived and real scarcity, Topidi suggests, can trigger inter-group competition, and work as powerful governance technologies by masking asymmetrical allocations of resources and fostering and justifying inequalities and domination towards vulnerable groups. The chapter shows that one of the most damaging instances of scarcity for minorities remains the attempts by local governments and global economic forces to hamper the productive capacity of segments of populations and lands in the Global South to meet the consumption demands of the Global North, as exemplified by the conflict between the Ogoni and multinational oil company Shell. Polycentric designs for governance, Topidi affirms, can become a helpful tool to "unlearn" scarcity patterns and tackle potential conflicts arising from scarcity scenarios.

In Chapter 2, "Understanding Scarcity 'in the Land of Abundance': Mexican Migrants in Tulsa, Oklahoma (USA)", Ana Gutiérrez Garza engages with symbolic aspects of scarcity by critically examining how narratives of scarcity vindicate and rationalise uncertain and precarious journeys for undocumented Mexican women seduced by the promises of the American Dream escaping poverty, violence, and hardship. The chapter shows how the interplay between the dual and oppositional notions of scarcity and abundance shapes

4 Whereas the concept of minorities refers to national, ethnic, religious, and linguistic groups coexisting with a more dominant group, minorisation speaks to the state of being or becoming a minority and relates to the processes through which such minorities are constructed. Here, we look at minorisation in terms of "productive" likeness or similarities. In this book, some authors argue that certain groups rarely defined as minorities can be fruitfully analysed as if they were one.

the aspirations, hopes, and desires of personal and family upward mobility for women enrolling their children in early education programs funded by philanthropic organisations in the United States. Here, scarcity narratives about Mexico and promises of abundance in the United States are intrinsic to accepting and complying with models of motherhood as well as embracing new American values and ideals geared towards creating neoliberal American subjectivities and notions of deservingness.

In Chapter 3, " 'The Story of My Father': Life Narratives and Memories of Scarcity of a Spanish Gitano Family", Antonio Montañés Jiménez and Gory Carmona explore the interface between memory and scarcity, introducing the notion of "memories of scarcity" as an analytical device to comprehend the recollection of self-recorded life narratives produced by Gitano communities in Spain. Gory and his recently deceased father, the protagonists and leading voices featured in the text, vividly recount stories, struggles, and personal experiences stretching back to the aftermath of the Spanish Civil War. The chapter interrogates whether, or to what extent, scarcity can become a fruitful analytical framework to understand minorities' ideas and descriptions of their past and present selves. Scarcity is presented here as a double-edged sword, as by using it, researchers, perhaps inadvertently, could reinforce negative perspectives about Gitanos and re-victimise them.

In Chapter 4, "The Rise of Fabricated Majoritarianism: How Nationalism Based on "Othering" in Democracies at Times of Scarcity Is Exacerbating Existential Threats to Minorities", Joshua Castellino engages with critical political theories on the state and democracy to reflect on how "times of scarcity" characterised by climate emergency and growing global inequalities creates a push for resources that further fragments societies along ethnic, religious, racial, linguistic, and indigenous lines. This chapter presents scarcity as a political and economic context created by elites to impose and justify social orders and privileges in modern states that are remarkably damaging to minorities. In so doing, the chapter continues and furthers a well-established tradition of critical studies revealing how scarcity conditions and narratives maintain and reproduce the status quo. Castellino also examines how the historical imposition of the Europeanised State model onto diverse communities in non-Western contexts effectively condemned many societies to a "majoritarianism" that permanently favours access by a dominant group to governance systems and how the myth of the exaggerated threat posed by identity politics is helping to exacerbate scapegoating climates against minorities.

In Chapter 5, "Beyond the Western Idea of Scarcity. Contributions to a Relational Theory of Law From Indigenous Cosmovisions", Silvia Bagni tackles the current capitalism-driven climate and environmental predicaments by arguing that indigenous cosmovisions, interpreted here as a form of minority's knowledge and epistemology, may provide fundamental ideas and cultural models to tackle ecological crises, mainly through their holistic way of conceiving the relationship between human beings and other non-human entities.

The chapter questions Western societies' ever-expanding desire to produce abundance, calling for an ecological conversion of dominant lifestyles and legal systems. In other words, Bagni argues in favour of a radical shift from resource-based cultural legal and economic paradigms based on organising against scarcity to one sympathetic to indigenous knowledge and based on intra- and inter-species relationality.

In Chapter 6, "Diversity Governance, Minoritizing Processes and Concerted Solutions for Rural Scarcities: Learning Lessons and Tackling marginalisation in Northern Italy", Roberta Medda-Windischer and Federica Maino analyse the role of scarcity in furthering situations of vulnerability, minorisation, and depopulation among resilient rural communities in the north-east of the Italian Alps. Based on an action research approach, Medda-Windischer and Maino explore community-oriented concerted solutions to emerging rural vulnerabilities in contexts that expose people inhabiting mountains to risks and asymmetric access to resources vis-à-vis urban dwellers.

Chapter 7, "Emotional Scarcity and Well-Being Among International Students at Times of Crisis in South Africa During the COVID-19 Pandemic" by Faith Mkwananzi, Patience Mukwambo, Matome Winter Seshoka, and Nomzingisi Notenga investigates how the COVID-19 health crisis led to a politically constructed scarcity in South African universities. As a result of emerging conditions of material scarcity, an equally harmful emotional scarcity ensues in university settings for international students. By focusing on students' emotional experiences of scarcity and unmet needs, the chapter provides empirical insights crucial to understanding educational arrangements and broader socio-political relations shaping mobility between countries in the Global South.

In Chapter 8, "A People Without a Land: Scarcity, Biopolitics, and Romani People in the Middle East", Arpan Roy engages with the idea of scarcity of land. Reframing Marxist theories, Roy investigates how economic scarcity, difficulties in accessing property and lack of land access have shaped the lives and labour of two Romani groups (Doms and Aptal Turkmen). Roy claims that the incapacity to acquire land and property, the basis for permanent settlement, is an instance of constructed scarcity, a politically manufactured situation injuring the trajectory of a particular group in a way oddly experienced by the landed elites of the Arab Levant. The main argument of the chapter is that historical and political trajectories of dispossession are inscribed in Romani consciousness and model Romani lifestyles and ethics through the biopolitical reproduction of kinship.

In the final chapter, "Epistemic Violence From Silencing to 'Scarcity of Empathy': The Experience of Indigenous Scholars in Brazil", Camila Ferreira Marinelli focuses on indigenous academics' experiences in universities in Brazil, placing scarcity of empathy as a prerogative of epistemic violence perpetuated by colonialist standardisation of knowledge and Western ideas of what it is to be "civilized". Departing from material understandings of scarcity, Ferreira Marinelli interrogates the value of reconsidering emotional interpretations of scarcity as a lack of immaterial resources and empathy to understand the pain-riddled journeys of indigenous scholars navigating colonial structures and neglect in higher education spaces.

Some additional thoughts: looking at minorities through the lens of scarcity

Scarcity aligns with a set of cognate terms, such as poverty, inequalities, vulnerability, hardship, deprivation, precarity, or adversity, repeatedly utilised by scholars, political analysts, and social justice activists to emphasise salient existential and socio-economic challenges that minorities encounter in contemporary societies. Because of the overlapping similarities and entanglement of minorities' experiences rooted in marginalisation and disadvantage and the vast repertoire of scholarly terminology to address minority issues, the term *scarcity* risks adding to terminological confusion in the literature. Worse, scarcity may come across as a fuzzy catch-all notion for violence, power, or colonial interactions. While remaining aware of the potential perils of refashioning concepts, we also trust there are enough reasons to refresh our conceptual apparatus in minority studies.

Unlike other concepts, due to its strong historical resonance with natural resources, scarcity is well equipped to bridge the natural and the social (Wilk, 2019), and its usage favours multidisciplinary approaches. Literature on scarcity shows different forms of scarcity can be found in contemporary and historical processes, including naturally produced goods, assets, and commodities, as well as social benefits and economic opportunities. The scarcity of natural resources heightened by the ongoing climate crises (water, clean air oil, fish stocks, grazing land) affects disproportionately poor, underprivileged, and minorities, initiating refugees' movement. The scarcity of petrol, energy, or gas not only fosters international political tensions, wars, and conflict but it could also cause price inflation and economic recession. The scarcity of commodities in poor or economically less developed countries and promises of abundance in the West shape global imaginaries and aspirations, too. Migrants' journeys and choices are often informed and shaped by these representations of scarcities, which act as "push and pull" factors in their decision-making processes.

The scarcity of social and economic resources, or the social perception of the limited availability of goods such as jobs or state aid, plays a prominent role in shaping inter-group relationships under neoliberal structures and hegemonic discourses. Although immaterial and emotional approaches are seldom incorporated into the literature on scarcity, it can be argued that the recent rise of the far right and anti-migration, refugee, and women rhetoric, along with the growing dismantling of the welfare state since the 1980s, can be partially attributed to the scarcity of empathy vis-à-vis minorities and vulnerable populations. Menacing threats indeed are coming to define emerging contexts of radicalisation and uncertainty aggravated by resurfacing cultural and political radical views of Otherness. Against this background, we propose scarcity can capture the entanglement of specific material and immaterial risks and hazards minorities face in this unwelcoming post-pandemic world.

The book attempts to answer some critical questions regarding the interface of scarcity and minorities: Is scarcity a valuable concept to capture the specific circumstances and challenges minorities face in the contemporary world? What sort of scarcities are relevant in each scenario? What areas of minorities' social reality are most critically modelled by scarcity conditions? How are conditions of scarcity resisted, reimagined, or navigated by minorities?

Minorities, Scarcity and Conflict thus aims to unpack the social life of "scarcity" as both concept and experience. Whereas previous work offers remarkable insights into the production of social thinking regarding scarcity, we propose an alternative way of looking at scarcity, one able to bring together different understandings and overlapping dimensions of scarcity and capitalise by placing them into a productive analytical focus for studying minorities. Minorities face manifold scarcity conditions specific to their position in ethnic, linguistic, racial, and social stratification systems: minorities face multiple scarcities. Multiple scarcities refers to the diverse and intertwined social and existential conditions producing a shortage of goods, care, empathy and opportunities that affect the well-being, needs, and demands of minorities. The concept of multiple scarcities can help to capture the interactions between multidimensional aspects of structural power relationships and the numerous scenarios ensuing from the unequal distribution of goods, care, empathy, and opportunities that affect the well-being, needs, and demands of social minorities.

Solutions to scarcity, as Castellino claims in Chapter 4, require recalibrations of global financial systems, changes in consumption patterns, and better distribution of value across commercial supply chains but also a further cultural shift, with an emphasis on educating majorities about the nature of their privileges as well as the racial and ethnic structures in place preventing minorities from accessing resources. Polycentric designs for governances, as proposed by Topidi in Chapter 1, and action research methodologies, as suggested by Medda-Windischer and Maino in Chapter 6, can be excellent forms of organising decision-making practices to alleviate scarcity and foster awareness and local solutions to advance democratic ways of dealing with scarcity scenarios for minorities. As with the concept of "minority", scarcity risks overemphasising one-dimensional damaging aspects of people's experiences and identities. Gory Carmona, a Romani/ Gitano contributor to Chapter 3, noted, "Scarcity . . . must not be the only lens through which you scholars look at Gitano people". Here, Gory pointed to the sometimes-inescapable tensions between scholars' interests and views and minorities' ever-changing self-representation and needs. In this book, we respond to Gory that scholarship must underscore and examine injustice in detail to spread awareness and challenge it. However, we recognise that discussions about the political implications involved in academic representation, participatory/ collaborative approaches in research design, and ultimately, becoming aware of the consequences of using specific terminology and perspectives are excellent starting points for progressing debates about, and perhaps solving, this dilemma.

References

Achterhuis, H. 1993. Scarcity and Sustainability. In W. Sachs (ed.) *Global Ecology: A New Arena of Political Conflict*. London: Zed Books.

Anand, P. B. 2010. *Scarcity, Entitlements, and the Economics of Water in Developing Countries*. Edward Elgar Publishing.

Appadurai, Arjun (ed.). 1986. *The Social Life of Things: Commodities in Cultural Perspective*. Cambridge: Cambridge University Press.

Barbier, Edward B. 2015. *Nature and Wealth Overcoming Environmental Scarcity and Inequality*. Palgrave Macmillan.

Bar Sadeh, Roy and Lotte Houwink ten Cate. 2021. Toward a Global Intellectual History of 'Minority'. *Comparative Studies of South Asia, Africa and the Middle East (2021)* 41 (3): 319–324.

Bataille, Georges. 1991. *The Accursed Share, Volume I: Consumption*. New York: Zone Books.

Bissell, W. C. 2005. Engaging Colonial Nostalgia. *Cultural Anthropology* 20 (2): 215–248.

Bíró, Anna-Mária and Dwight Newman. 2022. *Minority Rights and Liberal Democratic Insecurities: The Challenge of Unstable Orders*. Routledge.

Campbell-Stephens, Rosemary. 2021. *Educational Leadership and the Global Majority: Decolonising Narratives*. Cham, Switzerland: Springer International Publishing.

Collins, E. and V. Türk. 2023. Foreword. In *Protecting Minority Rights: A Practical Guide to Developing Comprehensive Anti-Discrimination Legislation*. New York and Geneva: Office of the United Nations High Commissioner for Human Rights (OHCHR), and the Equal Rights Trust.

du Boulay, Juliet and Rory Williams. 1987. Amoral Familism and the Image of Limited Good: A Critique from a European Perspective. *Anthropological Quarterly* 60 (1): 12–24.

Edsall, Thomas B. 2012. *The Age of Austerity: How Scarcity Will Remake American Politics*. Anchor Books.

Eichler, Jessika and Kyriaki Topidi. 2022. *Minority Recognition and the Diversity Deficit Comparative Perspectives*. Bloomsbury.

Fassin, Didier and Richard Rechtman. 2007. *The Empire of Trauma: An Inquiry into the Condition of Victimhood*. Princeton, NJ: Princeton University Press.

Foster, George. 1965. Peasant Society and the Image of Limited Good. *American Anthropologist* 67 (2): 293–315.

Gay y Blasco, P. and M. Fotta. 2023. *Romani Chronicles of COVID-19: Testimonies of Harm and Resilience*. Oxford: Berghahn Books.

Hartmann, B. 2010. The Ghosts of Malthus: Narratives and Mobilisations of Scarcity in the US Political Context. In L. Mehta (ed.) *The Limits to Scarcity: Contesting the Politics of Allocation*. London: Earthscan, pp. 49–66.

Hellberg, S. 2020. Scarcity as a Means of Governing: Challenging Neoliberal Hydro Mentality in the Context of the South African Drought. *Environment and Planning E: Nature and Space* 3 (1): 186–206.

Hobbes, Thomas. (1651) 1993. Leviathan. In Mark C. Rooks (ed.) *British Philosophy: 1600–1900*. Charlottesville, VA: Intelex Corporation.

Homer-Dixon, Thomas F. 1999. *Environment, Scarcity, and Violence*. Princeton, NJ: Princeton University Press.

Huff, Amber and Lyla Mehta. 2019. Untangling Scarcity. In Fredrik Albritton Jonsson, John Brewer, Neil Fromer and Frank Trentmann (eds.) *Scarcity in the Modern World History, Politics, Society and Sustainability, 1800–2075*. London: Bloomsbury Academic, pp. 27–46.

Jairath, J. 2010. Advocacy of Water Security: Leakages in the Argument. In L. Mehta (ed.) *The Limits to Scarcity*. London and Washington, DC: Earthscan, pp. 215–232.

Jonsson, Fredrik Albritton, John Brewer, Neil Fromer and Frank Trentmann (eds.). 2019. *Scarcity in the Modern World History, Politics, Society and Sustainability, 1800–2075*. London: Bloomsbury Academic.
Kahl, Colin H. 2006. *Environment, Scarcity, and Violence*. Princeton, NJ: Princeton University Press.
Kidron, Carol A. 2021. 'Rebirthing' the Violent Past: Friction Between Post-Conflict Axioms of Remembrance and Cambodian Buddhist Forgetting. *Anthropological Forum* 31 (3): 291–311.
Knight, Daniel. 2015. *History, Time and Economic Crisis in Central Greece*. Hampshire: Palgrave Macmillan.
Knight, Daniel and Charles Stewart. 2016. Ethnographies of Austerity: Crisis, Temporality, and Affect in Southern Europe. *History and Anthropology* 27 (1): 1–18.
Kugelmann, Dieter. 2007. Protection of Minorities and Indigenous Peoples. In A. Von Bogdandy and R. Wolfrum (eds.) *Max Planck Yearbook of the United Nations*, vol. 11. The Netherlands: Brill, pp. 233–263.
Luks, Fred. 2010. Deconstructing Economic Interpretations of Sustainable Development: Limits, Scarcity and Abundance. In *The Limits to Scarcity: Contesting the Politics of Allocation*. London: Routledge, pp. 93–108.
Macklem, Patrick. 2008. Minority Rights in International Law. *International Journal of Constitutional Law* 6 (3–4): 531–552.
Malinowski, Bronislaw. 1922. *Argonauts of the Western Pacific: An Account of Native Enterprise and Adventure in the Archipelagoes of Melanesian New Guinea*. London: Routledge.
Malthus, T. R. 1798. *An Essay on the Principle of Population*. Republished in: Malthus, T. R. 1970. *An Essay on the Principle of Population and a Summary View of the Principle of Population*. Edited by A. Flew. Harmondsworth: Penguin Books, pp. 61–217.
Marushiakova, Elena and Vesselin Popov (eds.). 2021. *Roma Voices in History: A Sourcebook*. Brill.
Meadows, Donella, Dennis L. Meadows, Jurgen Randers and William W. Behrens III. 1972. *Subtitled 'A Report for the Club of Rome's Project on the Predicament of Mankind'*. New York: Universe Books.
Mehta, Lyla. 2005. *Politics and Poetics of Water: Naturalising Scarcity in Western India*. Orient Blackswan.
Mehta, L. (ed.). 2010. *The Limits to Scarcity: Contesting the Politics of Allocation*. London: Routledge, pp. 31–48.
Montañés Jiménez, A. and D. Gómez Ávila. 2024. Moral Panic, Spanish Roma and Political Contestation During the COVID-19 Health Crisis. In Simone Maddanu and Emanuele Toscano (eds.) *Inequality, Youth, Democracy and the Pandemic*. London: Routledge.
Newman, Dwight. 2022. *Research Handbook on the International Law of Indigenous Rights*. Research Handbooks in International Law Series. EE Publishing.
Orgad, L. and R. Koopmans (eds.). 2020. *Majorities, Minorities, and the Future of Nationhood*. Cambridge: Cambridge University Press.
Pipyrou, Stavroula. 2020. Displaced Children, Silence, and the Violence of Humanitarianism in Cold War Italy. *Anthropological Quarterly* 93 (3): 429–459.
Pipyrou, Stavroula and Antonio Sorge. 2021. Emergent Axioms of Violence: Toward an Anthropology of Post-Liberal Modernity. *Anthropological Forum* 31 (3): 225–240.
Ricardo, David. 1817. *On the Principles of Political Economy and Taxation*. London: John Murray.
Richter, Brian. 2014. *Chasing Water: A Guide for Moving from Scarcity to Sustainability*. Island Press.

Robbins, L. 1932. *An Essay on the Nature and Significance of Economic Science.* London: Palgrave Macmillan.
Ross, A. 1996. The Lonely Hour of Scarcity. *Capitalism, Nature, Socialism* 7 (3): 3–26.
Santos Pereira, Luis, Ian Cordery and Iacovos Iacovides. 2009. *Coping with Water Scarcity: Addressing the Challenges.* Springer.
Schwartz, R. 1997. *The Curse of Cain: The Violent Legacy of Monotheism.* University of Chicago Press.
Scoones, Ian, Rebecca Smalley, Ruth Hall and Dzodzi Tsikata. 2014. *Narratives of Scarcity: Understanding the 'Global Resource Grab'.* Working Paper 076. Future Agricultures, PAAS.
Shafir, Eldar and Sendhil Mullainathan. 2013. *Scarcity: Why Having too Little Means so Much.* Times Books.
Shahabuddin, M. 2021. *Minorities and the Making of Postcolonial States in International Law.* Cambridge Studies in International and Comparative Law. Cambridge: Cambridge University Press, p. I.
Sen, Amartya. 1981. *Poverty and Famines: An Essay on Entitlement and Deprivation.* Oxford: Clarendon Press, Oxford University Press.
Topidi, Kiriaki and Eugenia Relaño Pastor (eds.). (2024). *Minority Rights and Social Change: Norms, Actors and Strategies.* Routledge Advances in Minority Studies. London: Routledge.
Townsend, Cathryn, Athena Aktipis and Lee Cronk. 2021. Does Scarcity Lead to Selfishness? *Anthropology News*, 23 June.
United Nations. n.d. *Minorities.* https://www.un.org/en/fight-racism/vulnerable-groups/minorities.
United Nations and Equal Rights Trust. 2023. *Protecting Minority Rights: A Practical Guide to Developing Comprehensive Anti-Discrimination Legislation.* New York and Geneva: Office of the United Nations High Commissioner for Human Rights (OHCHR), and the Equal Rights Trust.
Weszkalnys, Gisa. 2015. Geology, Potentiality, Speculation: On the Indeterminacy of 'First Oil'. *Cultural Anthropology* 30 (4): 611–639.
Wilk, Richard. 2019. *Rethinking the Relationships Between Scarcity, Poverty and Hunger: An Anthropological Perspective. Scarcity in the Modern World History, Politics, Society and Sustainability, 1800–2075.* London: Bloomsbury Academic, pp. 47–61.
Wutich, Amber and Alexandra Brewis. 2014. Food, Water, and Scarcity: Toward a Broader Anthropology of Resource Insecurity. *Current Anthropology* 55 (4): 444–468.
Xenos, Nicholas. 1989. *Scarcity and Modernity.* Routledge.

1 Unlearning scarcity within ethno-cultural minority groups

Between perceptions and reality

Kyriaki Topidi

Introduction: scarcity as a multidimensional concept for minority groups

From a minority studies perspective, our understanding of the concept of scarcity is far from being epistemologically uniform. Scarcity is commonly framed as the outcome of competition over resources among groups, likely to exacerbate inter-group tension, distrust and create discriminatory impact between them. *Perceived* scarcity refers to the use of artificially created conditions leading to the deprivation of goods and can also be at the root of hostility towards minority groups for similar reasons (Bianchi et al., 2018). For the purpose of introducing the concept within the frame of majority-minority relations, its consideration as both a material physical reality as well as an element of discourse are necessary to reveal its impact on minority groups.[1] The linkage between scarcity and minority groups becomes particularly evident in the use of the perception of scarcity as a means of oppression and exploitation of groups in predominantly colonial terms. The most characteristic illustration of this trend remains the attempts to cease through investments the productive capacity of segments of population and lands in the Global South to meet the consumption demands of the Global North (Dawson et al., 2018, at p. 2).

As a concept, material forms of scarcity carry in addition an inherent, internal 'duality': they can refer both to situations where resources are insufficient to cover everybody's needs but also to cases where resources are simply insufficient per se, as the object of scarcity may be indivisible (Häyry, 2022, at p. 48). A characteristic recent example of the latter kind draws from the recent experiences of the COVID-19 pandemic, where people have been exposed to shortages in the enforcement of their rights to health, liberty, culture and equality, highlighting the clash between the realm of individual freedoms with that of collective care ethics premised on group membership.

1 On the conceptual varieties of the notion see M. Dawson et al., 'Introduction: Resource scarcity between conflict and cooperation', in M. Dawson et al. (eds.) *Global Resource Scarcity: Catalyst for Conflict or Cooperation?* Abingdon: Earthscan (Routledge), 2018, 1–18.

DOI: 10.4324/9781032661780-2

To be clear, regardless of the type of scarcity (real vs. perceived, material vs. based on discourse), its impact on individuals as well as on groups is both material and immaterial. Illustrating the former type, according to the World Bank, 10.7 per cent of the world's population lives on less than 1.90 US dollars per day (*scarcity as poverty*). As importantly, scarcity of the latter kind elicits important psychological consequences (*scarcity as impairment*) that may 'hijack the cognitive system, triggering a focus on the urgent demands but also inducing a neglect of other information' (Zhao and Tomm, 2018). Such myopic decision-making can create a vicious cycle whereby by virtue of the neglect of useful information, victims of scarcity fail to save resources alleviating their condition due to diminished cognitive performance (Zhao and Tomm, 2018, at p. 6). Taken together, the types of scarcity lead to social stigmatization due to the (unjustified) linkage of poverty as the outcome of incompetence (Zhao and Tomm, 2018, at p. 13). This kind of 'causality' creates in turn self-fulfilling prospects of poverty as the justification of low/impaired cognitive performance through stereotypization of specific minority groups and their alleged lack of abilities.

In a more historical perspective, scarcity has also been instrumentalized to justify the unequal distribution of resources between dominant and non-dominant groups. Critical race theory (CRT)[2] is one prominent theoretical framework that aims to combat scarcity-based ways of understanding our world.[3] Conceiving race as a social construct designed to uphold stratification and hierarchization of groups, CRT asks, among others, the pertinent question for majority-minority group relations on the extent to which scarcity has become in essence a socialization process against marginalized (minority) identities permeating a variety of social structures (e.g. economics, labour market, education). A useful example in this respect from across the Atlantic, where the scarcity 'mentality' has been actively operationalized, concerns Asian Americans. Increasingly positioned as 'model' citizens against Black Americans, a minority myth is constructed that sustains a narrative of scarcity endangering any solidarity patterns against oppression, while obscuring the root causes of inequalities in our societies.

Seen in this light, in governance terms, the outcome of the uses and practices of scarcity is commonly connected to hidden economic agendas and projects of deprivation to maintain existing inequalities, with conflicts and violence being an integral part of these strategies. The underlying consideration in these attempts is to seek triggers that intensify tensions between groups

2 CRT is a framework developed in the 1970s and 1980s in the United States that 'argues, as a starting point, that the axis of American social life is fundamentally constructed in race' (*Encyclopedia of Diversity and Social Justice*). It also challenges openly the ability of law and law enforcement authorities to overcome white supremacy, while using colour-blind and post-racial approaches to do so.

3 For a European transposition of the theory, see for example Steve Rose, 'A deadly ideology: How the "great replacement theory" went mainstream', *The Guardian*, 9 June 2022.

that are culturally or ethnically distinguishable. The fundamental (though questionable) premise of such strategies of scarcity lies in the assumption that gains of one group will automatically entail the losses of others. As a governance concept, scarcity is therefore precisely constructed on the premise that individuals as well as groups coexist within a competitive environment, where resource allocation on egalitarian terms is de facto unattainable.

Given the multiple facets of scarcity analysis that concern minority groups, this chapter will focus on the concept from the perspective of diversity governance. The chapter will attempt to consider, first, the ways in which scarcity can disguise scenarios of abundance that are devised to create scenarios of 'constructed scarcity'. Second, it will briefly explore the main implications of perceived scarcity for minority groups through social exclusion and stereotypization to, then, third, unpack scarcity as a 'technology' of governing against minority groups. Additionally, a short case study on the conflict in the Niger Delta region of Nigeria involving the Ogoni and other indigenous peoples shall serve to illustrate some of the theoretical points raised throughout the chapter. Finally, some concluding remarks will reflect on governance approaches that could contribute to reverse scarcity, with particular emphasis on polycentric design frameworks.

Scarcity and abundance through a minority group lens

The conceptualization of scarcity is characterized by a number of common trends in the existing scholarly literature: first, it is qualified as resource related as already mentioned and connected to poverty, migration and social cleavages, all potentially conducive to conflict scenarios (Homer-Dixon, 1999). Typically, for example, within an environmental context, scarcity is linked to limited access to essential common goods (e.g. food/water) triggering competition among ethnic, religious and regional identity groups (De Juan and Hanze, 2021). Second, it is neatly distinguished from abundance in mutually exclusive terms (Bhavani, 2009). Abundance of resources, however, can still lead to scarcity through patterns of exploitation.[4] The interconnection between abundance and scarcity[5] is well illustrated in the case of the delta region of the Niger, discussed later in this contribution.

According to Homer-Dixon (1999), scarcity can intensify social segmentation by affecting social groups often across ethno-cultural lines. Still, exposure and vulnerability to scarcity affects groups in differentiated patterns and with asymmetric impact (De Juan and Hanze, 2021, at p. 155). The variations can be related to ethnic settlement patterns, pre-existing inequalities or livelihood

4 Bhavani (2009, at p. 71) cites the examples of Myanmar, Cambodia and Liberia in this respect along with the Chinese example where in areas of abundant resources, residents can have lower per capita incomes when compared to resource-poor residents.

5 See also Gutiérrez Garza, Chapter 2 in this volume.

strategies (von Uexkull, 2016). At the same time, however, scarcity can also be conducive to higher degrees of inter-group cohesion: as groups become confronted with existential threats, patterns of solidarity and cooperation emerge among their members (De Juan and Hanze, 2021, at p. 155).

In classical liberal terms, a passive relationship between rights and access to (limited) resources is tightly linked to the old question as to whether equality and productivity are compatible (Schofield et al., 2002, at p. 291).[6] The accumulation of capital out of fear of scarcity (and starvation) for a large segment of the labour force has been put forward historically as the basis for the maximisation of productivity, precisely to illustrate the connection between equality and productivity (Macpherson, 1973, at p. 17).

For marginalized or vulnerable minority groups, cultural and/or historic inequalities can also contribute towards the creation of conditions of scarcity in acute terms, particularly felt by segments within these groups such as women (e.g., through limitations of access to resources, leading to limitations in their livelihood activities and ultimately bringing about scarcity of resources towards subsistence). The practice of 'resource grabbing' is, for instance, a common feature of socially constructed scarcity and consists of powerful actors taking control of resources at the expense of local communities, characteristically eliminating their rights to land/water, often when access to resources in question plays an integral role in their informal and/or customary systems of governance. The political and economic dimensions of scarcity in such scenarios are hard to ignore and justify the basic classification of scarcity situations between those that are the product of biophysical shortages (akin to 'experienced scarcity') and those that result from socio-political processes that serve primarily the interests of actors with power (akin to 'constructed scarcity') (Mehta, 2018, at p. 32).[7]

Within a colonial context, minority groups that did not conform to the liberal theory of property acquisition became the primary targets of scarcity theories.[8] These groups had traditionally maintained a cultural and socio-economic lifestyle linked to nature and the environment and were categorized as economically unproductive (Appiagyei-Atua, at p. 74). At the same time, resources that were under the control of such groups, deemed unproductive, were forcibly removed from them, creating conditions of de facto scarcity. The main instruments used were the implementation of 'indirect rule' policies, often engaging the help among the more 'civilized' segments within these indigenous groups, the practice of settler colonialism, the creation of labour reserves in areas that were not profitable from the point of view of natural resources, and even the partitioning of ethnic groups when drawing colonial borders.[9] As

6 See J. Bentham in the volume arguing that the concepts are not compatible.

7 This typology is similar to the already mentioned distinction between material and perceived scarcity.

8 See Roy, Chapter 8 in this volume.

9 Appiagyei-Atua (2012, at pp. 75–76), stressing the limitations of access to resources for indigenous groups that considered them part of their cultural heritage.

a result, scarcity of resources (and access to political power), as an outcome of these processes, has later on became the main cause of civil wars in continents such as Africa, hidden behind the ethnicity factor.

Scarcity as social exclusion and stereotypization of minority groups

Scarcity, according to Mehta, is not a neutral condition, especially when socially generated (Mehta, 2018, at p. 21). To determine whether indeed scarcity is only perceived and essentially the product of a political strategy of domination, the questions that must be addressed concern the general conditions for access to goods, the critical appraisal of the presence of any entitlements to resources by specific groups and as importantly the modalities for resource allocation.

Looking at scarcity from the perspective of discriminatory access to resources is a valid trajectory for minority groups. In this case, both in the Global North and the Global South, scarcity becomes the outcome of low levels of socio-economic participation and can be largely the product of social hierarchies. In addition, the distribution and control of goods must be assessed and differentiated further according to gender, race, occupation, caste or culture/religion. Echoing Sen's work (Sen, 1993) and according to his entitlements theory, lack of access to goods is not synonymous with physical scarcity of the good per se. Rather, scarcity is rather contingent on the economic cost of good, on the necessary infrastructure to access it or can be simply due to social exclusion, leading as a result to 'entitlement failures'.

But should all goods be considered 'economic' goods?[10] Should access to these goods only depend on one's ability to pay? Amartya Sen's work on hunger serves as a useful illustration of such debates: in his study on starvation and famines of the early 1980s he made a fundamental distinction, when examining hunger, between scarcity as a result of lacking access to food due to socio-political conditions, as opposed to those situations where food was insufficient. He concluded that the former situation prevailed at the time.

The link between scarcity and socio-economic exclusion is not, however, always clearly spelt out: social exclusion, according to Sen, can 'substantially help in the causal as well as constitutive analyses of poverty and deprivation (Sen, 2000, at p. 47). Operationalizing social exclusion in empirical, quantifiable terms can allow the examination of how/why (justification and dynamics) individuals and groups are placed at the margins of societies (Good Gingrich and Lightman, 2015, at p. 99) measuring structural material deprivation in conjunction with case-based, individual subjective experiences.

In this respect, the UN 2030 Agenda includes the principle that every person should benefit from prosperity and enjoy minimum standards of well-being (UN, 2015). The connection between social exclusion and scarcity

10 Mehta (2018) considers water in this respect, noting how it shifted from a good and public service to a commodity adjusted to economic principles.

here lies in the fact that the former is characterized by material deprivation and lack of agency and control over important decisions. This dual condition is encountered often among minority groups on the basis of ethnicity, religion, socio-economic status or gender identity (UN, 2016, at pp. 18, 20). Characteristics related to identity and/or group belonging, in fact, tend to increase the risk of social exclusion: caste, ethnicity, religion and shared values or way of life are usual such characteristics.

It should be, nevertheless, clarified that while poverty should be seen as an outcome of scarcity, social exclusion can be qualified as both an outcome and a process leading to scarcity (UN, 2016, at p. 20). In the context of social exclusion, scarcity can also become multidimensional and overlapping: while largely context dependent, social exclusion becomes the result of the presence of discrimination, lack of personal safety or of participation in socio-economic and political life. The geographies of deprivation, furthermore, are considered to function largely on the preselected criteria already mentioned increasing the risk of exclusion and leading to scarcity (UN, 2016, at p. 24). Access to opportunities to enjoy public goods (e.g. education, health, infrastructures), access to employment and income and finally access to political/cultural participation constitute common indicators conducive to a study of one's 'scarcity positionality', as mirrored in and through exclusion (UN, 2016, at p. 26). In cases of limited political participation, more specifically, scarcity becomes visible through the limited influence in representation and decision-making on matters related to resource allocation.

Another most impactful implication of scarcity regarding inter-group relations concerns the link between scarcity and stereotyping processes. Stereotypization processes against ethno-racial minority groups grow in response to scarcity, when majority groups develop stereotypical perceptions of minority groups in order to protect their dominant status (e.g. characterizing minority group members as lazy or uneducated) (Berkebile-Weinberg et al., 2022, at p. 9). Moreover, the perception of threat by the majority of minorities can also be linked to efforts and motives to control and oppress the latter (Berkebile-Weinberg et al., 2022, at p. 10). Reactions of this kind are rooted in perceived resource competition, as mentioned, and ultimately have been found to strengthen racial disparities in society.[11] Thus, resource competition in the relevant literature is depicted as fostering distrust and discriminatory treatment between groups, while perceived scarcity can predict negative attitudes towards minority groups (Bianchi et al., 2018; Brewer et al. 1978; Stephen et al., 1999).

In sum, to some degree, the effect of scarcity on stereotyping is to 'mediate' the transition towards the 'justification' of discrimination against minority

11 Berkebile-Weinberg et al. (2022, at p. 10) explaining the connection of this finding with social dominance theory, which is founded on the aim of maintaining or establishing group dominance when hierarchy becomes threatened.

group members, regardless of whether scarcity is real or perceived. Furthermore, stereotypization is used to explain why, in the eyes of the dominant group(s), minority groups and their members are not deserving of resources (Berkebile-Weinberg et al., 2022, at p. 2).

Scarcity as a technology of governing

Scarcity, arguably, very often represents a socially constructed approach to govern the present socio-economic order. Unlike natural and neutral phenomena, scarcity can be connected to prevailing social hierarchies[12] and as such operate as a 'regulatory device' towards various groups. When approaching scarcity from a governance perspective, it is commonly connected to (neo-)liberalism in relation to their common approaches towards the organization of human life and the environment (Hellberg, 2020, at pp. 187–188).

The historical roots of scarcity as an instrument in the 'art of government' are described by Foucault in his work *Security, Territory, Population*. He explains how scarcity was used in the transition towards a free economy in the seventeenth and eighteenth centuries: from an outcome to be avoided through price control, storage and exports, it became tied to a system that promoted 'the free circulation of the grain', emphasizing the emergence of populations as both political subjects and objects of biopolitical regulation. Malthus, in his *Essay on the Principle of Population* (1798), went further by classifying populations according to their relationship to futurity and their ability to attain material progression (Tellmann, 2013, at p. 135). Such hierarchization is difficult to separate from colonial binary imaginaries of the 'savage' and the 'civilized' life. Digging deeper, Tellmann in his analysis of Malthus' work connects the population thesis with a fear that underdeveloped groups will 'eat up the future for all',[13] placing emphasis on conditions of resource scarcity. Overall, Malthus' work has steered the debate on and around scarcity in a classical economic liberalist sense by arguing, among other points, that population growth can only be compatible with the available means of subsistence 'by the periodical or constant action of misery or vice' (Malthus, 1789, at p. 144). Scarcity thus is part of natural law based on the inevitability of human needs and desires which are deemed socially acceptable at a given point in time.

More contemporary conceptualizations of scarcity have added to Malthus' 'scarcity postulate' as described above, an additional layer to the term as a permanent feature of socio-economic systems within societies that live

12 On the 'manufacturing of scarcities', see J. R. Johnston, 'The political ecology of water: An introduction', *Capitalism, Nature, Socialism*, 14(3), 73–90 (2003); J. Linton, *What Is Water? The History of Modern Abstraction*. Vancouver: ABS Press, 2010, p. 68; L. Mehta, 'The manufacture of popular perceptions of water scarcity: Dams and water-related narratives in Gujarat, India', *World Development*, 29(12), 2025–2041 (2001); L. Mehta (ed.), *The Limits of Scarcity*. London and Washington, DC: Earthscan, 2010.

13 Tellmann (2013, at p. 151).

in perpetual scarcity (Xenos, 1987, 2010). Moving beyond a situation where available resources lack the demand for them, scarcity has been gradually transformed to a 'regulatory device' that is premised on the hierarchization of groups and their needs. In simpler terms, the concept has been used to create an artificial sense of limitation based on uncertainty and apprehension while relying on the key concepts of privilege and deprivation. Such a differentiated relationship to resource use for different categories of population is not sustainable insofar as it connects entitlement and access to resources with socio-economic criteria (e.g., the ability to pay for them).

In response to this last development, Mehta developed the distinction between scarcity as lived experience as opposed to constructed scarcity (Mehta, 2010, at p. 23; 2001). The former resonates an understanding of the term that describes shortage of resources while the latter, of particular relevance for the present analysis, looks at scarcity as an obstacle to the more equitable distribution of goods. Modern scarcity, based on the conflation between need and desire, stands in an almost paradoxical relationship with abundance, as two sides of the same coin, where continuously increasing desires for resources create perpetual perceptions of scarcity (Dawson et al., 2018, at p. 4).

Ideological responses to this approach have been of three kinds, according to Homer-Dixon (Homer-Dixon, 1999): the first response is based on the idea that having finite resources will in deterministic terms lead to poverty, once the resources have been exhausted. The second, more optimistic, response is based on the idea that markets and institutions should work towards the goals of conservation, substitution and investment in order to prevent scarcity. The third response, useful for the understanding of the nexus between scarcity and minority groups, claims that at the basis and source of scarcity lies the unequal distribution of resources, and not the other way round. In this light, scarcity, apart from a material consideration, can be also understood as a socially constructed concept, describing the tendency of powerful groups to present certain resources as scarce, in order to maintain their own position through solutions to the scarcity problem that primarily serve them.

From the perspective of minority groups, and without neglecting the materiality of resource availability, questions concerning the source/justification for scarcity and the actors that are most affected both positively but also negatively through conditions of scarcity may guide the assessment as to whether one is looking at *lived* as opposed to *constructed* situations of scarcity. Discursive framings of resources that maintain fragmentation of groups are not uncommonly used to justify their unequal distribution. Often, however, scarcity is not constructed on the basis of racial/ethnic criteria but rather on the relationship of the group(s) to the use of the resource in question, across socio-economic criteria (Hellberg, 2020, at pp. 197, 199).[14] A closer look at

14 In this particular case, water scarcity in South Africa is used to increase the value of water while increasing at the same time competition between its users.

the situation in the delta region of the Niger river in Nigeria illustrates aptly these points.

The delta region of the Niger as an example of constructed scarcity

> What we wanted—as subsistence farmers and fishermen—all we wanted was to continue to fish, to continue to farm. We don't want our means of livelihood to be taken away from us. We are not employees of Shell. Very few of our people are employed by the government. So, if we don't farm and we don't fish, then we die of hunger.
>
> (Minority Rights Group, 2019)

The modern state of Nigeria originated with British colonialization in the nineteenth century and gained full independence from the United Kingdom in 1960. Today, Nigeria is divided along religious lines: Muslims dominate the north, whereas Christians dominate the South. Despite being a secular state, the rapid insurgency of extremist religious groups such as Boko Haram or Daru Islam in northern Nigeria intending to enforce Sharia as a legal system has led to the persecution and displacement of communities and citizens, particularly religious and sexual minorities. Also, ethnic groups and minorities here are particularly vulnerable to post-colonial economic exploitation and environmental degradation ensuing from unsustainable mineral and oil extraction by British and other multinational companies.

In 1956, oil was discovered in commercial quantities in Bayelsa State (Oloibiri). It has constituted a considerable resource ever since, bringing Nigeria to the top of the list of oil-producing African states.[15] At the same time, the Niger Delta region is home for more than 20 ethnic and linguistic minority groups (Omeje, 2006, at pp. 44–45). And yet, the region in question offers a striking example of a context where unprecedented wealth in terms of resources coexists with extreme poverty and conflict between rival ethnic groups, the government and organs within the government itself. With vast oil reserves, this region has been devastated over the years from oil spills, soil and water pollution, gas fires and global warming (Bhavani, 2009, at p. 73). The delta's inhabitants have been confronted with daily survival struggles while private companies and subsequent Nigerian dictators and rulers have accumulated extreme wealth. In addition, resource-driven conflict along with environmental destruction have left many of these communities in the areas where the oil is produced marginalized and in perpetual infrastructural deficit.

15 According to data from the Organization of the Petroleum Exporting Countries (OPEC), Nigeria produces oil representing 95 per cent of its export earnings and 70 per cent of government revenue (cf. Igwe, 2020).

During the 1990s the Nigerian government, joined by the British/Dutch company Shell and other multinational oil companies, adopted a repressive approach related to the disruption of the work of the company by minority groups. The groups in question were protesting fuel shortages and attempted to take out fuel from leaking pipes. The situation escalated causing the death of thousands of people through explosions, only to deteriorate further by extrajudicial executions and the mobilization of military task force personnel to control the revolts (Human Rights Watch, 2000).

Shell claimed the loss of crude oil barrels as theft, and the Nigerian government attempted in vain to control the situation. The solution found was to agree to make payments as compensation to local communities via traditional leadership positions, fuelling further conflict under the weight of scarcity as well as the emergence of a thriving black market trade in stolen crude oil (Minority Rights Group, 2006). Therefore, despite the immense oil wealth in the region, ethnic groups like the Ogoni, along with 40 other ethnic groups, continued to live in extreme poverty. The eruption of a pro-violence stance against the multinational corporations exploiting the resource led to full-blown militancy, particularly between 2007 and 2009.

Indicatively, in 2009, Shell settled a case brought by the Ogoni community (*Kiobel v. Royal Dutch Petroleum Co.*) for alleged complicity in extrajudicial murders of Ogoni community members in 1995; Shell denied complicity. The amount of the settlement rose to US$ 15.5 million (Horsfield, 2012). In terms of environmental scarcity, however, according to the 2011 UN Environment Programme the effects of the oil pollution required a quarter of a century of efforts to reverse them, given that over 60 per cent of the local population relied on the environment for its livelihood (Horsfield, 2012). Environmental pollution of the scale described in that region had in fact destroyed the means of survival for the minority communities in question for the coming years. In 2014, Shell was further found responsible under English law for three devastating oil spills, awarding the affected communities US$ 55 million in compensation and ordering the clean-up of the environment along with remediation and restoration measures. The compensation was paid in 2015, but the environmental cleaning did not occur. In 2017 and again in 2018, Shell returned to court to reverse the decision concerning the clean-up with no success. By virtue of a Nigerian government decree, as of 1 March 2019 Shell, along with other companies, could resume oil exploration in Ogoniland (Minority Rights Group, 2019).

The Niger Delta conflict has been analyzed as 'a mixture of greed and grievance', opposing the Nigerian government and the oil companies with militants and local communities.[16] A Presidential Amnesty Programme (PAP) in 2009 offered monthly stipends and training to ex-militants in exchange of the

16 Igwe (2020) notes that the production of crude oil in Nigeria in 2009 diminished from 2.2 million barrels per day to 700,000 as a result of militancy.

surrender of their weapons, within a disarmament, demobilization and reintegration programme. Despite this initiative, daily crude oil loss to oil thieves in Nigeria continues to range between 250,000 and 400,000 barrels per day, with a number of Nigerian security agencies hired to protect oil infrastructure being complicit in this activity.[17]

Resource-related scarcity and abundance have consequently become interwoven, creating multiple levels of conflicts between local communities and the government but also within and between the minority communities themselves. The scarcity framework has been thus successfully operationalized and maintained due to the failure of the Nigerian government to compel oil multinationals to engage in environmental protection, also in light of the damage caused exposing the local communities to multidimensional poverty and lack of access to basic resources such as water. At the same time, competition for the limited available resources among traditional community leaders has led to vandalism and theft.

Retrospectively, the domination of ethnic majority elites in the Nigerian political landscape relies on a broader scarcity logic that is connected to a predisposition against ethnic minorities, including those in the Niger Delta region. The dominant economic elites in the country operate with the aim 'to maintain a fundamentally compromised and dysfunctional state conducive to high-stakes accumulation', dividing the population between 'aggrieved acquisitors', struggling for day-to-day survival and 'oppressive amassers' that acquire resources creating conditions of scarcity of the other category of stakeholders (Omeje, 2006, at p. 47). In this sense, scarcity is used as a technology of governing that systematically excludes minority groups from a fairer distribution of resources and in addition impacts their ability to maintain their traditional forms of livelihood by damaging the environment.

Concluding remarks: reversing scarcity through polycentric designs for governance

The literature focusing on resource abundance and conflicts has identified in the 2000s how conflicts tend to arise due to control of a resource of one group at the expense of others (Le Billon, 2008). At best, however, scarcity, even when only of a perceived kind, operates as a contributing factor to the creation and escalation of such conflicts, not as their main justification (Goldstone, 2001). In other words, a study on scarcity without the consideration of the unequal growth experienced by ethno-cultural minority groups or its social and cultural components, including history and perceptions (Timura, 2001), can evoke only a partial picture of the link between structural inequalities and access to resources.

17 Igwe (2020), citing a 2019 Report of the Civil Society Legislative Advocacy Centre.

One of the possibilities studied within governance that could reverse scarcity patterns against minorities relies on polycentric design. Polycentric thinking is based on the acknowledgment that it is only through the involvement of a multitude of actors (e.g., states, civil societies, social movements) that governance arrangements are likely to reach effective solutions towards the fairer redistribution of goods. This is mainly because polycentric governance considers and reflects on complexity (Voss and Schroth, 2018). Polycentric governance arrangements are precisely based on the understanding that a variety of independent actors come together and decide to coordinate through a general system of rules.[18] Escaping more classic forms of governance that distinguish between centralized and decentralized approaches, polycentric approaches to resource governance imply more efficient governance schemes as decision-making and implementation happen at the level of users, where conflicts arise (Amaruzaman et al., 2022).

Tested in research exploring climate change and ecological system, polycentric governance can be useful when applied in contexts of asymmetric power relations, similar to those prevailing in (perceived) scarcity conditions. In its theoretical development in this particular field, it has been characterized by decentralization, local embedding and responsiveness to specific contexts. The co-production of norms and interests among resource users reflects contextualization. In relation to scarcity, this particular governance approach posits an understanding of poverty of minorities as the result of the lack of space given to them to reverse their situation. This space would be dedicated to the consideration of the groups' interacting interests and considerations outside bipolar oppositions (e.g. 'civilised' vs. 'uncivilised'). As importantly, it encourages capacity building of local actors, who are often members of minority groups, in order to become involved in decision-making concerning resource management. By supporting and balancing the needs for goods with the conservation of essential resources, perceived forms scarcity can be eliminated. To 'unlearn' scarcity, therefore, as an inevitable governance path, resource management necessitates transparency both from governments and the private entities involved in the management of public goods. Social exclusion and government non-responsiveness flourish when local communities are cut from abundant resources or when resources are distributed along ethnic lines.[19]

As some resources become increasingly socially constructed around perceptions of scarcity, non-excludability (i.e. the open access to areas/resources for all) becomes a more pressing claim, especially in environmental governance terms. This is because global sustainability is framed more and more along the lines of interdependence as local claims, usages and property structures gain in

18 Appiagyei-Atua (2012, at p. 85), citing the Canadian case of *Pushpanathan v Canada* (1998) 1 SCR 982, at para. 36 as an illustration of the approach.

19 Bhavani (2009, at p. 75) cites the example of Kenya in this respect, where ethnic voting has been found to be a response to competition for land rights.

visibility. National interests and security issues often thus disguise hierarchies based on disadvantage.

In addition, scarcity is premised on an antagonistic understanding of the liberal conception of human rights as instruments of exclusion of those that are deemed undesirable, as opposed to the social and redistributive aims of justice. This implication can only be reversed through plural governance schemes. Political, cultural and economic exclusion in practice reinforce scarcity by amplifying the patterns of human rights violations, when invalidating the claims of those whose identities deviate from majorities and/or the mainstream. While there are no conclusive responses available on the way(s) that scarcity affects group membership within and between minority groups, it is becoming increasingly clear that high levels of inequality formulated through scarcity risk triggering and perpetuating inter-group competition and conflict.[20]

As the short discussion on the Niger Delta region has shown, scarcity can ultimately become the consequence of a so-called resource curse, where a central actor (in this case the Nigerian government) enables conflict through a 'rentier state model' behaviour that aims to maximize natural resource exploitation (here, oil) as a source of revenue. How the lines of exclusion and conflict are drawn is not always clear-cut. In situations like this one, the lines between abundance and scarcity can become essentially blurred, illustrating the need for fresh approaches on the management of resources especially when linked to cultural difference and social justice aims.

References

Amaruzaman, S. et al. (2022) 'Polycentric environmental governance to achieving SDG16: Evidence from Southeast Asia and Eastern Africa', *Forests*, 13(1), 68, https://doi.org/10.3390/f13010068.

Appiagyei-Atua, K. (2012) 'Minority rights, democracy and development: The African experience', *African Human Rights Law Journal*, 69–88.

Berkebile-Weinberg, M. M. et al. (2022) 'Economic scarcity increases racial stereotyping in beliefs and face representation', *Journal of Experimental Social Psychology*, 102, 104354.

Bhavani, R. (2009) 'Scarcity, abundance and conflict: A complex new world', *The Whitehead Journal of Diplomacy and International Relations*, 65–80.

Bianchi, E. et al. (2018) 'Re-examining the link between economic downturns and racial antipathy: Evidence that prejudice against blacks rises during recessions', *Psychological Science*, 29(10), 1584–1597.

Brewer, M. B. et al. (1978) 'Ingroup bias as a function of task characteristics', *European Journal of Social Psychology*, 8(3), 393–400.

Dawson, M. et al. (2018) 'Introduction: Resource scarcity between conflict and cooperation', in M. Dawson et al. (eds.) *Global Resource Scarcity: Catalyst for Conflict or Cooperation?* Abingdon: Earthscan, Routledge, 1–18.

20 De Juan and Hanze (2021, at p. 152) in the field of environmental scarcity and climate change.

De Juan, A. and Hanze, N. (2021) 'Climate and cohesion: The effects of droughts on intra-ethnic and inter-ethnic trust', *Journal of Peace Research*, 58(1), 151–167.
Goldstone, J. A. (2001) 'Demography, environment and scarcity', in P. Diehl and N.P. Gleditsch (eds.) *Environmental Conflict*. Boulder: Westview, 84–108.
Good Gingrich, L. and Lightman, N. (2015) 'The empirical measurement of a theoretical concept: Tracing social exclusion among racial minority and migrant groups in Canada', *Social Inclusion*, 3(4), 98–111.
Häyry, M. (2022) 'Scarcity, justice, and health crisis leadership', *Philosophies* 7(3), 48, https://doi.org/10.3390/philosophies7030048.
Hellberg, S. (2020) 'Scarcity as a means of governing: Challenging neoliberal hydromentality in the context of the South African drought', *Nature and Space*, 3(1), 186–206.
Homer-Dixon, T. (1999) *Environment, Scarcity and Violence*. Princeton, NJ: Princeton University Press.
Horsfield, N. (2012) 'Corporate irresponsibility in the Niger Delta, minority rights group', 27 February, https://minorityrights.org/2012/02/27/corporate-irresponsibility-in-the-niger-delta/ [last accessed 10.11.2022].
Human Rights Watch (2000) 'Update on violations of human rights in the Niger Delta', https://www.hrw.org/news/2000/12/14/update-human-rights-violations-niger-delta [last accessed 09.11.2022].
Igwe, U. (2020) 'A political economy perspective on oil and conflict in Nigeria's Niger Delta', *LSA Blog*, 16 September, https://blogs.lse.ac.uk/africaatlse/2020/09/16/political-economy-perspective-oil-conflict-security-nigeria-niger-delta/ [last accessed 23.11.2022].
Johnston, B. R. (2003) 'The political ecology of water: An introduction', *Capitalism, Nature, Socialism*, 14(3), 73–90.
Le Billon, P. (2008) 'Diamond wars? Conflict diamonds and geographies of resource wars', *Annals of the Association of American Geographers*, 98(2), 345–372.
Linton, J. (2010) *What Is Water? The History of Modern Abstraction*. Vancouver: ABS Press.
Macpherson, C. B. (1973) 'Politics: Post-liberal democracy?' in R. Blackburn (ed.) *Ideology in Social Science*. New York: Vintage Books, 17–31.
Malthus. (1789) *An Essay on the Principles of Population as It Affects the Future Improvement of Society*. London: John Johnson.
Mehta, J. (2018) 'Taking the scare out of scarcity: The case of water', in M. Dawson et al. (eds.) *Global Resource Scarcity: Catalyst for Conflict or Cooperation?* Abingdon: Earthscan, Routledge, 21–38.
Mehta, L. (2001) 'The manufacture of popular perceptions of water scarcity: Dams and water-related narratives in Gujarat, India', *World Development*, 29(12), 2025–2041.
Mehta, L. (ed.) (2010) *The Limits of Scarcity*. London and Washington, DC: Earthscan.
Minority Rights Group (2006) 'More than a decade after the death of Ogoni activist Ken Sano-Wiwa Niger Delta's ethnic groups continue to pay the high cost of oil extraction', 10 November, https://minorityrights.org/2006/11/10/more-than-a-decade-after-the-death-of-ogoni-activist-ken-saro-wiwa-niger-deltas-ethnic-groups-continue-to-pay-the-high-cost-of-oil-extraction/ [last accessed 09.11.2022].
Minority Rights Group (2019) 'Interview of Lazarus Taman, It's Ogoniland today, but it could be your home tomorrow', 18 July, https://minorityrights.org/2019/07/18/ogoniland-today-your-home-tomorrow.
Omeje, K. (2006) 'Oil conflict and accumulation politics in Nigeria', ECSP Report 12, 44–49, https://www.wilsoncenter.org/publication/oil-conflict-and-accumulation-politics-nigeria [last accessed 23.11.2022].
Rose, S. (2022) 'A deadly ideology: How the "great replacement theory" went mainstream', *The Guardian*, 9 June, https://www.theguardian.com/world/2022/jun/08/a-deadly-ideology-how-the-great-replacement-theory-went-mainstream [last accessed 25.04.2024].

Schofield, P., Pease-Watkin, C. and Blamires, C. (eds.) (2002) *The Collected Works of Jeremy Bentham-Rights, Representation and Reform: Nonsense upon Stilts and Other Writings on the French Revolution*. Oxford: Oxford University Press.

Sen, A. (1993) 'Poor, relatively speaking', *Oxford Economic Papers*, 35(2), 153–169.

Sen, A. (2000) *Social Exclusion: Concept, Application and Scrutiny*. Manila: Asian Development Bank.

Stephen, W. G. et al. (1999) 'Prejudice towards immigrants', *Journal of Applied Social Psychology*, 29(11), 2221–2237.

Tellmann, U. (2013) 'Catastrophic populations and the fear of the future: Malthus and the genealogy of liberal economy', *Theory, Culture & Society*, 30(2), 135–155. https://doi.org/10.1177/0263276412455830 (Original work published 2013).

Timura, T. (2001) '"Environmental conflict" and the social life of environmental security discourse', *Anthropological Quarterly*, 74(3), 104–113.

United Nations (2015) '17 sustainable goals—the 2030 agenda for sustainable development', https://sdgs.un.org/goals [last accessed 25.04.2024].

United Nations (2016) *Leaving No One Behind: The Imperative of Inclusive Development*. New York: Department of Economic and Social Affairs, Report, https://www.un.org/en/desa/report-world-social-situation-2016.

Von Uexkull, N. et al. (2016) 'Civil conflict sensitivity to growing-season drought', *Proceedings of the National Academy of Sciences*, 113 (44), 12391–12396.

Voss, J.-P. and Schroth, F. (2018) 'Experimentation: The politics of innovation and learning in polycentric governance', in A. Jordan et al. (eds.) *Governing Climate Change: Polycentricity in Action?* Cambridge: Cambridge University Press, 97–228.

Xenos, N. (1987) 'Liberalism and the postulate of scarcity', *Political Theory*, 15(2), 225–243.

Xenos, N. (2010) 'Everybody's got the fever: Scarcity and US national energy policy', in L. Mehta (ed.) *The Limits of Scarcity: Contesting the Politics of Allocation*. New York: Earthscan, 31–48.

Zhao, J. and Tomm, B. (2018) 'Psychological responses to scarcity', *Oxford Research Encyclopedia of Psychology*, https://zhaolab.psych.ubc.ca/pdfs/Zhao_Tomm_2018.pdf [last accessed 09.11.2022].

2 Understanding scarcity in "the land of abundance"

Mexican migrants in Tulsa, Oklahoma (USA)

Ana P. Gutiérrez Garza

> I came here eight years ago. I came directly to Oklahoma, and I crossed through the desert but the first time we crossed the *migra* (migration officers) caught us and sent us back to Mexico. The second time we passed also through the desert, but it was really bad, really dangerous, they were snakes and they told us that the drug cartels were kidnapping people. Thank God nothing happened. Back in Mexico I was struggling a lot to sustain my children. I did not have money for diapers or food, and you know that in Mexico you have to pay for schoolbooks and uniforms. That's when I talked to my brother, who was already here and decided to come.

Carmen from Ciudad Juarez tells me while we sit on the sofa in her living room. Her home is extremely clean (chlorine scent) and nicely decorated with photos of the family and various children. While sharing with me her migration journey, she tells me that she has two more children, but they are not with her; they are in Mexico. She has not been able to bring them but makes sure to send remittances every week and save money to pay for coyotes (smugglers) to bring them at some point in the future. She feels remorse for having left them, but, as she explained, her life in Mexico was very difficult due to poverty and the experience of violence in the hands of her ex-husband. She did not have a choice but to migrate to the United States in order to make enough money to support her children and escape the abusive relationship.

The possibility to have a better future for Carmen and other migrants like her is provided by the promise of economic success that the "American Dream" offers to Mexican migrants who are willing to leave behind a life characterised by an overall precarity and scarce resources. The United States offers dreams of abundance and promises of success, promises of fair compensation for one's hard work, and access to material resources. However, the American Dream for undocumented migrants is filled with obstacles as it is based on a liberal and racial capitalist model that rests on claims of individual self-governance, meritocracy, and white supremacy. As soon as migrants face the legal liminality in which they must exist, which restricts the dreams of achieving upward social mobility and economic success, they find themselves adapting and learning how to access resources that might help them achieve their migration goals.

DOI: 10.4324/9781032661780-3

In this chapter, I consider the question of how Mexican migrants in Tulsa, Oklahoma, navigate and engage with different institutions/programs in order to access various resources that include legal aid, medical care, and education among others to advance their aspirations of socio-economic success. I am particularly interested in their experience with and perceptions of early education programs, particularly Educare, a pre-kindergarten (pre-K) program dedicated to ensuring readiness of children most at risk for school failure. For Mexicans in Tulsa, having access to these programs conveys the opportunity of having a proper education that would grant them social and economic mobility, but most of all, that will help them become American subjects. In examining these experiences, I want to show how aspirational paradigms and narratives of progress that emerge at a personal and community level coexist with perceptions of scarcity and abundance and how these become manifested throughout migrants' journeys. These perceptions are connected to migrants' past experiences of poverty, lack of opportunities, and an overall precarity back in Mexico. Migrants described in their life stories, narratives of scarcity, as reasons to migrate to the United States. Their journeys and expectations of the future illustrate the ways in which people think of migration as a life project that with hard work would provide abundance. In this regard, abundance is manifested in the access to economic and material resources, in abundance of opportunities for their children, which includes the possibility to access and accumulate educational, social, and cultural capital. These notions of abundance are an intrinsic part of the so-called American Dream, a life project that offers millions of migrants the possibility to break the poverty chain (as they call it, *romper la cadena*) in which they were born, a cycle that is structured and sustained not only along class but racial lines in Mexico (Solís, Avitia y Güémez, 2020). The American Dream is also, as my interlocutors explained, shaped by the possibility to speak English, have a car, get good education for their children, and being able to consume goods that they could not access back in Mexico (Mahler, 1995; Menjívar, 2000, 2006). It entails the realisation of economic dreams and aspirations in which migrants would not have to deal with scarcity, but instead have access to a life in which the fruits of their hard labour can be materialised in resources for them and their children. Felipa from Zacatecas tells me:

> It is very different for my children in Mexico and for my children here. Here my girls can learn English, back in Mexico they cannot. My girls here they have an American passport therefore they could get any job, my boys back in Mexico cannot. There's a big difference. My girls are in a better country because back in Mexico there's a lot of poverty and you have to work a lot all the time. My two girls here, I think they are going to get a good job, or a degree, for example they can become teachers. In Mexico that does not happen.

The American Dream, as Mahler (1995) explains, is filled with contradictions as it can be a way in which people are able to bear fruits from hard work and sacrifice; however, it is also a disillusion, as it can become a source of abuse and pressure to generate cash for remittances. The conditions under which migrants labour to generate money are among the most exploitative, not only because undocumented migrants occupy the lowest rung of the economic ladder but also because their status as "illegal" leaves them vulnerable to abusive practices. As Mahler notes, "people pay dearly for their own exploitation" (1995, p. 70), and even though first-generation migrants might experience downward status mobility, several studies have suggested how in spite of poverty, high levels of discrimination and often modest parental human capital, second generation "Latino" young people have experienced substantial educational success and upward mobility (Kasinitz, 2008, p. 254).

My research was based on fieldwork in Tulsa, Oklahoma, among Mexican women who participated in the early education program Educare.[1] The women I interviewed came from poor backgrounds in Mexico, had no or very little education, and had migrated to the United States by crossing the border (via the river and the desert) without any documents.[2] Some of them brought their children with them (the so-called 1.5 generation), therefore they were not citizens; others had children in the United States, and some of them had a combination of both (citizens and undocumented). I collected the life stories of 35 women migrants and used semi-structured interviews to gather data on care arrangements and forms of cooperation around childcare. The interviews aimed to investigate *emic* notions of care and well-being of children, good parenthood, and notions of social and economic success. I interviewed women actively participating in early education programs and hence were involved in the various programs that the state and non-profits have to alleviate poverty and create self-reliant neoliberal individuals. Most of my interlocutors either worked as community lay advisors, called *Promotoras*, at the Center for Family Resilience in the Department of Human Development and Family Science at Oklahoma State University, a center funded by the George Kaiser Family Foundation (founders of Educare), or were recipients of the services of community advisors.

During my conversations with women, it became clear how they had ideas about their roles as mothers that were related to their own cultural values (or cultural obstacles, as some put it) that existed in sharp contrast to the model that early education programs like Educare promoted. Regardless of these differences, women understood what they had to do to fit the model of the deserving liberal subject to get access to these programs. Being a particular type of mother who fit this model was, as I will show, informed by their racialised and gendered

1 I did short stints of fieldwork in Oklahoma in 2014, 2015, and 2016.

2 According to Portes and Rumbaut (2014, p. 113), the largest foreign group—Mexicans—has the lowest level of schooling according to both indicators. This result is not due to Mexico's having a singularly bad educational system but to the more than 2,000-mile border with the United States, allowing peasants and workers of modest origins to come in search of work.

neoliberal subjectivities: sometimes they were successful at fitting the right type of parenting, and sometimes they were not. On this chapter, drawing on the voices that I collected during my interviews, I also analyse transnational representations of scarcity and abundance through the study of women's involvement in Educare as a way to access what they perceive as "abundant resources" to advance the lives of their children who, if undocumented, live within a socio-legal structure that deny them a subject of rights. By participating in these programs, which offer the promise of socio-economic success and upward mobility for their (second-generation) children, women attempted to counteract a life dominated by the experience of scarcity and lack of opportunities.

Narratives of scarcity

Scarcity refers to the fundamental economic concept where the resources available to meet human wants and needs are limited in comparison to the unlimited wants and needs that people have. In other words, it's the condition of having insufficient resources to fulfil all the desires and demands of a population. Robbins argued that economics was not about "material welfare: the provision of goods to further prosperity and development", but rather it was about "scarcity: the provision of goods to fulfil all wants" (1932, pp. 12–15). Scarcity is as one of the basic problems encountered in most aspects of economics (Lipsey, 1971, p. 50). In many ways, poverty has been the key domain to which scarcity has been applied to explain how it affects economic decisions and behaviours. Within economic anthropology, the formalist approach "defined economics in terms of the choices made by individual actors under conditions of scarcity" (Hart and Hann, 2012, p. 66). This approach, according to Stafford, "is premised on a psychological assumption: that under conditions of scarcity humans will on aggregate behave as rational maximisers of utility" (2020, p. 15). This rationality assumption, as Stafford further argues, is adopted by economists purely for the sake of model building: they believe that economic life is psychological. "Economic agents may be rational or not, by some definition, but they are definitely thinking and making crucial choices about how best to live their lives" (2020, p. 15). By contrast, the substantivist approach assumes that economic life is embedded in socio-cultural historical contexts and is not detached from religion, politics, or kinship institutions. Under this approach, economic choices are heavily constrained by social and cultural variables; in other words, human choices are only free in a restricted sense (Chibnik, 2011). This approach also erases the focus on utility maximisation under conditions of scarcity, which as Stafford argues cancels the possibility to consider how economic life involves calculations, feelings, thoughts, judgment, and decisions that shape people's lives (2020, pp. 16–17).

My analysis of migrants' limited access to socio-economic resources within a state that rejects their existence takes into consideration how economic life is embedded in wider social, cultural, and historical contexts. However, I also consider how people confronted by myriad philanthropic projects, which have abundant resources, make utility-maximising choices (which may considered rational or not) due to their own experiences of scarcity back in Mexico. As I will show, people make choices and manage conflicting demands that include emotional considerations, such as caring for their families, and practical considerations, such as engaging in migration journeys. When resources are scarce, my interlocutors were forced to prioritise certain needs and goals (socio-economic) over others. These choices involve balancing emotional attachments that they have towards kinship and ideas of care and practical considerations. For the general impoverished communities in Tulsa, the abundance of early education resources offers the opportunity to improve, to become a deserving subject and fit citizen; for Mexicans, it also represents the promise of achieving the American Dream.

For Mexican migrants in Tulsa, scarcity has different meanings: it is more than an economic condition attached to their poverty back in Mexico; it also relates to an overal lack of opportunities to improve oneself through hard work. During the interview, Sara commented:

> We come from a ranch (*somos del Rancho*) but it was very difficult for us to survive there, if it rains you can actually make and have food but if it doesn't it's very difficult because there's no work. There were times when we could not feed our children and we would travel to the city of Zacatecas to find some work in construction or cleaning for me. But it does not matter how much you work, or how much you try, for people like us there are very little opportunities in Mexico to provide for your children.

Although the children helped the parents during the harvest season and the two boys accompanied the father whenever he had a job in the city, there was never enough money to support the family. In this regard, scarcity relates to the lived experience of poverty and the allocation of resources; it is also one of the reasons that drove migrants to make the choice to migrate and improve their economic situation. In their migration narratives, people talked about their poor backgrounds and the scarcity that they and their families have experienced in Mexico over several generations. Scarcity in this case underlies the existence and experience of racialised poverty created by the unequal distribution of resources and lack of opportunities. Teresa from Zacatecas explained:

> I come from a poor background, my father was a salesman, he used to buy vegetables and fruits and then sold them in the ranches. My mother didn't work but stayed at home she needed to take care of eight children. But my father had an accident and he started having some economic troubles therefore some of my brothers started migrating to the US. I came later on, illegally but I am here.

While talking about migrating to the United States, my interlocutors talked about the contrasting lives they have in the United States. As she proudly shows me a cabinet in her living where she keeps her collection of teacups, Amalia from Guanajuato tells me:

> We can eat much better here than we did back in Mexico. Here you can have your fridge full of things, not there. My life here has improved a lot because back in Mexico we worked a lot, and we could not save anything. It was very difficult; life in Mexico was very difficult especially when you have no education. We came here to offer my children a better life.

Women expressed that the United States, in contrast to Mexico, is a place where they are able to bear fruits from their hard work and sacrifice. In Mexico, according to most women, people remain poor despite their efforts and hard work: there simply are not enough opportunities for people with little education. In their narratives, women asserted that, regardless of their undocumented status, migrants in the United States could afford renting or buying a good house for the family, have a car, get free education for children and jobs, and be able to consume things that they did not have access to back in Mexico.

The United States is perceived as a site of abundance, particularly when it comes to material gain and a place where people with ambitions, self-made subjects who are willing to work hard, and to slowly adapt and become new subjects can have access to the life they always wanted. Rosa from Puebla tells me: "I always tell my husband, there are two types of ambitions, you know I am very happy here in my house, this is what we have right now, and everybody has what they have worked for. If you have a nice car, it is probably because you are a hard worker". Her home is a three-bedroom home, with an open living room attached to a small kitchen. The house also has a big porch with a hanging chair where we had our conversation. Across the yard, there was a shiny new pickup truck that according to her was the main thing that her husband desired; she explained that it had been expensive, but he deserved it as he was a hardworking man who provided for this family. Overall, people were convinced with the choice of having migrated; and despite the sacrifices, people believe it had been the right choice it to take care of the family, to offer a better future for their children, and to escape from poverty. In this sense, their choice was easily justified based on the socio-economic advantages that they had already gained. Above all, their decision to migrate was expressed as completely rational; by doing it, they were maximising their choices and opportunities in life. By saying this, I am not trying to hide the fears that surrounded their lives as undocumented migrants. Families live with the constant fear of deportation, and their social personhood is structured around being deportable; as a result, they must endure the anxiety of the prospects of losing everything they had sacrificed themselves for. Still, the colossal compromises that they had made were based on a wider ethics of care towards kinship relations, hence morally justified.

Overall, Mexican migrants embody two contrasting figures in the United States. On the one hand, they are perceived as hardworking people capable of sustaining forms of manual labour unwanted by most and also as people willing to make huge sacrifices for their families. Their recognised and added value—even among the most conservative circles in Tulsa—is erected upon their labour, upon their capacity to become docile subjects, malleable and potentially disposable. George, a 78-year-old white man, told me when we talked about the presence of Mexicans in Tulsa: "They are hardworking people who care about their families. They do not hesitate to take any jobs, they are not lazy and are not scared to do jobs that others would not do". In his view, Mexicans were different from African Americans and Native Americans, who were overly reliant on welfare and therefore had become "lazy". On the other hand, there is a contrasting figure that depicts the migrant person as a usurper who deprives other citizens of the rights acquired by their ancestors (i.e., Native Americans, African Americans, but most importantly white settlers). Stacey, a poor, young white woman from Oklahoma, was convinced that her children were not advancing in their learning at school because of the number of Mexican migrants in the classrooms who did not speak English and needed special attention.

Regardless of their achievements, shortcomings, or in some cases even citizenship, Mexicans remain part of a community that is characterised by being racially different, by being non-white (although in comparison with African Americans and Native Americans, they think of themselves as white). These contrasting figures exist in what De Genova calls the social space of illegality defined as an "erasure of legal personhood—a space of forced invisibility, exclusion, subjugation, and repression that materializes around [the undocumented] wherever they go" (Coutin, 2000, p. 30) in the form of real effects ranging from hunger to unemployment (or more typically, severe exploitation) to violence to death—that is nonetheless always already confounded by their substantive social personhood" (De Genova, 2002, p. 427). In other words, the social personhood of migrants cannot be detached from migrants' embodiment of illegality and with it the possibility of deportability (Martinez and Slack, 2013; Rugh and Hall, 2016). This implies that migrants' lives are crosscut by a constant threat of deportation, of being forced out and physically removed from the nation-state. If this is the case, and migrants' experiences of abundance and opportunities in the United States are no more than temporary stages in which their labour is rendered invisible but nonetheless exploited, then how do they construct dignified lives? How do they access resources in a social landscape in which they are racialised and impoverished subjects? How do people living in a state of conflicting perceptions of scarcity and abundance manage to navigate a system that pigeonholes them as a racial minority that is unfit?

Mexican migration to Oklahoma

Before I move on to my analysis of the ways in which women access educational resources for their children, I want to explain how my discussion on accessing scarce resources for Mexican migrants is not necessary about traditional narratives on the ways in which migrant communities try to "steal" resources from citizens, although this narrative is part of the anti-immigration discourse regarding Hispanic migrants in the United States. It is more complex than this. In this case I refer to a community that lives within a series of restrictions that have been historically imposed throughout decades of complex and draconian immigration laws and labour relations between Mexico and the United States. In the particular case of Oklahoma, the migration of Mexicans started in the aftermath of the 1910 Mexican revolution. Mexicans were escaping from the threat of war and pulled by the expansion of the railroad, agriculture, and work in the coal mines (Smith, 1980). This migration flow was largely unchecked by immigration officials until 1929 due to the great demand for labour in burgeoning industries in the Southwest. During the shortages of World War II, Mexican migrants were brought back to Oklahoma to work on the railroads, cotton fields, and industry under the Bracero Program,[3] a farm labour program created in 1942 that permitted millions of Mexicans to work legally in the United States on short-term labour contracts. However, the continuing demand for agricultural and unskilled labour pulled a significant number of unauthorised workers. In the 1960s, Mexican nationals and Mexican Americans moved to Oklahoma from agricultural jobs in the Rio Grande Valley of Texas in search of more stable, year-round employment.

The numbers of Mexican-born residents of Oklahoma grew by 1980, even when the economic crisis pushed a large number of native-born Oklahomans out of the state. By 1986, more than 20,000 unauthorised residents of Oklahoma legalised their status following the passage of the Immigration Reform and Control Act (IRCA). These immigrants were in turn able to sponsor the legal immigration of family members who came into the country with or without authorisation. The 1990s witnessed a rapid growth of the population of Mexican immigrants; according to Dent, the number of Mexicans and Latinos residing in Tulsa County reached nearly 12,000 (2008, p. 35). By 1996 the government developed the Illegal Immigration Reform and Immigrant Responsibility Act 1996 (IIRIRA), which enhanced border controls and penalties for unlawful entry to or presence in the United States. Paradoxically, instead of preventing the flow of unauthorised migration, the Act generated further attachment and settlement among immigrants who were disincentivised to return home and be caught by authorities in the process. By 2006, roughly three-quarters of the approximately 85,000 Mexican immigrants residing in Oklahoma had

3 Upon its termination in 1964, the Bracero Program had brought more than 4 million *braceros* (arms) to work in US agriculture and on railroads. Available at: https://guides.loc.gov/latinx-civil-rights/bracero-program#:~:text=An%20executive%20order%20called%20the,on%20short%2Dterm%20labor%20contracts.

entered since 1990, and as many as 54,000 of these were estimated to be unauthorised (McCormick, 2009, p. 316).

The Mexicans who lived in Tulsa during the first half of the twentieth century usually worked in industry and agriculture; hence they followed a seasonal pattern and high turnover rate. Now, most Mexicans and Latinos work in construction and hotel/restaurant industry or have their own businesses. Many of these businesses (approximately 3,000 in 1992) operated and prospered in low-income neighbourhoods, revitalising once declining areas (McCormick, 2009). Most of these migrants tend to stay for as long as they can. This, according to Taylor Dent, is surprising considering that in 2007 the government designed and implemented House Bill 1804, which "allows law officers to check the legal status of immigrants, ends public assistance to undocumented immigrants, and applies a harsh penalty for employers that employ illegal immigrants" (2009, p. 36). Although H.B. 1804 mirrored existing federal law provisions, it created a sense of heightened vigilance, suspicion, and intolerance amongst private citizens, public employees, business owners, and officers. H.B. 1804 created fear and panic among the immigrant communities. Many undocumented parents with children who were US citizens made arrangements for the care and custody of their children in the event that they were arrested and deported; individuals in the community were afraid to go to hospitals and seek medical care; there was even a drop-off in patient visits to clinics serving Hispanic clients. There was an increase in racial profiling by the police, who were accused of making pretextual traffic stops of Hispanic drivers (Jones, 2008). As of October 2016, Oklahoma did not allow lawfully residing immigrants to enrol in Medicaid. The state also required most public employers and contractors to use the E-Verify system when hiring employees, even though the system is a breach of privacy. On top of this, the state stopped issuing driver's licences to individuals residing in the country without legal permission.

Immigration law in the United States has been historically a mechanism used by the state, not only to control the movement of people who are undocumented, but to create the figure of the "illegal" and the deportable person as a socio-political condition. In this regard, De Genova (2004) explains that the production of illegality provides an apparatus for sustaining Mexican migrants' vulnerability and tractability—as workers—whose labour power, inasmuch as it is deportable, becomes an eminently disposable commodity (Chavez, 2007, 2013; Coutin, 2003; Menjívar, 2006). There is nothing matter-of-fact about the "illegality" of undocumented migrants.

> "Illegality" (in its contemporary configuration) is the product of US immigration law—not merely in the abstract sense that without the law nothing could be construed to be outside the law; nor simply in the generic sense that immigration law constructs, differentiates, and ranks

> various categories of "aliens"—but in the more profound sense that the history of deliberate interventions.
>
> (De Genova, 2004, p. 173)[4]

Despite the legal restrictions and the surveillance and criminalisation of undocumented migrants, places like Oklahoma still attract migrants who are finding it increasingly difficult to survive in other states. Oklahoma was, for most of my interlocutors, a second migration destination that offered good opportunities in terms of jobs (construction, roofing, factory work, and service sector jobs) and, more importantly, affordable housing. Jose, from Guerrero, told me how 30 years ago there were a few Mexicans in Oklahoma but there was a lot of work in construction.

> I think that many people were coming here because houses were really cheap, they were only $4000 or $5000, you could buy one, fix it and sell it quite easily. It was very cheap. They were many houses that nobody wanted to repair so we did. Sometimes you can actually find some houses like that now, it is not as it was before, but you can find some. In contrast, in California you would have to pay $1000 rent for a one-bedroom flat, it is crazy. When I lived to California I lived in a house where I paid $1500 a month and we were 15 people living in there.

Most of my interlocutors had initially migrated to California or Texas where they had family and wide social networks. Those who moved to Oklahoma confirmed that in Tulsa they were able to afford to rent, or even buy two- to three-bedroom houses where the family could live without sharing rooms with strangers. According to the American Immigration Council there are 245,500 immigrant residents in Oklahoma, of which 42.1% are from Mexico and 5.7% from Guatemala. The Council also accounts for 98,000 undocumented migrants. https://map.americanimmigrationcouncil.org/locations/oklahoma/. The increasing presence of Mexicans in Oklahoma is also reflected in the number of community-based institutions serving them. There are numerous Catholic and Protestant churches offering spiritual and material assistance. The Hispanic American Foundation of Tulsa promote ethnic pride and sponsor celebrations commemorating such events as *Cinco*

4 Recent scholarship has focused on the construction and production of "illegality" and the "illegal" person as a juridical status and a socio-political condition. These scholars have been interested in studying the mechanisms that sustain and produce migrant illegality. Some of these studies pay particular attention to the role of history and the state in the construction of the so-called illegal migrants (Mexicans) in the United States (e.g., Rosas, 2007; De Genova, 2005; Boehm, 2009, 2012). These studies emphasise the processes in which migrants are not only constructed as the "illegal" but how they are constantly controlled and excluded from different states despite multicultural rhetoric of integration.

de Mayo and 16 de Septiembre (Mexican Independence Day). There are other organisations across the state, such as Oklahoma City's Latino Community Development Agency and Legal Aid of Western Oklahoma, which offer social, economic, educational, and legal assistance (Smith, 1980). These organisations have created a sense of community in the state that contrasts sharply with the conservative ideology of the people in power.

On top of the organisations that help Hispanic migrants, there are myriad organisations in Tulsa that work towards the alleviation of overall poverty. Many of these organisations are funded by vast wealth originating from oil and banking industries in Tulsa. Billionaires like George Kaiser, whose wealth derives from oil and banking, or the Schusterman and Zarrow families who have founded philanthropic organisations intended to fill the gap created by welfare cuts created by conservative governments. These foundations cover services ranging from education and housing to health care and public parks. Hundreds of millions of dollars stream from private donors to fill the service gaps but do not manage to replace equitable service distribution provided by the state. For instance, the Charles and Lynn Schusterman Family Philanthropies focus on the prevention, intervention, and treatment of child abuse and neglect in Israel and Tulsa. They are involved in reforming Tulsa's public education system and provide development opportunities for teens and professional development for teachers through various coaching and mentoring programs.

Similarly, the Anne & Henry Zarrow Foundation targets poverty by supporting housing and shelter resources, social services, mental health, and indigent healthcare initiatives. The George Kaiser Family Foundation works on the Criminal Justice Reform and Women in Recovery programs after incarceration, community health projects and Tulsa Educare, a pre-K program partly subsidised with federal Head Start grants. This range of organisations helps mitigate the poverty that surrounds these communities; at the same time these organisations educate, train, and manage people to become respectable neoliberal subjects. For instance, the Catholic and Pentecostal churches have programs designed to help migrants in the process of acculturation to the new American culture by reminded them of the importance of values around family, community, and work. Lucia tells me: "As our pastor says, we have come to a new country, where things are different, here we need to behave in a good way, respect the rules, we need to prove that we deserve to be here". Organisations like Educare not only help the poor communities in the provision of education for their children but provide particular programs and special training to turn mothers and children into respectable and successful subjects who would eventually succeed in life.

Early education: Educare and families

According to the foundation, Educare is a "research-based program with a foundation in the best of early childhood practices that ensure school readiness of children most at risk for school failure." https://www.tulsaeducare.org/.

The program involves partnerships between Tulsa's public school officials, Head Start,[5] and other partners dedicated to narrowing children's achievement gap in their communities. Pre-K efforts focus on at-risk children, but Oklahoma (as well as Florida and Georgia) offers voluntary, universal pre-K (UPK) to all 4-year-olds regardless of family income and documented status. Oklahoma's penetration rate of 71 per cent is the highest in the nation (Barnett et al., 2008). "Both UPK and Head Start seek to prepare children for the cognitive and socio-emotional demands of formal schooling" (Lowenstein, 2009, p. 2). These programs exist thanks to the partnerships between philanthropists and the local Tulsa government; they seek to narrow the achievement gap through a curriculum that develops school readiness for disadvantaged children. According to Lowenstein (2009), these programs put an emphasis on early learning in the context of an array of goals, including healthy social, emotional, and physical development, as well as parent involvement.

The curriculum developed by these programs is based on the assumptions that poverty and low socio-economic status have an impact on emotional and behavioural problems in children (Bradley and Corwyn, 2002; Ripke and Huston, 2006). "Factors like harsh inconsistent parenting, parental conflict, maternal depression and overcrowding seem to be important mediators of the relationship between poverty and children's socio-emotional development" (Lowenstein, 2009, p. 4). Some studies also report higher rates of emotional and behavioural problems among racial minorities, as they are likely to live in low-income households (Douglas-Hall and Chau, 2008). In this regard, Hispanic children have been found to experience higher rates of unmet mental health needs but have not been using any mental health services due to language barriers, challenges of acculturation, and restrictions on access to government assistance (Douglas-Hall and Koball, 2004). Early education programs put an emphasis on the need to provide children with the tools to have a proper socio-emotional development[6] that would prevent them from engaging in antisocial disorders, violent and non-violent delinquency in adolescence, and long-term unemployment in adulthood (Kokko and Pulkkinen, 2000).

5 Head Start is a federally funded comprehensive child development program that annually serves close to 1 million low-income young children and their families). The program's goal is to promote the school readiness of low-income children by enhancing their social and cognitive development through the provision of comprehensive services, including preschool education; medical, dental, and mental health care; nutrition services; and parent-involvement efforts (US Department of Health and Human Services, 2004). Founded in 1965, Head Start serves children between the ages of 3 and 5. Early Head Start was created in 1994 for the purpose of serving pregnant women and children birth to age 3 (National Head Start Association, 2025).

6 Socio-emotional development involves the acquisition of certain skills. These include the ability to identify and understand one's own feelings, accurately read and understand others' emotional states, manage strong emotions and their expression constructively, regulate one's own behaviour, develop empathy for others, and establish and sustain relationships (National Scientific Council on the Developing Child, 2005).

Among my interlocutors, early education programs like Educare represented the possibility to offer their children the best chances to succeed in the new country despite their illegality. Migrants' illegal status rendered them as "criminals", therefore they are not deserving of the help that the state offers. When it comes to accessing resources, Mexican migrants must prove they are self-reliant subjects who deserve the help provided by charities, organisations, and the Church. Along with other communities living in poverty, like African Americans (Lewis, 2022; Lewis and Gutierrez Garza, 2023), Mexican migrants must engage in self-fashioning practices to change their own social and economic circumstances. In the case of my informants, these self-fashioning practices range from learning the American way and working hard as individuals, to shed Mexican cultural traits that get in the way of successfully becoming American (i.e. part of the white middle class). As Cacho argues, "claiming deservingness through demonstrating respectability assumes that we can make a clear distinction between people of colour who are criminal and people of colour who are respectable, but this distinction is far from being fixed or stable" (2012, p. 119). Early education programs like Educare offer Mexican migrants the tools to raise good, honest children; they are a gateway to achieve the respectability they had lost due to their "illegality" and to become American. Elsa tells me:

> Yes I think Educare is very good because [my daughter] has learned a lot, for instance, she did not know how to behave around other kids, if we did something here at home with other kids she used to fight a lot because she was not used to having kids around. It was all about her. She did not like to share her toys with other kids, now at Educare she has learned how to share her toys, she has learned the alphabet, colours. I think that Educare has been a very good influence in her education.

When talking about her daughter, Elsa mentioned that she had also received the benefits of Educare, as parents need to have an active involvement in the school. Mothers must become teachers of their children; they have to constantly participate in the education and provide positive stimulus to their children once they leave the classroom. This is part of the Parent as Teacher (PAT) program, which is a family support program for families with young children. Parents learn about child development and early learning; for Mexican mothers, this program was a way to prove that they, as mothers, were also willing to improve along with their children.

As Cacho suggests, in the case of families, and particularly Hispanic mothers, people are required to provide evidence of their heteronormative morality and domesticity (Cacho, 2012, p. 117), and in the case of early education, the will to learn and improve (Li, 2007). While describing a similar program to

Educare, called EvenStart, Delia from Guadalajara explained to me how the program educated mothers.

> Mothers could not work because they had to come with their children to those lessons, they were taught parenting skills. The good thing about this programme is that not only children were learning but also mothers. It was a very good programme, every Thursday we had some time for mothers to come to the class with their babies and applied what they had learned in the parenting classes and we would observe them and supervise them and see how they interacted with their kids, because you know many times we are busy with domestic chores and we really do not pay any attention to our children, or we just left them to play on their own, or do whatever is more convenient for us. We also visited the mothers at their homes to check on them and see how they were doing.

This explanation resonates with the experiences of some of the *Promotoras* that I followed during fieldwork. As I mentioned at the beginning, some of the women that I interviewed were *Promotoras*; this means that they were not only recipients of the programs but also supervisors. They were in charge of visiting women's homes once or twice a month in order to check that they were doing their "homework". The visits included asking women about how much time they had spent with their children after school, how many activities they were doing, and diet checks; on some occasions, women were given a checklist of physical exercises they had to do with their children to improve motor skills. *Promotoras* were employed by Oklahoma State University and the Center for Family Resilience, which was funded by the George Kaiser Family Foundation. Part of the *Promotoras'* jobs was also to convince mothers to send their children to Educare or another early education program.

Overall, women thought that Educare was the best thing that could happen to children because most of the time, parents do not dedicate enough time to their children. Parents—particularly mothers—who are considered responsible for their children to turn out well and to transmit good moral values, must learn how to learn and how to teach as part of being good parents, and the same time how to unlearn their own cultural conceptions of care, motherhood, and kinship. Sara from Zacatecas says:

> As Hispanic people we have this tradition, this custom of keeping the child with us because they are too young. Mothers usually said that children are too young to go to school, I used to think like that, however I was working and left my daughter with my grandmother who was here back then. I used to think that my grandma was the best person to take care of my child, but she really did not teach my daughter anything of what is taught in a school. A child in a house only watches television. So, I started thinking about bringing her to the school, if she was already

> staying with grandma, I would rather take to a place where she would learn. I then took the decision to put her in school.

The women who attend these programs must constantly reflect on their roles as mothers and as teachers to improve the lives and prospects of their children. Through these programs, children can learn how to be American, advance, and prepare for school. The process also involves monitoring the continuous efforts that parents must make to self-fashion new subjectivities as parents.

However, these new subjectivities often clash with cultural notions and conceptions of motherhood. Although women praised early education, they talked about the conflicts they experienced the moment they needed to make the decision to send their children to these programs. Elsa, who had her daughter at Educare and was about to have a baby, told me that she was still not sure about sending her baby to the program: "I know it is quite difficult because they are really young, they are babies, and it makes you feel guilty about leaving them when they are this young". Patricia explained: "I think it should be an obligation, but when my children were babies, I did not want to detach myself form them. If God had given me opportunity to be a mother, I would take care of them". When asking Amelia about sending her 1-year-old to Educare, she told me that she was not ready yet,

> because I feel that he still needs me, he is too young. I think that those programs are fundamental for children, but I don't think they provide what a mother can give, what I can teach him because those are people who do not have the same connection that I have with my own child. I think that's very important. Maybe he'll go to Educare once he is four.

Women have heard and learn from others that children who had been in pre-K had learned English, learned social and motor skills, and overall were more developed than other children; still, their notions of what a good mother should be, or good parenting, sharply contrasted with the requisites of the programs. Before standing up to pick up her baby boy, who was crying in his cradle, Amelia remarked:

> I think I am not going to think about it and *tentarme el corazón* (literally touch my heart, an expression that is used when people have to make a tough decision) I am just going to put him in Educare. It is really difficult, even sometimes when I leave him with his dad, I feel bad and guilty about it.

For them, a good mother was someone who took care of her children, someone who is focused on her children and educates them—someone who is aware of their needs and is attentive 100 per cent of the time. Whenever children misbehave, women expressed that it was the mothers' fault, "I am 200% sure that it relates to the mothers", Patricia told me. The presence of mothers is absolutely necessary in the making up of good children; still, most women have to find work in order to survive in the United States, therefore they must leave their children in the care of others. They relied on the help of their families (nuclear and extended), and those who did not have any kinship networks were required to pay other women within the community. However, not being able to care for their children produced feelings of guilt and inadequacy. Maria tells me, with tears in her eyes:

> In California I had to leave them alone, I didn't even know if they were actually going to school or not. I think they started to meet people that we're not good for them and then they decided to leave school and start working. I think that they preferred to earn money than to go back to school. For example, the youngest one used to hang out with gangs since we were in California. He stopped going to school sometimes my husband would take him to school and five minutes later the police were calling him to tell him that they've caught him. Can you believe that? I did not have time to be with them because I had to work, I know it is my fault that they got involved with the wrong people. Now they are both in Mexico, they were deported and banned from coming back.

She was convinced that it was fault, her absence, what pushed her sons to get involved with gangs and drug dealing in California and Tulsa. "Now is different for Elsa and Rocio (the youngest daughter). Elsa is a promoter and is aware of the benefits of Educare. I am still trying to convince her to send the baby as soon as possible". The most important thing that a mother needs to do, is to help their children to adapt to the new culture, to *ser alguien en la vida* (become someone in life), to leave scarcity behind. After all, migrants' reasons to migrate are grounded on the prospects to *romper la cadena*, to break the poverty chain through the acquisition of a proper education that will provide, in their minds, stability, abundance, success, and security that resembles a white middle-class model or family.

Conclusion

Early education programs promise the alleviation of poverty through the teaching of strategies or liberal self-fashioning, self-reliant subjects that can change their circumstances despite of their culture, economic status, or race. Paradoxically, by participating in these programs, women find themselves trapped in a moral dilemma, that of not being able to be there for their children and the guilt of not being good teachers helping in the development of their children. The result is that they are never enough, that despite their efforts they will never be fully American. These contradictions could be argued to be a result of the nature of these programs as "one size fits all", particularly when working with racialised impoverished communities. It could be argued that is a problem of cultural relativity, but this conclusion only takes us so far. On the one hand, these programs have proven to be effective and have a positive impact in the development of children (Gormley, Phillips and Gayer, 2008; Gormley et al., 2011; Garces, Thomas and Currie, 2002). On the other hand, these programs hardly account for the particularities of such communities or try to understand and consider the rationalities and structural conditions that keep these communities poor. There is a lack of in-depth assessment of the needs and realities of a community that has no legal rights in the United States, that has been historically maintained as a disposable community whose relative value relies on the power of their labour, on their capacity to be exploitable, but most importantly, on the fact that they can be deportable (De Genova and Roy, 2020). As Lewis and I have argued elsewhere, it is important to reveal the complex ethical-moral terrains in which such programs and policies are played out. Doing so will show how such programs are at odds with historically and culturally produced ethics of the raced poor by understanding their agency, rationalities, and moral orders of the factors that keep them poor (2023, p. 43).

The Mexican migrants in Tulsa escape from poverty and scarcity in Mexico to find an abundance of resources offered by philanthropic organisations that are in charge of helping the poor via programs, like Educare, that promote forms of personhood shaped and reproduced through discourses and practices of liberal self-governance. These discourses are at odds with the social control of my interlocutors (along with other impoverished communities) as racialised subjects who are denied full citizenship. They are at odds with a liberal and racial capitalist system in which "racialized and impoverished subjects cannot be incorporated into liberal orders—precisely because those very orders depend on their difference and subordination" (Lawson et al., 2023, p. 3), and in the case of Mexican migrants, on their designation as illegal and deportable.

References

Barnett, W. S., Epstein, D. J., Friedman, A. H., Boyd, J. S., and Hustedt, J. T. (2008) *The State of Preschool 2008: State Preschool Yearbook.* New Brunswick, NJ: National Institute for Early Education Research.

Boehm, D. A. (2009) '"¿Quien Sabe?": Deportation and temporality among transnational Mexicans.' *Urban Anthropology and Studies of Cultural Systems and World Economic Development*, 38(2/3/4), 345–374.

Boehm, D. A. (2012) *Intimate Migrations: Gender, Family, and Illegality Among Transnational Mexicans.* New York: New York University Press.

Bradley, R. H., and Corwyn, R. F. (2002) 'Socioeconomic status and child development.' *Annual Review of Psychology*, 53, 371–399.

Cacho, L. M. (2012) *Social Death: Racialized Rightlessness and the Criminalization of the Unprotected.* New York: New York University Press.

Chavez, L. R. (2007) 'The condition of illegality.' *International Migration*, 45(3), 192–196. Available at: https://doi.org/10.1111/j.1468-2435.2007.00416.x.

Chavez, L. R. (2013) *The Latino Threat: Constructing Immigrants, Citizens, and the Nation*, 2nd ed. Stanford University Press.

Chibnik, M. (2011) 'Anthropology, economics, and choice.' In *Anthropology, Economics, and Choice.* University of Texas Press. Available at: https://doi.org/10.7560/726765.

Coutin, S. B. (2000) *Legalizing Moves: Salvadoran Immigrants' Struggle for U.S. Residency*. Ann Arbor: University Michigan Press.
Coutin, S. B. (2003) 'Illegality, borderlands, and the space of nonexistence.' In Warren, R. P., and Maurer, B. (Eds.), *Globalization Under Construction: Governmentality, Law, and Identity*, pp. 171–202. Minnesota: University of Minnesota Press.
De Genova, N. P. (2002) 'Migrant "illegality" and deportability in everyday life.' *Annual Review of Anthropology*, 31, 419–447. Available at: https://doi.org/10.2307/4132887.
De Genova, N. P. (2004) 'The legal production of Mexican/migrant "illegality".' *Latino Studies*, 2(2), 160–185.
De Genova, N. P. (2005) *Working the Boundaries: Race, Space, and "Illegality" in Mexican Chicago*. Durham: Duke University Press.
De Genova, N. P. and Roy, A. (2020) 'Practices of illegalization.' *Antipode: Radical Journal of Geography*, 52(2).
Dent, T. (2008) *The Latinos of Tulsa: Their Place in Space and Patterns of Migration*. ProQuest. Dissertation Publishing. Oklahoma State University. Available at: https://www.proquest.com/openview/6dbc47bc80f06a249299610f3271b693/1?pq-origsite=gscholar&cbl=18750.
Douglas-Hall, A., and Chau, M. (2008) *Basic Facts About Low-Income Children Birth to Age 6*. New York: National Center for Children in Poverty.
Douglas-Hall, A., and Koball, H. (2004) *Children of Recent Immigrants: National and Regional Trends*. New York, NY: National Center for Children in Poverty. Available at: https://doi.org/10.7916/D8K64ST5.
Garces, E., Thomas, D., and Currie, J. (2002) 'Longer-term effects of head start.' *The American Economic Review*, 92(4), 999–1012.
Gormley Jr., W. T., Phillips, D., and Gayer, T. (2008) 'Preschool programs can boost school readiness.' *Science*, 320, 1723–1724.
Gormley Jr., W. T. et al. (2011) 'Social-emotional effects of early childhood education programs in Tulsa.' *Child Development*, 82(6), 2095–2109. Available at: https://doi.org/10.1111/j.1467-8624.2011.01648.x.
Hart, K., and Hann, C. (2012) *Economic Anthropology*. Cambridge, UK and Malden, MA: Polity.
Jones, R. C. (2008) *Immigrants Outside Megalopolis: Ethnic Transformation in the Heartland*. Lexington Books.
Kasinitz, P. (2008) 'Becoming American, becoming minority, getting ahead: The role of racial and ethnic status in the upward mobility of the children of immigrants.' *The ANNALS of the American Academy of Political and Social Science*, 620(1), 253–269. Sage Publications Inc.
Kokko, K., and Pulkkinen, L. (2000) 'Aggression in childhood and long-term unemployment in adulthood: A cycle of maladaptation and some protective factors.' *Developmental Psychology*, 36(4), 463–472.
Lawson, V., Elwood, S., Daigle, M., Herrera, J. A., Gutiérrez Garza, J., Kohl, E., Lewis, J., Ramirez, M., Reddy, C., and Valencia, Y. (2023) *Abolishing Poverty: Towards Pluriverse Futures and Politics*. Athens, GA: University of Georgia Press.
Lewis, S. J. (2022) *Violent Utopia: Dispossession and Black Restoration in Tulsa*. Durham and London: Duke University Press.
Lewis, S. J., and Gutierrez Garza, A. P. (2023) 'Of promise and problem: The poverty politics of recognition, race, and community in Tulsa, Oklahoma.' In Lawson, V., Elwood, S., Daigle, M., Herrera, J. A., Gutiérrez Garza, J., Kohl, E., Lewis, J., Ramirez, M., Reddy, C., and Valencia, Y. (Eds.), *Abolishing Poverty: Towards Pluriverse Futures and Politics*. Athens, GA: University of Georgia Press.
Li, T. M. (2007) *The Will to Improve: Governmentality, Development, and the Practice of Politics*. Durham, NC: Duke University Press.

Lipsey, R. G. (1971) *An Introduction to Positive Economics.* London: Weidenfeld and Nicolson.
Lowenstein, A. E. (2009) *Fostering the Socio-Emotional Adjustment of Low-Income Children: The Effects of Universal Pre-Kindergarten and Head Start in Oklahoma.* Department of Psychology, Doctoral Dissertations. Thesis, Georgetown University.
Mahler, S. J. (1995) *American Dreaming: Immigrant Life on the Margins.* Princeton University Press.
Martinez, D., and Slack, J. (2013) 'What part of "illegal" don't you understand? The social consequences of criminalizing unauthorized Mexican migrants in the United States.' *Social & Legal Studies*, 22(4), 535–551. Sage Publications Ltd.
McCormick, E. (2009) 'The Oklahoma taxpayer and citizen protection act: Blowing off stream or setting wildfires.' *Georgetown Immigration Law Journal*, 23, 293.
Menjívar, C. (2000) *Fragmented Ties: Salvadoran Immigrant Networks in America.* University of California Press.
Menjívar, C. (2006) 'Liminal legality: Salvadoran and Guatemalan immigrants' lives in the United States.' *American Journal of Sociology*, 111(4), 999–1037.
National Head Start Association. (2025) *Head Start Services.* Office of Head Start. https://acf.gov/ohs/about/head-start. Accessed 28 March 2025.
National Scientific Council on the Developing Child. (2005) *Children's Emotional Development Is Built into the Architecture of Their Brains* (Working paper II). https://developingchild.harvard.edu/wp-content/uploads/2024/10/Childrens-Emotional-Development-Is-Built-into-the-Architecture-of-Their-Brains.pdf
Portes, A., and Rumbaut, R. G. (2014) *Immigrant America: A Portrait, Updated, and Expanded.* University California Press.
Ripke, M. N., and Huston, A. C. (2006) 'Poverty: Consequences for children.' In Balter, L., and Tamis-LeMonda, C. S. (Eds.), *Child Psychology: A Handbook of Contemporary Issues*, 2nd ed., pp. 521–544. New York: Psychology Press.
Robbins, L. C. (1932) *An Essay on the Nature and Significance of Economic Science.* London: Macmillan.
Rosas, G. (2007) 'The fragile ends of war forging the United States–Mexico border and borderlands consciousness.' *Social Text,* 25(2(91)), 81–102.
Rugh, J., and Hall, M. (2016) 'Deporting the American dream: Immigration enforcement and Latino foreclosures.' *Sociological Science*, 3, 1077–1102.
Smith, M. M. (1980) *The Mexicans in Oklahoma.* Norman: University of Oklahoma Press.
Solís, P., Avitia, M., y Güémez, B. (2020) *Tono de piel y desigualdad socioeconómica en México.* Reporte de la Encuesta Proder # 1. México: El Colegio de México. Available at: https://discriminacion.colmex.mx/wp-content/uploads/2020/07/info1.pdf.
Stafford, C. (2020) *Economic Life in the Real World: Logic, Emotion and Ethics.* Cambridge University Press.

3 "The story of my father"

Life narratives and memories of scarcity of a Spanish Gitano family

Antonio Montañés Jiménez with Gory Carmona

Introduction

Some months before his father passed away to the COVID-19 virus in 2020, my Romani/Gitano interlocutor and friend Gory Carmona shared with me an audiotape titled "The story of my father", in which his father narrated some of the roughness and economic struggles of his childhood and youth years after the civil war in Spain (1936–1939). In a dramatic and heartbreaking manner, Gory's father's[1] narration recalls a past dominated by poverty, violence and racism. The account of his life was, fundamentally, a chronicle of and about scarcity.

Gory intended to share his father's life narrative with the public, so I suggested he include some excerpts of the recording in this chapter. I also proposed Gory replicate[2] his father's account using his own urban life experiences as a Gitano man born and raised in the south of Madrid. What follows is the product of an experimental idea, one that has taken Gory and me[3] to explore scarcity as a theoretical tool to investigate Gitanos' memories and self-perceptions as well as the political affordances of memory-sharing practices.[4]

On an empirical level, the chapter documents and examines the production of life narratives[5] and memories of Gory and his father in a historical period

1 Name-avoiding regarding beloved deceased is a cultural trait among Gitanos and other Roma groups, especially in the presence of non-Roma or nonrelated Roma. Out of respect for Gory's father's memory and Gitanos' cultural norms, Gory and I decided against including his name in this piece.

2 Gory's father's original audio lasts 21 minutes and 21 seconds, and Gory's original audio lasts 20 minutes and 14 seconds.

3 I (Antonio) wrote the chapter and transcribed, translated, and edited the fragments of the recordings. Gory recorded his and his father's audio and helped to select passages from the audio tapes. Gory's comments about the chapter's content shaped its analytical framework.

4 The material used in this chapter results from my continued ethnographic engagement with Gory (Montañés Jiménez, 2022; Montañés Jiménez and Carmona, 2023) and my academic attempt to enhance the voices and involvement of my Gitano interlocutors in the production of scholarly knowledge.

5 Although life narratives are usually in-depth accounts of one's life, and Gory's and his father's narrations are relatively short summaries of some significant events of their lives, I categorise them as such because they were produced with the purpose of presenting their audience with key life-defining moments and a linear storyline regarding their life trajectories.

DOI: 10.4324/9781032661780-4

spanning from the aftermath of the Spanish Civil War to the present. On a theoretical level, the chapter interrogates whether, and if so, to what extent, scarcity can become a fruitful analytical framework to understand Gitanos' ideas and descriptions of their past and present selves. To that end, the chapter introduces the concept of "memories of scarcities": the act of producing life narratives around ideas of shortage and insufficiency.

The term scarcity (*escasez* in Spanish), or akin terms such as hardship, privation or necessity, are frequently used among Gitanos in the south of Madrid, especially among those living in disadvantaged neighbourhood areas, when describing their collective, family and individual experiences. Locutions such as *Los Gitanos siempre lo pasamos mal* (We Gitanos always have it bad) are indeed common currency among Gitanos I met doing anthropological fieldwork in the city of Madrid. Gory's father would use the word *fatigas* (struggles) to describe much of his life experiences, and Gory often claims *estar en apuros* (to be in a tight spot) when asked about his financial situation. Against this backdrop, thus, the notion of scarcity—one of this book's main analytical foci—may offer a suggestive lens to unpack the negative socio-economic consequences of ethnic stratification patterns for Gitanos in Spain.

Economists usually distinguish between "relative scarcity", which describes a situation where something is limited in supply compared to demand, and "absolute scarcity", which represents a context in which something is limited, regardless of demand. Further, some scholars have distinguished between "lived scarcity", as "something that some people may experience due to the objective biophysical shortage of resources", and "constructed scarcity", as "something that is manufactured through sociopolitical processes to neglect the interests of unprivileged people and reinforce the privileges of dominant groups" (Mehta, 2001). As I will show, absolute and lived scarcity concepts seem appropriate to capture Gory's father's childhood experiences in postwar Spain in the '50s and '60s. The notion of constructed scarcity is also suitable for analysing the life stories provided by Gory and his father from the '70s onward in the context of the growing unequal distribution of resources in the modern capitalist Spanish society. Like many other minority groups, Gitanos are often subject to politically constructed narratives of scarcity. According to Scoones and collaborators, political economists, sociologists and political ecologists frequently understand scarcity relationally as something that "can be manufactured, both politically and discursively" (Scoones et al., 2014, p. 9). The problem of scarcity here, thus, is one of "access, inequality and historical relations of power" (Scoones et al., 2014, p. 9). In a similar vein, Ross (1996) distinguishes between socially generated scarcity (insufficient necessities for some people and not others) and absolute scarcity (insufficient resources, no matter how equitably distributed) and argues that despite resources being available, and abundant, neoliberalism has encouraged a pro-scarcity climate reinforcing austerity measures against people experiencing poverty. In the Gitano context, discussions about constructed scarcity are relevant because, under climate and fear of scarcity, Gitanos are consistently accused of benefiting from State subsidies to a greater extent than other groups in Spanish society. The notion that Gitanos are privileged by the Spanish State is predicated on preconceptions shared by many Spanish people about Gitanos being free riders who exploit and take advantage of social welfare schemes and resources (Montañés Jiménez and Gomez Ávila, 2024).

However, while acknowledging that economic notions of scarcity may prove insightful in exploring the entanglement of class-related struggle and cultural marginalisation for Gitanos, this chapter takes a somewhat unusual and perhaps counterintuitive approach to scarcity. The chapter approaches scarcity not as an economic concept but as an *aide-mémoire* and a notion intrinsically related to producing life narratives, experiences and stories. I begin the chapter by discussing some methodological aspects of self-recorded practices and how Gitanos usually deal with or are represented to deal with the past as a group. Then, I present Gory's father's biographical account to, finally, present Gory's own life narratives and reflections. I intersperse some historical notes and observations between Gory and his father's accounts to provide context for their life narratives.

Some introductory reflections: minorities, self-recorded life narratives, and the Gitano past

The Spanish legal system lacks a definition of, and even a mention of, the idea of national minorities. The 1978 Spanish Constitution, which gathers the fundamental legal principles of the contemporary Spanish State, favours the term *pueblo* (people/communities) in the preamble to its articles and order to "protect all Spaniards and peoples of Spain in the exercise of human rights, of their culture and traditions, languages and institutions". Although most Gitanos may not use the word *minority* to define themselves, they conspicuously possess many attributes and fit sociological depictions of a minority group, especially ethnic or cultural minorities (see introduction). As a cultural group, Gitanos can claim a historical collective identity shaped by particular culture, traditions and language and a long history of discrimination on a cultural basis. Most importantly, Gitanos' collective life is defined by power imbalance vis-à-vis the Spanish non-Gitano majority.

Accounts of Romani groups facing rejection are ubiquitous in European scholarship (Fox and Vermeersch, 2010; Gay y Blasco, 2016; Grill, 2012: 43; Nacu, 2012; Powell and Lever, 2017). Due to oppression and cultural racism, Spanish Romanies/Gitanos have historically and consistently performed worse than the non-Gitano Spanish population in key well-being indicators such as health, education, housing, or integration in the labour market. Many Gitano families survive on the margins of the capitalist productive system by carrying on low-profit informal economic activities such as scavenging and selling goods on streets and in flea markets. While this general portrayal cannot accurately describe the heterogeneity of Gitano communities' living conditions and class positions, it rings true for many.

Anthropologist have devoted attention to how Romani groups deal with the past (Gay y Blasco, 2001; Montañés Jiménez, 2022; Stewart, 2004; Williams, 2003). Discussing Gitano social memory, shared identity and sources of Gitano distinctiveness in an impoverished urban setting in Madrid, Gay y Blasco affirms that her informants

> consistently downplay the past in their accounts of themselves as part of *el pueblo Gitano* (the Gitano people), and do not look to a historical or mythical past for explanations of their way of life or their difference from the dominant society.
>
> (1999: 13–14)

According to Gay y Blasco, Gitanos' disregard for their past—a force that nevertheless is always threatening to spill over into the present—is expressed in practices of containment and obliteration, which remove ancestors from communal memory and go hand in hand with a performative cultural identity organised around a lack of structural political organisation other than kinship and shaped by the need to comply with the Gitano ways in the present (Gay y Blasco, 2001). While I do not intend to engage with Gay y Blasco's theoretical underpinnings at length in this chapter, I wish to elaborate briefly on her insights regarding *la vida de antes* (the life of before), the descriptions of "life as it used to be" (2001: 634).

By "the life of before", Gay y Blasco refers to an imagined distant past, a period in which most Gitanos alive today did not participate and is understood by them as an ahistorical, changeless period of unknown duration shaped by persecution, poverty, marginality and adversity (2001: 634). "The life of before" includes no origin stories, no accounts of how the Gitanos came to be what they are and where they are (Gay y Blasco, 2001: 635). Discussions about the origins and history of Romani groups and Gitanos, an aspect that has obsessed gypsilorists and non-Gitanos scholarship for centuries, are far from being, according to Gay y Blasco, essential to understanding the current lives of Gitanos in the south of Madrid, who often look disinterested in the topic and dispute the value of such questions when ethnographers ask them (Gay y Blasco, 1999; see also San Román, 1997: 69). Instead, Gitanos in the south of Madrid "produce only highly schematic and comparatively underdeveloped accounts of their past as a group', and these accounts are very rarely brought to the fore within the context of everyday life" (Gay y Blasco, 1999). Negative specificities of "life of before" predicated on privation echo persistent critical aspects of the current experiences of Gitanos, yet neither their stories nor their protagonists' identities, according to Gay y Blasco, are elaborated or transmitted actively. When forcedly narrated, undeveloped accounts of the past draw on notions of progress and modernity, which "works as a counterpoint to present conditions" and signals the relative improvement conditions of Gitano people in current times (Gay y Blasco, 2001: 640).

Spanish anthropologist Teresa San Román presents similar views to Gay y Blasco's, when she notes that

> Gitanos in general are not friends of speaking using the preterit, they get easily tired, they get anxious and pass to talking of the most immediate present that they can, making it difficult to reconstruct their past, even the most recent one.
>
> (San Román, 1997: 69; not my translation)

Cañete Quesada, whose work focuses on Gitanos' oral testimonies during the Spanish Civil War, adds a much-needed reflection about power in the conversation regarding the lack of written/oral sources and generational transmission of knowledge, by stating that "Gitanos' reaction to silencing their own past, although perhaps responding to a specific aspect of group idiosyncrasy, also reflects the traumatic experience in an obscure past that is still difficult to evoke and unlikely to be shared" (2020: 22).

Departing from the present-oriented ethos and practices of obliteration that anthropologists persistently associate with Roma and Gitanos, in this chapter Gory and his father actively strive to remember and share their views and experiences about their past with the firm intention that they be shared outside of their close kin. Such an "open" attitude is significant because there is a scarcity of (Gitano) memories in the Spanish public sphere. Even in academia, with some notable exceptions (Gamella, 1999; Wang, 1996; Fernández Fernández and Rodríguez Padilla, 2010; Fernández Fernández et al., 2009), historical and anthropological work including genuine Romani voices and life narratives in Spain are sparse. Šūpulis (2019) has noted that Roma are willing to engage and narrate their past and ethnicity through life stories in academic interviews in Latvia to navigate identity ambivalence. On the one hand, Latvian Roma define themselves "as everyone else" in national contexts, restraining the narration of cultural differences driven by the anxiety of returned Nazi and communist persecution. On the other hand, Latvian Roma also recognise the existence of ethnic differences pertaining to their cultural heritage and traditions (Šūpulis, 2019). Such ambivalence between cultural differences and national belonging will also become apparent in Gory's and his father's narratives. However, albeit using different narratives plots, Gory and his father will criticise the use of cultural differences as justification for the episode of racism and xenophobia they encountered in the past.

Before presenting Gory's and his father's self-recorded material, I would like to add some observations regarding the production and presentation of their life narratives.

Life narratives can be defined as subjective accounts of significant events, experiences and stories narrators consider relevant to situate their identity, sense of self and individual trajectories. Life narrators draw on selected memories within temporal frameworks limited by their lifespan and personal storytelling to construct a particular image of themselves and their relationship to the world before a real or imagined audience, binding autobiographical memory and the self over time (Bluck and Habermas, 2000). Paradoxically, forgetting and remembering are mutually constitutive when producing life stories. Because of the selective nature embedded into the act of bringing experiences and memory into discourse, oblivion and omission are intrinsic to creating biographical narratives. Life narratives include a selection of stories emerging in a context in which narrators' interests and intentions, expectations from real or imagined audiences, and the perceived agendas of story collectors intersect to create and co-produce the practice of storytelling. In anthropology, biographical accounts often raise questions around accuracy, intentionality and the influence of anthropologists—by their presence or actions—in shaping the outcome, words and ideas used by narrators to present their former selves. Whereas Gory's father's account was spontaneously produced, Gory used his father's original narrative as a model for his storytelling. Therefore, they are intrinsically tied. Admittedly, memories of scarcities emerging from Gory's and his father's life accounts in this chapter are largely subjective. Facts, however, are not inevitably fictitious but rather ingrained in personal memories and reconstructed within a broader narrative that provides meaning and guides the selection of facts themselves. Furthermore, because of word-limit restrictions, the material here presented is a recreation of their life narratives, shorter, more concise and adapted to academic style and writing.[6] The selective engagement with few episodes of their lives, as well as the restricted selection of extracts featured in this chapter, was a deliberate decision made by Gory and me to tell a story we think follows in the footsteps of his father's original purpose. According to Gory, his father recorded his life story "primarily to denounce the injustice we Gitanos and our families suffered in the past." Gory himself, triggered by my suggestion, replicated his father's story to honour his memory and build upon his father's original intention to denounce injustice.

Gory's father's life narrative and memories

Gory's father was born in Andalucía, a region in the south of Spain. He was raised as a Gitano man by his Gitano parents, who survived the Spanish Civil War. Gory's grandparents defined themselves as "Gitano *canasteros*" (basket-weaver Gitanos). Gitanos *canasteros* have captured the imagination of Andalucians due to their itinerant lifestyle, trade skills and craftmanship talent, as well as with their symbolic association with romanticised bohemian and freedom ideals in a period of technological advancement and tradition erosion in the Spanish countryside. Highly renowned poets and flamenco singers, such as Federico García Lorca and Camarón de la Isla, honoured and exalted the

6 I adapted and translated the original content of Gory's and Gory's father's accounts to make them more readable in formal English. I summarised some stories, tried to improve the flow of some sections and deleted some parts to avoid iterations. However, quotes remain relatively unaltered in meaning and reflect the original content.

figures of *canasteros* in their poems and songs. To this day, Gitanos *canasteros* are often featured in Spanish songs, traditional Spanish romance, and popular culture as a symbol of Gitano purity and an expression of longing for an idealised and lost past.

Gory's grandparents were poor and struggled with *fatigas* (hardship), and their children faced extreme economic deprivation when growing up. Gory's father moved to Madrid in his twenties, where he met and married his Gitana wife and fathered his four sons. I briefly met Gory's father in an Evangelical Pentecostal Gitano Church when he was an older man. He converted to Pentecostalism in the 1990s, when Pentecostal Gitano churches started a spectacular expansion across the south of Madrid. Gory describes his father as a people person, capable of charming and establishing friendships with payo (non-Gitano) and Gitano people alike. He struck me as a shy and agreeable Gitano man. Gory, however, defines him as a man with a "strong personality" who "always stands up for himself". As some of the quotations show, this description accurately reflects his life attitude before personal injustice and discrimination, as narrated by Gory.

Gory's father was born in the 1940s, a historical period defined by a fratricidal civil war (1936–1939), widespread extreme poverty and economic collapse. Fascist General Francisco Franco, the brand-new head of the Spanish State following the coup that ended up overthrowing the left-leaning II Republic in 1939, imposed a climate of political persecution that led to the triumph of authoritarian values. Franco's economic policies were inspired by autarkic ideals that sought to reduce foreign economic, political and cultural influences by promoting national self-sufficiency. Thus, in the '40s and early '50s, Spain remained isolated from liberal Western Europe after the Second World War (1939–1945) and benefited little from the financial and industrial development driven by the European postwar economic growth.

In a war-devastated country, and not unlike most Spanish people, many Gitanos faced woes and endured economic hardship. We know little about the lives and experiences of Gitanos during the Spanish Civil War and the subsequent dictatorship of General Francisco Franco, as they were rarely documented in schoolbooks, chronicles or historical monographs (Cañete Quesada, 2020; See also Martín Sánchez, 2017, 2018). Those Gitanos living in Andalucía, an already poverty-stricken region before the civil war, confronted a particularly salient difficult life. Gory's father's life story account begins in the year he was born (1943) and introduces us to his childhood struggles with poverty, racial discrimination and Gitanos' economic survival practices during the postwar period. Whereas Gory's father's account is a linear, non-segmented storyline, here it will be split into three parts to facilitate its analysis.

Material scarcity following the Spanish Civil War

Like many other Spanish families, Gory's father's family faced a scenario of absolute material scarcity in the years following the Spanish Civil War.

Andalucía was one of the first regions attacked by the fascist rebel troops. In 1937, hundreds of thousands of Andalusians were forced to flee the region in a refugee movement known as *la desbandá* (the stampede). In the aftermath of the Civil War, Republicans, as well as the general population, were intimidated, retaliated against and murdered if accused of having republican links, not collaborating with or plotting against the brand-new Spanish fascist regime. Gory's family remained in Andalucía during the war and its aftermath and suffered the devastating socio-economic consequences of the massive economic recession ensuing from the military battle. Many Gitano families, who were already in a highly vulnerable position before the start of the war, lived in conditions of absolute misery but managed to survive. Gory's father's memories vividly illustrate this dark period of the Spanish past:

> I was born on the 29th of June in 1943 in a small town called San Roque in Cadiz. We lived in a hut made out of stones and branches with my parents and brothers. We did not have money to buy bricks, so the house was made of materials we found in the area. Keeping the house standing using strings was a lot of effort. Guardia Civil often came to the area to dismantle the house because we were not allowed to stay there. They were very aggressive and beat the adults. When our home was destroyed, we were forced to construct it again; meanwhile, we lived underneath some sheets we used as roofs. I remember winters were especially harsh on us. The rain leaked inside, and it felt freezing. We usually slept together to keep us warm. We lived like dogs!
>
> We were extremely poor, and food was scarce. Gitanos coming to town was as if we were the plague! People excluded us and rarely offered us any job. We were *gitanos canasteros* (basket-makers). My dad would make baskets, and my mother would sell them. She would go to Gibraltar and sell them to English women. Despite being illiterate, she was able to learn some sentences in English to sell stuff. Sometimes, we stole fruits and animals to eat. It was very sad my father had to steal food to feed his children, but it was the only way we could survive. As a child, I worked for some people, keeping, feeding and caring for their animals. I spent days barefoot in the field, enduring heavy rains and hot days. All of it for a piece of bread and some olive oil. I usually stole food from the pigs.

Gory's father's account reveals intimate and heartbreaking experiences and prove that national experiences of absolute scarcity do not necessarily forge solidarity between suffering subjects and communities. Several passages merit special attention. The narrated scarcity of a semi-nomadic life in a postwar, deprived Spain contrasts with the strong resilience shown by Gory's father. The iterative mention of animals—dogs, pigs, horses—in Gory's father's account not only shows the prominence of agricultural activities in Andalucía but also blatantly reflects the powerful feelings of dehumanisation he harboured during his childhood. Notably, Gory's father's account also offers context and provides some ethical justifications to understand petty thieving in the postwar context. Gitanos, by no means, were alone in suffering traumatic experiences of scarcity, extreme poverty and deprivation in Spain in the aftermath of conflict. However, adding to an already gloomy situation, many Gitanos, like Gory's family members, faced ethnic persecution and harassment from neighbours, the State and military law enforcement agencies.

Police brutality, cruelty and violence

The first section of the narration by Gory's father briefly spotlights police brutality as performed by the Spanish Guardia Civil, the oldest law enforcement agency in Spain and one of two national police forces operating in the country. In this second portion, he elaborates on his dramatic encounters with Guardia Civil growing up in the Cadiz countryside. Gory's father recounts his encounter with this police force as follows:

> When I was little, I feared Guardia Civil. I remember they were extremely violent. They were violent towards everyone, but especially Gitanos. My father was beaten up before our eyes many times. We were very little and could not do anything about it but cry. Guardia Civil was ruthless without remorse. In the summer, we Gitanos would gather around the river near my hometown and have parties. Guardia Civil did not like it, so they would come riding their horses and beat us up, including women. Everyone then ran and cried; it was very sad, and I still get emotional remembering those episodes. Sometimes, they would come with scissors to give us bad haircuts and laugh at us. I have seen movies about Hitler, and I feel they were very similar to him and the way he treated people. Franco and Guardia Civil were awful to Gitanos. Maybe not every Gitano suffered the same as my family did, but I honestly think most Gitanos living in rural areas back then have similar stories to share.

As part of its daily duties, the Guardia Civil patrols and investigates crimes in rural areas, including highways and ports, whilst the National Police usually deals with safety in urban situations. During the postwar period, the Guardia Civil grew a reputation as a heavy-handed police force. The fact that the Guardia Civil largely operated—and still does—in primarily rural and isolated parts of Spain during the postwar era increased the risk of police violations of individual civil rights through lack of supervision and accountability. In addition, a social and political climate defined by fascist ideals and authoritarian values facilitated abuse and the proliferation of hate-based practices. Gory's father's horrifying memories speak to themes of cruelty and abuse of power. They are also a testament to the long-term emotional scars that victims and witnesses of extreme violence carry during their lifetime. The feeling of impunity and entitlement by the Guardia Civil, as described in the extract above, saturating the recount of memories is both heartbreaking and infuriating. Particularly telling is the narrative opposition between the joy associated with Gitano communal life—and its parties—and the presence of the Guardia Civil, associated with persecution and malice. As a result of his traumatic childhood experience, Gory's father portrays and narrates the Guardia Civil in the Francoist era as the personification of evil.

Overcoming material scarcity, Madrid and a new life

Gory's father resumed his life story in the early '60s when he was a young man in his late teens. The year 1959 was key for Spanish economic development. That year, the Francoist government approved *El Plan de Estabilización de 1959* (the Stabilisation Plan of 1959), a series of financial measures whose main goal was the economic liberalisation of the Spanish markets, marking a turning point from previous autarkic policies. The plan's implementation led to industrialisation, economic growth, job losses in rural areas and mass migration movements towards urban areas, hollowing the rest of the country. Gory's family followed many other payo and Gitano families who emigrated to urban areas, such as Madrid, the capital of Spain. Similar to non-Gitano working-class people internal migrants, Gitanos in urban capitals were habitually allocated in deprived neighbourhoods under construction, many of which lacked essential equipment and infrastructure.

> My life was filled with hardship until I was sixteen years old. In 1959, I moved out to Madrid with my family. In the beginning, my life was not better. My mother had to beg in the street to get some money. We ate bread other people threw into bins—my possessions amounted to a pair of shoes and trousers. We lived in an impoverished neighbourhood in the city, filled with rats and bugs. It was hard for everyone at that time, not only us. I prayed every night to God for help. I was very good-mannered and humble, so payo people liked me. Two payo friends I made in the neighbourhood let me construct a small house in one of their land possessions. Some years later, someone in Villaverde offered me a job in a second-hand store. I had to carry a lot of weight moving the clothing around, but I was thrilled I had a job.[7] Then I met a gitana woman I married and had four beautiful kids. Later on, I found a house in Orcasitas, a neighbourhood in the south of Madrid, and my life changed for the better. Now I have grandkids! I am very thankful to God my life changed for the better.

Gory's father's account exemplifies the chaotic nature of Madrid's city's rapid expansion and reception of massive internal migration flows from rural areas.

7 Subsequently, he became a gardener and then retired.

Notably, the portrayal of non-Gitano people here changes. From remarking discrimination, he focuses on the intervention and generosity of two non-Gitano friends who made a difference in his quality of life. The overall approach also changes. From a negative, pitiful account of his relationship with his surroundings emerges a more positive undertone, one that is grateful to life, Madrid and God for offering him a loving family and a home. The experiences of poverty, hope and uncertainty intertwine to describe a subjective account defined by a positive linear narrative. From a place of sadness and poverty to relative material comfort and emotional fulfilment, Gory's father recounted his journey, which ended happily.

Gory's life narrative and memories

When writing the present chapter, Gory is in his late-40s and is a father of two. He was born and raised in the south of Madrid. Gory lives in Villaverde, a working-class and marginalised area. I met Gory while conducting ethnographic fieldwork among Pentecostal Gitanos, and soon our friendship grew. Gory claims his character is remarkably similar to his father's. He takes pride in being a people person and his ability to make friends, especially with non-Gitano individuals. His father's passing was an excruciating moment for Gory, as he felt exceptionally close to him.

Gory defines himself as a songwriter. Indeed, Gory is related to *Los Carmona Habichuela*, a celebrated Spanish gitano flamenco family, and writes songs for flamenco singers and pop music artists. Despite his musical talent, he lacks stable wages and finds it challenging to make ends meet. Gory has been a flea market vendor and has worked on temporary contracts as a garbage collector, gardener and ticket officer for sporting events. Moreover, his family rely on the *Renta Mínima de Inserción,* an emergency minimum income allowance granted by the Madrid Regional Government.

Like his father, Gory is a devoted Christian believer. For nearly two decades, he was a member of the Iglesia Evangélica de Filadelfia (IEF), the foremost Gitano-led church in Spain. Recently, Gory left the IEF church to join a multicultural church led by a non-Gitano pastor and mainly frequented by Christian immigrants and a few other Gitano families. Gory does not hold any ministry position, but he is a highly active church member. Interestingly, as this development ties religious worldviews with discussions about scarcity, Gory has recently shown an appreciation for prosperity gospel ideas. The prosperity gospel (PG) is a Christian movement predicated on controversial beliefs advocating that it is God's will for Christians to be wealthy, healthy, and successful. Interestingly, PG ideas have recently spread across Gitano families and communities (Montañés Jiménez, 2016). PG leaders often consider themselves messengers of God, whose mission is to transform the world and lead believers to social and financial prominence. Consequently, access to positions of power, high status or influence is a divine mandate, and the success of a Christian is a clear sign of being blessed. As put by Gory, the IEF church he used to attend claims God is a "provider", meaning God will supply spiritual nourishment and material comfort to meet believers' basic needs. In line with PG ideas, his new non-Gitano Pentecostal church takes one step further, claiming God is, primarily, a "God of abundance". Gory takes issues with PG churches that speak bluntly about money or demand large sums of money in form of tithing or donations from their congregation members, but he firmly believes that Christians should follow individual ambitions, hold aspirations toward upward mobility and pursue success in their professional careers.

Gory was born in the '70s, a historical period in which Franco's fascist regime gave way to the arrival of representative democracy (1978) and the emergence of consumerist capitalism in Spain. He grew up in a Madrid socio-economic context shaped by rapid industrialisation, a steady improvement of communication and transport infrastructure, and increased investment in the health and education system by the Spanish State. However, he has also lived through the early 1990s recession, the 2008 financial crash and the 2020 COVID-19 pandemic emergency. Gory's account follows his father's steps as it touches upon themes such as his childhood, relationship with payo people and work life. To create analytical and formal symmetry, the text selection featured in this chapter replicates the three-section structure first introduced to analyse Gory's father's life memories.

Madrid and the growth of peripherical urban areas

Gory's family journey from decaying rural areas to emerging urban peripheries under construction mirrors the path of hundreds of thousands of Spanish payo working-class and Gitano families in the second half of the twentieth century. Technological improvement in the agricultural sector rendered traditional professions obsolete, and industrialisation acted as a pull factor for economic migrants like Gory's parents. Poor Spanish migrating families were located in the city's most neglected areas and makeshift barracks, most of them located in the south. To this day, Madrid's city social hierarchies shape the capital city's space. Affluent families and individuals reside mainly in the north, whereas the south is mostly home to working-class inhabitants. Most Gitano families still reside in the south.

Against that backdrop, Gory starts his account by chronicling a childhood life experience defined by some degree of scarcity but also by a strong sense of local identity and emotional attachment to emerging working-class barrios. In Gory's words:

> I was born in 1977 in Orcasitas, a neighbourhood in the city of Madrid. I have three brothers, two of them older than me. I am the one who is more similar to my father in terms of character. Sometimes, we had arguments, but we were close. Soon after I was born, we moved to Villaverde, another area close to Orcasitas. I have very fond memories of my childhood. We played in the streets with other children, and no cars were on

> the roads. The streets were safe for us children. Streets lacked pavements, so we played in the mud; it was a lot of fun. I remember my parents and others planted some trees back then, now those trees are enormous! I was not aware back then, but surrounding my neighbourhood, some areas were home drug markets and drug selling points. However, it felt very safe to me. When I grew up and was older, I realised our barrio was poor compared to others. Everything was under construction. Sometimes, we had no running water or electricity at home. I remember we lived in an illegal shack for some time, but then we moved into public housing. Our neighbourhood was made up of Gitano and non-Gitano families. We did not have much back then, but food was always on the table. I remember fondly when they opened the 12 de Octubre Hospital, one of the best medical centres in Europe.

Gory describes his childhood using an apparent dualism. Externally, Gory portrays Villaverde as a place of poverty and lurking dangers (such as drugs), yet he insists on depicting his experience positively. As a child, Gory felt he was safe and taken care of. Clearly, the hospital is here an idiom of progress signalling modernity, institutional presence and care. Gory's jolly, nostalgic and (perhaps) idealised recollection of his childhood contrasts remarkably with his father's. From a postwar scenario in rural Andalucía to an urban environment beginning to grow economically in the country's capital, pairing descriptions of Gory's and his father's childhoods shows an intergenerational improvement, one that Gory is very aware of.

Neighbours, police and barrios

Despite Gory's rosy description of his childhood, Villaverde was—and to some extent still is—a hostile environment for Gitanos. Not unlike the rest of the Spanish people, many Villaverde payo inhabitants in the '80s had deep-seated prejudices and stereotypes regarding Gitanos (Buhigas Jiménez, 2024; Montes, 1986). Gitanos were often scapegoated for wider class-based and spatial marginality–related social problems they faced. Back then, and still to his day, Gitanos became a master symbol of drug dealing and the marginality and social decay that threatened payo Villaverde's neighbourhoods, which led to recurrent collective anti-Gitano collective mobilisation by payos (Buhigas Jiménez, 2024; Gay y Blasco, 1999: 34; see also Gamella, 2002). However, the way Gory narrates his family's relationship with non-Gitano people in his childhood is diametrically opposed to his father's account in the '40s. Gory's account reads as follows:

> People are very fond of my family in my barrio. I have a lot of payo friends. When I was little, and my father was still alive, we frequented a bar, and the owner would lend us chairs and tables to have flamenco parties. Gitano flamenco singers often came by to sing and dance with us.

> I have relatives that are very well-known in the music world. I compose and play music, too. Police would often stop by to keep an eye on us, and sometimes, they would join the party. We had a good relationship with them. We cleaned up the street after we finished, and they appreciated it. People often think of Gitanos as troublemakers, but that is far from the truth.

In opposition to the widespread representation of Gitanos as isolated and excluded neighbours, Gory's account interweaves a sense of barrio community with feelings of warmth, affection and closeness. The police also feature in a positive light, not as a heavy-handed institution but as an amicable force. Gory's account thus chooses to engage with positive aspects of inter-group dynamics by collapsing or playing down ethnic borders as he firmly believes this harmonic scenario is accurate to his memories about the past.

Work-life experiences

In this last section, Gory narrates his work-life experience, shaped by difficulties securing jobs and a desire to keep composing music. As I write this chapter, he still suffers from regular migraines, fatigue and occasional respiratory problems. His medical conditions make it difficult to access and secure jobs. Gory recounts his past and current job access situation as follows:

> When I finished primary school, I spent years without studying or working. I never finished secondary school. I feel I lost some years of my life, although, to be honest, I was very happy back then. I would hang out with my friends and family, which was a lot of fun. I signed up for a training course on carpentry offered by Fundacion Secretariado Gitano, an NGO [non-governmental organisation] specialising in providing aid for Gitanos. Then, when I was seventeen years old, I worked in a supermarket, but unfortunately, my boss bullied me. When he discovered I was Gitano, he made my life impossible. He assigned me the heaviest task and repeatedly farted when he was close to me to make me feel uncomfortable. Of course, he did not renew my contract. Some years later, I worked with some relatives in flea markets. I also broadcast some radio in Villaverde. Most importantly, I have always composed music for artists. Making music is what I like the most, and I am very good at it. In fact, I consider myself a musician. I make some money with music, but it is a tough and competitive industry. Lately, I have worked as security for Atletico de Madrid's football games and as a garbage collector. Unfortunately, I have been suffering from chronic migraines for the last decades, and that is preventing me from working in regular jobs. Every other day, I get headaches, and it is excruciating. I had COVID-19, and that made things worse; I still have some respiratory problems. Even though

> I have some clinical diagnoses from doctors for my chronic migraines, I am struggling to get recognition for my illness from the State. I have long been applying for disability retirement income to no avail. It is very frustrating. However, although I have it bad, I think the future is bright for new Gitano generations. My youngest daughter wants to become a criminologist, and I know many young Gitanos in primary and secondary schools are keen on acquiring university and professional training. I honestly believe this young generation of Gitanos will make a difference and demonstrate that, with the help of God, we Gitanos can contribute to society and get good jobs and education. You will see!

Like his father, Gory has faced discrimination in the workplace because of his cultural identity. Whereas Gory narrates his efforts to navigate a Spanish job market where he finds it difficult to find permanent wages and struggles to be recognised as a functional, diverse worker with a right to a State stipend, he also harbours hope for future generations. For him, young generations of Gitanos hold high aspirations for themselves and aim to acquire qualifications and better jobs. Against a backdrop of a high Gitano school drop-out ratio and enormous difficulties in accessing university qualifications in Spanish society, Gory's statement shows he trusts new generations will be able to overcome structural barriers and ethnic inequalities.

Conclusion

The juxtaposition between Gory and his father's memories presents a captivating overview of their narrated life trajectories. Read together, both accounts indicate significant disparities in the degree of difficulties Gory and his father encountered but also shed light on the multiple scarcities they have faced as Spanish Gitano men living in rural and working-class environments. Gory's father's memories are remarkably similar to the sketchy descriptions Gay y Blasco associates with how Gitanos often narrates "the life of before", as they take place "in the countryside, moving from village to village", describe a life in which "they were very poor and stole from the non-Gypsies", and "suffered at the hands of the Guardia Civil", and are negatively assessed as "hard, miserable, low" (Gay y Blasco, 2001: 634). Whereas Gory's life memories differ significantly from his father's in the degree of experienced poverty, violence and racism, the content of both accounts speaks to experiences of shortage around various sorts of resources often associated with discussion about scarcity, including housing, welfare, jobs and goods.

Departing from economic and development approaches to scarcity, this chapter has explored memory-related dimensions of shortage, testing the hermeneutic and anthropological value of the notion of memories of scarcity against self-recorded life narratives produced by Gory and his father. The use of memories as a measuring rod to evaluate the value of scarcity is endorsed by the fact that life narratives are excellent methodological tools to explore self-perceptions, narratives about the self and, more generally, the expression of subjectivities and values.

As a general analytical framework, the notion of memories of scarcity indeed captures critical experiences pertaining to ideas of shortage and insufficiency shaping the production of memories by Gory and his father. Memories of scarcity, as a concept bridging and connecting individual experience with structural inequalities, enable us to bring to the analytical forefront experiences of shortage. Most human beings share such experiences at some point, but they are particularly harmful when affecting the lives of minorities and vulnerable populations. Despite Gory's and his father's narratives being first-person accounts and telling individual stories, they express and are embedded in a collective experience shared by many Gitanos in the city of Madrid and, therefore, are likely resonant with the struggles and life experiences of Gitanos in Madrid and beyond. Notably, their memories and life events are similar to those of other Gitano and non-Gitano individuals living in Madrid's urban peripheries in the twentieth century.

The complexities of life experiences and narrative turns taken by both to represent and depict their life trajectories exceed the boundaries of scarcity. Gory and his father's narratives encapsulate stories about how Gitanos endure scarcity but also prompt reflections about what it means to share and circulate those stories about the past in a context of cultural marginalisation and stigma. Instead of confining and forcefully fitting life experience narratives into frameworks of scarcity, we must emphasise the idea of scarcity as a generative and productive tool.

When taking the form of autobiographies, critics argue that life narratives over-celebrate individuality, signalling the dominance of Western sensibilities predicated on individualism, accomplishment, notoriety or desire to impress. However, life narratives can also give voice to people and individuals who remain marginalised, invisible and invalidated by society. Life narrators chronicle personal and historical events, and their memories can serve to create historical records, complement existing archival sources or question hegemonic historical readings of some historical periods. In that sense, by recounting their own lives and intimate experiences, and by omitting or forgetting others (Gemignani, 2014), narrators are making "history" while also "performing several rhetorical acts: justifying their own perceptions, upholding their reputations, disputing the accounts of others, settling scores, conveying cultural information, and inventing desirable futures, among others" (Smith and Watson, 2002: 13).

The chapter argues that far from being neutral and detached recollections of one's past, life narratives and memories can become intentional political research devices. They are political because they can be used to reveal and denounce injustice. Also, in contexts of marginalisation, they may be used to contest negative representations about a category of people, empowering narrators to own their voices and ideas about how they should be perceived. Gory's and his father's narratives are politically divergent, though. It seems apparent Gory's father intended to create a record of his life experiences and the hardships he encountered as a Gitano man. Perhaps driven by his new-found religious beliefs about prosperity and abundance, Gory's recollection speaks to a new historical moment in which, fortunately, Gitanos have better socio-economic prospects than past generations in the south of Madrid.

Gory firmly believes Gitanos, or any community for that purpose, cannot be defined by what they lack. It is the inherent tension and gap between life as a whole and the necessary reductionist narratives about one's life in tandem with concerns about representation that ultimately triggered Gory to indicate, after recording some of his memories, that his life, and by extension, that of his father, are not and cannot be exclusively defined by scarcity. Scarcity, he pointed out, "must not be the only lens through which you scholars look at Gitano people". In so doing, Gory shifted my attention from scarcity to broader debates regarding (self-)representation, adding layers of complexity to the conversation about the entanglement of scarcity and minorities taking place in this book.

Some scholars, indeed, have criticised how scholarly work on Roma/Gypsy usually approaches them *only* as a marginal group (Cantón Delgado et al., 2019: 462; Chinoy and Lagunas Arias, 2022; Marushiakova and Popov, 2011: 102). When Gory recounts his life story and analyses his father's, he firmly departs from one-dimensional and damaged-centred approaches. Even though he focused on a few negative experiences, Gory strived to portray his experiences in a positive light and gently refused to engage with overarching negative frameworks. Gory critically engages practices of scholarly knowledge production by providing an alternative and positive narrative of Gitanos' life in his account. Furthermore, Gory's effort to refashion society's perspective of Gitanos engages further issues regarding Romani (mis)representations in public fora. Thus, the analytical potential of scarcity, Gory cleverly notes, may be overshadowed by its potential impact in reinforcing undesirable trends in a context of abundant scholarly work that focuses on the negative aspects of scarcity in Gitanos' lives.

References

Bluck, Susan and Tilmann Habermas. 2000. 'The Life Story Schema'. *Motivation and Emotion* 24 (2): 121–147.

Buhigas Jiménez, Rafael. 2024. '¡La periferia arde! Violencia y hostigamiento urbano contra los gitanos de Madrid en los años 80'. *AREAS. Revista Internacional de Ciencias Sociales* 46: 5–23.

Cañete Quesada, Carmen. 2020. 'The Memory of Spanish Gypsies: Scholarship, Oral History, and Archive Research'. *Romani Studies* 30 (1): 15–47.

Cantón-Delgado, Manuela, Marco Toyansk and Javier Jiménez-Royo. 2019. 'Suspicion and Prejudice: The Role of Ideology in Studying Christian Revival Among the Roma'. *Social Compass* 664: 455–470.

Chinoy, Clara and David Lagunas Arias. March 2022. 'One Route to Respectability: An Historical View of Socio-Cultural and Economic Reproduction Among the Gitanos of Lebrija'. *Journal of Gypsy Studies* 4 (1): 3–26.

Fernandez Fernandez, Dolores, Monica de la Flor Heredia and Eusebio Rodriguez Padilla. 2009. *El pueblo gitano en la Guerra Civil y la Posguerra: Andalucia Oriental.* Granada: Asociacion de Mujeres Gitanas ROMI.

Fernández Fernández, Dolores and Eusebio Rodríguez Padilla. 2010. *Mujeres gitanas represaliadas en la provincia de Granada durante la Guerra Civil y la Posguerra: 1936–1950.* Granada: Arráez/Asociación de Mujeres Gitanas ROMI de Granada.

Fox, Jon and Peter Vermeersch. 2010. 'Backdoor Nationalism'. *European Journal of Sociology/Archives Européennes de Sociologie* 51 (2): 325–357.

Gamella, Juan F. 1999. 'En sus propias palabras. Historia de vida de tres abuelas gitanas'. In *Los gitanos andaluces. Demófilo: Revista de Cultura Tradicional de Andalucía.* Sevilla: Fundación Machado, pp. 233–276.

Gamella, Juan F. 2002. 'Exclusión social y conflicto étnico en Andalucía. Análisis de un ciclo de movilización y acción colectiva antigitana (1976–2000)'. *Gazeta de Antropología* 18.

Gay y Blasco, Paloma. 1999. *Gypsies in Madrid: Sex, Gender and the Performance of Identity.* Oxford: Berg.

Gay y Blasco, Paloma. 2001. '"We Don't Know Our Descent": How the Gitanos of Jarana Manage the Past'. *The Journal of the Royal Anthropological Institute* 7 (4): 631–647.

Gay y Blasco, Paloma. 2016. '"It's the Best Place for Them": Normalising Roma Segregation in Madrid'. *Social Anthropology* 244: 446–461.

Gemignani, Marco. 2014. 'Memory, Remembering, and Oblivion in Active Narrative Interviewing'. *Qualitative Inquiry* 20 (2): 127–135.

Grill, Jan. 2012. 'It's Building Up to Something and It Won't Be Nice When It Erupts': The Making of Roma/Gypsy Migrants in Post-Industrial Scotland'. *Focaal* 2012 (62): 42–54.

Martín Sánchez, David. 2017. 'El pueblo gitano y la guerra civil Una historia desconocida de la contienda del 36'. *Andalucía en la historia, dossier Gitanos la historia olvidada* 55: 24–27.

Martín Sánchez, David. 2018. 'Los gitanos en la guerra civil: Atrapados entre dos bandos'. *La Aventura de la Historia* 235: 30–33.

Marushiakova, Elena and Vaselin Popov. 2011. 'Between Exoticisation and Marginalisation: Current Problems of Gypsy Studies'. *Behemoth: A Journal on Civilisation* 41: 86–105.

Mehta, Lyla. 2001. 'The Manufacture of Popular Perceptions of Water Scarcity: Dams and Water-Related Narratives in Gujarat, India'. *World Development* 29 (12): 2025–2041.

Montañés Jiménez, Antonio. 2016. *Etnicidad e identidad gitana en los cultos pentecostales de la ciudad de Madrid.* El caso de la' Iglesia Evangélica de Filadelfia' y el 'Centro Cristiano Vino Nuevo el Rey Jesús'. Papeles del CEIC, vol. 2016/2, Papel 158. CEIC.

Montañés Jiménez, Antonio. 2022. 'Death, Commemoration and Grief in the Age of COVID-19: The Case of Christian Pentecostal Gitanos in Spain'. *Anthropology Now.*

Montañés Jiménez, Antonio and Gory Carmona. 2023. '"COVID-19 Is a Trial from God": Gitanos, Pentecostal Imaginaries and Compliance'. In P. Gay y Blasco and M. Fotta (eds.), *Romani Chronicles of COVID-19: Testimonies of Harm and Resilience.* Oxford: Berghahn Books.

Montañés Jiménez, Antonio and D. Gómez Ávila. 2024. 'Moral Panic, Spanish Roma and Political Contestation During the COVID-19 Health Crisis'. In Simone Maddanu and Emanuele Toscano (eds.), *Inequality, Youth, Democracy and the Pandemic.* London: Routledge.

Montes, Juan. 1986. 'Sobre el realojamiento de los Gitanos'. In T. San Román (ed.), *Entre la marginacion y el racismo: Reflexiones sobre la vida de los gitanos.* Madrid: Alianza Editorial, pp. 155–170.

Nacu, Alexandra. 2012. 'From silent marginality to spotlight scapegoating? A brief case study of France's policy towards the Roma'. *Journal of Ethnic and Migration Studies* 38 (8): 1323–1328.

Powell, Ryan and John Lever. 2017. 'Europe's Perennial "Outsiders": A Processual Approach to Roma Stigmatisation and Ghettoisation'. *Current Sociology* 655: 680–699.

Ross, Andrew.1996. 'The Lonely Hour of Scarcity'. *Capitalism, Nature, Socialism* 7 (3): 3–26.

San Román, Teresa. 1976. *Vecinos gitanos*. Madrid: Akal Editor.

San Román, Teresa. 1997. *La diferencia inquietante: Viejas y nuevas estrategias culturales de los gitanos*. Madrid: Siglo XXI.

Scoones, Ian, Rebecca Smalley, Ruth Hall and Dzodzi Tsikata. 2014. *Narratives of Scarcity: Understanding the 'Global Resource Grab'*. Working Paper 076, Future Agricultures, PAAS.

Smith, Sidonie and Julia Watson. 2002. *Reading Autobiography: A Guide for Interpreting Life Narratives*. University of Minnesota Press.

Stewart, Michael. 2004. 'Remembering Without Commemoration: The Mnemonics and Politics of Holocaust Memories Among European Roma'. *The Journal of the Royal Anthropological Institute* 10 (3): 561–582.

Šūpulis, Edmunds. 2019. 'A Community Without History? A Life Story Approach to Romany Memory and Ethnicity'. *Romani Studies* 29 (1).

Wang, Kristen. 1996. *The Story of Tío Carlos: The Autobiography of a Spanish "Gitano"*. Frankfurt and Maine: Peter Lang.

Williams, Patrick. 2003. *Gypsy World: The Silence of the Living and the Voices of the Dead*. Chicago: University of Chicago Press.

4 The rise of fabricated majoritarianism

How nationalism based on 'othering' in democracies at times of scarcity is exacerbating existential threats to minorities

Joshua Castellino

Introduction

The establishment of the State in Europe in the post-Westphalia phase (from around 1648 onwards) ushered in a number of international treaties as those of a lesser status within these new units sought protection guarantees. This was an early indicator of the significant impact that would fall on minorities through the establishment, consolidation and gradual acceptance of the sovereign State. The emergence of the territorially centred sovereign State often based on the idea of a single 'nation' within its frontiers as the *only* legitimate governing entity, had significant consequences for those that did not bear allegiance to that nation. The development of 'national identities' and accompanying jingoism around nationalism were designed to convince polities that the ties that bound them were meaningful. But these were often achieved by accentuating differences with neighbouring polities, portraying one culture as superior and distinct to another. Continuous human migratory processes mostly driven by trade and commerce made communities heterogenous, heightening difficulties in maintaining singular uniting narratives, or in framing new, imagined, sometimes contested identities along commonly accepted lines. European expansion into the Americas, Africa and Asia in the name of bringing 'civilization, commerce and Christianity' which simultaneously exploited resources, territories and peoples not only created the blueprint for the contemporary extractive economic model and its deep consequences for contemporary climate change: it also set the physical frame for the determination of global political governance by establishing the State as the primary unit recognisable in international society (Castellino, 2024). Thus, lines drawn upon maps 'where no white man's foot had ever trod' became crystallised national frontiers with the communities trapped within forced to imagine and accept themselves as a community in the image of its colonial masters. Celebrated as the sovereign unit in international law through its coronation in the Montevideo Convention of 1934, the overall governance of these States often passed to the dominant group within, or to one with significant proximity

DOI: 10.4324/9781032661780-5

to the departing colonial ruler who could maintain its privileged access to resources.

The effective privatisation of an asset, i.e. the former colony, and its transfer to proxies or those who had the blessing of the former colonial powers was celebrated with fanfare drawing on Enlightenment-era ideas of self-determination. In its most famous guise this process is referred to as decolonisation, which is believed to have—and did—yield freedom from colonial subjugation. In its revolutionary sense, the transition generated a sense of freedom from oppression and, despite its incorporation flaws, was the precursor for the emergence of a new type of entity. In most cases though, this post-colonial independent State simply ran on the same socio-economic contours of its predecessor: its new rulers occupied the same palaces, often maintained the same institutions and adhered to the same laws that were deemed sacrosanct, especially those protecting property. Faced with relative poverty due to the systematic transfer of its wealth, the new post-colonial State often found itself escalating the exploitation of resources, land and peoples along the lines of the inherited economic model. Minorities and any other dissenters were often perceived as 'the enemy within' or the 'fifth columnists'. With minorities in particular, any pre-colonial trans-border links to kin communities divided by random boundary drawing was seen as an added threat. The establishment of constitutions accompanied by erection or consolidation of institutions as part of State-building processes were designed to reassure those within and outside the State that the gains of freedom would accrue in an ordered and just manner.

At a global level, the impacts of this transition vary widely: from genuine attempts at inclusion, protection and promotion, to active steps taken to make invisible, marginalise, exclude or in extreme cases, exterminate populations whose identity (real or imagined), ethnicity, religion, language or culture were deemed deviant from the norm. The development of the inherited colonial principles concerning the rule of law, democracy and human rights, all deigned to be of fundamental importance by the United Nations, were offered as a counterfoil to the worst of these excesses, creating external pressure ostensibly to promote better behaviour among the new additions to the expanded club of sovereign States. Compromises were forged in post-colonial States over the last 80 years which have begun to come under serious pressure in the current context of multiple crises.

Minority rights could be said to pre-date the development of public international law itself. Concern for the vulnerability of the few in the face of the potential tyranny of the many has occupied progressive thinkers throughout history. With global history books dominated by narratives of war it is unsurprising that genocide, ethnic cleansing and crimes against humanity feature prominently. That these disproportionately impact communities that may be more vulnerable than others meant that progressive systems thinkers throughout the ages have sought to focus attention to building normative frameworks, mechanisms and institutions in a bid to eradicate this element of human behaviour. Not always identifying the primary victims as minorities—perhaps for fear of reifying divisions within human families—this has nonetheless given rise to a strand of activity that could be recognised as the genesis of minority rights protection. Regular migration, the interspersing of populations of different lineage and the potential challenge that different customs and beliefs presented required thoughtful policy decisions if conditions of peace and order were to prevail in societies that were becoming increasingly diverse.

The *millet* system under the Ottoman Empire was an early precursor to finding ways to accommodate difference within communities, while many treaties commencing from the Promise of St. Louis of France to the Maronites in 1250 were also indicative of the need to engender protection for populations at times of particular vulnerability—such as along a migrant trail or when faced with mass expulsions after war. While early antecedents may exist elsewhere including within the waxing and waning of Chinese influence across the Silk Road, there has been inadequate attention devoted to this topic. Similarly inter-ethnic relations in other parts of the world, notably in pre-colonial Latin America, Africa and South and South-eastern Asia have not merited adequate attention. Instead, the literature, especially in the Western world on this topic, appears to reflect a standard Eurocentricity that may be familiar to readers with a wider historical ambit, in the suggestion that the subject of minority rights first emerged in Europe (Constantinides, 2022). Suffice to say there is adequate evidence in current narratives that suggests that the discipline of minority rights as a sub-field of law, political science, anthropology, sociology and history itself has had salience, irrespective of its inadequate documentation by those with power to control the narrative.

Building upon this impetus to challenge Eurocentricity in minority rights studies, this chapter seeks to challenge hegemonic narratives enforcing colonial assumptions and hierarchies in our contemporary global societies against the backdrop of current social, climate and moral crises. Driven by the growth of the climate emergency in conjunction with political systems that have been unable to tackle growing inequality, emerging scarcities have generated fierce competition for resources that are fragmenting societies along their ethnic, religious, racialised, linguistic and indigenous fault lines. Scarcity is driving migration from post-colonial entities towards the gleaming cities on the hill built in rich countries of the Organisation for Economic Co-Operation and Development, largely on the back of wealth exploited from the destruction of circular economies elsewhere. Rather than accepting this trail as an inevitable consequence of past and current exploitative socio-economic practices actions, the new arrivals are painted variously as 'criminals', 'scroungers' or 'economic migrants' and used as scapegoats to reify jingoistic nationalisms that had become suppressed in the previous era of relatively plenty. A collective and systematised lack of education about their own histories has endowed populations in former colonial countries with an unsubstantiated belief that their wealth was built on hard work and ingenuity while those seeking shelter within it are criminals. The idea that the systematised (and continuing) transfer of wealth that decimated circular economies and disrupted cultures may be criminal is simply dismissed with a variety of excuses.

This chapter is divided into four subsections. The first examines how the global imposition of the Europeanised State model onto diverse communities effectively condemned many societies to a 'majoritarianism' that permanently favours access by a dominant group to governance systems. The second contests the myth of the exaggerated threat posed by identity politics, highlighting their goal as designed to obscure other threats suggested as more legitimate. The third offers commentary on how democratic States are increasingly being governed with the attendant risks to this trajectory, while the final section will identity key questions germane to recalibrating a future in times of scarcity that may nonetheless contribute to establishing peaceful and ordered societies.

Importantly, this chapter presents scarcity as a political and economic construct generated by elites to impose and justify social order and maintain a conscious or subconscious ethno-religious privilege in modern States. Whereas scarcity is real or narrated—or a mix of both—this notion is understood as a pivot for the unjust capture and distribution of resources through an anthropocentric overexploitation of nature. In focusing specifically on how fabricated or artificial majoritarianism has historically harmed and undermined minorities, this chapter furthers a well-established tradition of critical studies revealing how scarcity conditions and narratives maintain and reproduce the status quo.

The modern exploitative democratic State: a caricature

The Creole claimants to power of the former archdioceses erected by Spain and Portugal in Latin America declared themselves independent of their ancestral homelands between 1810 and 1825 but feared Iberian *reconquista* of the Americas. They drew upon their European education to set about using law to guarantee their newly claimed possessions. Two rules were adopted that became the foundation for subsequent global decolonisation. The first, *uti possidetis juris*, legitimised the boundaries of the former colonial territories as political entities; the second established the European nation-state as the only recognisable form of governance in the Americas. This second self-declared phenomenon simply ignored other forms of governance that had existed since time immemorial across the American continents. These were relegated in importance by the first decision on boundaries which created the exclusive territorial frame within which the new political units were deemed to have exclusive jurisdiction, annulling every other exercise of sovereignty and re-subjugating native populations in the name of emancipating their new rulers.

The Montevideo Convention referred to earlier even sanctified this in international law. This was later to be elevated to becoming accepted at a global level. In the document enacted in Montevideo on 26 December 1933, the governments that attended the Seventh International Conference of American States identified a 'state' to constitute 'a sole person in the eyes of international law' (article 2), with the entity itself defined as possessing the following 'qualities': (1) a permanent population; (2) a defined territory; (3) government; and (4) capacity to enter into relations with other states.

This straitjacket placed upon incredibly diverse societies with myriad governance patterns that had existed in the Americas for centuries effectively channelled history in a particular direction that created the space in which majoritarianism, natural or coerced, could flourish. In addition to the summary dismissal of indigenous territories and governance systems, it also effectively expropriated all assets and put them at the behest of the sovereign State, to be claimed anew by those who agreed to shelter under its umbrella. Thus, pre-existing indigenous ancestral domains were annulled as new claims processes annihilated these titles on the self-declared basis that the land was *terra nullius* (i.e. owner free) until it came under the sovereignty of the new State. To exacerbate the caricature the self-declared sovereigns had their newly claimed sovereignty externally verified, including on the basis that their legitimacy stemmed from being the ones that reflected the majority political consensus of their populations—a validation of the principle of 'democratic consent' that was echoed in the American and French declarations of independence in 1776 and 1789, respectively. This was despite the lack of any attempt to determine the wishes of the *original* population. The newly minted States also drew on masculine nationalist narratives, framing their histories as successful quests whereby vast territories and scattered *uncivilised* tribes (Barsh, 1994) were now brought under order, with the lands put to good economic use, i.e. being made productive to serve humanity. Thus cultivation, in other words the anthropocentric exploitation of nature by human beings to serve human need, became the norm in the new world, with other lifestyles that were semi-nomadic or nomadic deemed to be wasteful and pre-modern. When viewed from a global lens this decision required all non-sedentary communities, including in Europe (Roma/Sinti Traveller) and others such as the Tuareg, Bedou or Saharawis to justify or claim they 'belonged' to a State. Indigenous communities all around the world, many who never had to think about—let alone 'prove'—that the ancestral domains were 'their' territories throughout their long-standing histories, were now expected to 'evidence' their claim to their lands, with this measured against the trappings of settlement such as cultivation or the holding of centrally issued land title deeds.

This anthropocentric vision was widely sold through education and mythology as being good for humanity, even though it was a very small portion of that humanity exploiting other human beings. While more progressive strands of Enlightenment-era thinking may have grudgingly conceded rights to some of these communities, no protection was envisaged for the natural world: for flora and fauna (Hamilton et al., 2015). Neither the land and waters nor other life forms were considered as subjects in this quest; their sole purpose was deemed to exist for the benefits of the new colonial powers. Sophisticated-sounding economic theories developed in the most venerated institutions of learning justified such exploitation, accounting processes deemed the value of nature itself to be negligible when measuring costs, supply chains became constructed to enable the value of the exploitation of the lands to generate wealth for those that came in contact with it, and the ensuing bounty—or goods and the monetary value they generated through commercial activity in them—was seen as such a significant virtue that statutes were built to the 'entrepreneurs' with the 'foresight' to construct such systems (Forrester, 2019). Indigenous resistance to the destruction of circular economies that were more in harmony with the natural environment were deemed threats to be eradicated through force; indigenous spirituality justifying harmony with nature was declared as backward and superstitious; their forced assimilation into what from then became the modern economy was assessed post facto as being consensual.

This process of forced assimilation had three major impacts in terms of the current discussion around scarcity. First, it systematised what was deemed to be the only form of legitimised political governance. Second, it discarded the rights of any competition or threat to that sovereignty from indigenous populations or from the existence of nature itself. Third, it provided the new sovereign with unlimited licence in perpetuity to exploit natural resources and to determine how the gains from this process would accrue. The schema adopted in the Americas in the early part of the twentieth century was reproduced in every part of the globe where European colonisation occurred. In most there were no automatic offspring to claim power, but in nearly all, with few exceptions, the lines drawn on maps to delineate interest between competing European sovereigns became sanctified as official boundaries for the new States that emerged. With the lines often paying little attention to the historical contours of the various communities, tribes or peoples, these artificially generated political units graduated to Statehood on the back of UN decolonisation from 1945 onward, drawing on the now established principle of self-determination. The new incumbents to power were often hand-picked by the departing power, and the transition process, sometimes portrayed as altruistic, nonetheless had a hard edge: seeking to guarantee continued influence on and access to the resources in the newly independent State. Faced with the prospect of seeking to unite multiple entities (e.g. tribes, nations, communities, ethnic groups) within the new boundaries of a single sovereign State, the new incumbents faced numerous challenges, some derived from historical communitarian antagonisms carefully nurtured and stoked through divide-and-rule policies of the colonial era. The legacies of cross-border territorial claims made life on the boundaries precarious—justifying the procurement of arms for self-defence, often helpfully supplied by the former colonial power to both sides for significant profit. The thirst for freedom among the population, built on a notion of being 'masters in their own lands' came with significant hope of material alleviation of their situation. Yet overexploitation of resources during the colonial period and continued ownership of assets in very few hands meant that poverty was often the default position for much of the newly independent populations. Faced with pressure to ameliorate these socio-economic challenges and to construct the foundations for prosperity—guarantee health and education; access to resources and the ability to become economically self-sufficient—the new State simply turned to its inherited wealth-generating source, namely exploitation of natural resources. Once again economics came to the forefront: the belief was that the generation of national wealth was compulsory, while its distribution would occur through a process of trickle-down economics. On the one hand this justified greater attention to wealth generation than its distribution, itself the cause of entrenched and ossified structural discrimination. On the other hand, the imperative of generating ever greater growth and wealth as an end in itself meant that limitless exploitation of resources was now justified. With minimal costs associated with the resource itself and no thought given to replenishing reserves, cost and value could simply be generated all along a supply chain, with the original labour costs kept very low. This overexploitation of primary products has in and of itself generated scarcity, if it were not for the additional fact that the nature of the use of some of these commodities, namely fossil fuels, have further hastened the approach of planetary boundaries while exacerbating other forms of scarcity.

The real threat to the modern (democratic) State

The identification of the link between colonial activities and climate change in the Intergovernmental Panel on Climate Change report (2022) is merely overdue recognition of the multifaceted impacts of the widespread colonial adventures of European superpowers that gained momentum commencing in the eighteenth century. This point was made often in the literature (e.g. Grove, 1997; Das, 2016), but was merely tolerated in the same way that many 'subaltern' perspectives seem to be addressed: as points to be noted in preambular phrases of introductions rather than in attempts to frame responses. Discussions on colonial adventures and State formation seem beyond the realms of many academic disciplinary boundaries. Thematic engagement with colonial crime is ignored in law, foreclosed by technical statutes of limitations. Histories continue to trumpet victors' justice ignoring legitimate stories of loss, damage and exploitation. Inequality is studied as an economic problem of distribution rather than a steady process of the untrammelled accumulation of wealth. Meanwhile, indigenous beliefs and systems find no meaningful echo in any formalised education system. Even scientists whose discipline is based on wide research into addressing natural phenomena appear to ignore traditional indigenous knowledge, though the lucrative use of patents generating wealth for the first 'discoverer' of ancient customs may be a less well-celebrated outcome of such recognition.

Significant other allies are implicated in perpetrating the myth of 'progress' through 'growth': historians in framing odes to adventurers, producing singular male-oriented narratives of entrepreneurship; economists justifying resource exploitation as 'growth and development'; lawyers explaining why established principles on title to territory reserved for the part of the world where perpetrators originated could be ignored elsewhere; adventurers and profiteers who in the name of free trade and finders' principle seized what they determined was theirs by their own rules; and leaders within and outside who attempted to construct societies and international economic systems with mere veneers of fairness.

Of course, the status quo hegemonic worldview is maintained not by colonial powers but by new post-colonial sovereign States that intrinsically support the current structure of international society which views them as the only legitimate holders of jurisdiction over their inherited territories. This bestows new sovereigns with 'exclusive rights' to benefit from extractive economic systems in place, often enabling rapid increase in exploitation rates to ostensibly generate wealth to aid State-building. That much of the wealth exploited and the monetary benefits generated do not accrue to the communities facing the loss and damage does not feature centrally in discussion over accountability. Questions over what percentage of the sale of 'national' assets' ends up in private rather than public hands is also obscure.

Indigenous leaders have voiced vehement opposition to the environmental destruction perpetrated by the extractive economic model via every platform to which they have had access and through intensive resistance to such forces. Where successful, such resistance has had a dramatic impact on scarcity, notably in the preservation of biodiversity, a stark contrast to places where the resistance was broken through a combination of guns, germs, steel (Diamond, 1998) and subterfuge. As if to prove that the colonial era mindset has not been completely relegated to the history books, the attempt to frame a global 30×30 protected areas initiative 'to preserve biodiversity' (Castellino, 2021) shows how one voiceless constituency—the environment—can be used as a blunt instrument to further relegate the second ignored constituency, i.e. indigenous populations. The idea that indigenous communities living in symbiosis with their environment protecting global biodiversity against all-comers through the ages while contributing nothing by way of a climate footprint (ICCA, 2021) should now be deemed collateral to the rest of the population's desire to protect an environment destroyed by its wanton quest for profits is not just morally dubious. It is likely to be deeply ineffective as the emerging scientific consensus has begun to show (e.g. Reyes-García et al., 2022 or O'Bryan et al., 2021; Hoffman et al., 2021). Its persistence as an idea that may nonetheless be implemented does not just heighten injustice and deepen structural discrimination; it is a potentially disastrous step for urgently needed climate mitigation. A far greater more tangible environmental impact could be achieved by transitioning any one of the world's megacities to sustainable energy sources over the next decade. Once again, the ability to bully one category of human population by another has given rise to this so-called 'green solution'.

The sub-prime crisis of 2007 had already revealed the extent to which the speculative insidious global financial model could have far-flung consequences. Rather than finding ways to increase vigilance and regulate such activity, the decade and a half since then appears to have energised them. While COVID-19 demonstrated the impact of scarcity in a very dramatic, globalised way, the fact is that societies had already shifted towards what would seem the natural consequences of its fundamentally extractive tendencies: the accumulation of vast wealth in the hands of the few at the cost of the disenfranchisement of the many. However, rather than this igniting French Revolution–style forces, the reverse happened: the wealthy found ways to engineer electoral victories that upheld their ideologies, channelling seething anger directed at the failures of traditional governance towards alternatives that were designed carefully to yield electoral majorities. Built on a neoliberal model of growth that derives from the same forces that justified worldwide exploitation, the subtle push against State regulation of corporations was achieved by relative stealth against headline grabbing statements critiquing the social democratic model (Mayer, 2017) and the attention paid to human rights. Helped by misdirected internal criticisms from within the human rights community, populists seized the opportunity to drive home their agendas. With democracy turning into a game of superior numbers, elections were won, and internal system changes commenced to guarantee pursuit of the extractive economic model. Thus, rather than tackle scarcity, scarcity formed the backdrop through which the anger derived as a consequence of it could be redirected using minorities as scapegoats, to consolidate the unfettered continuation of the very forces that instigated it.

This served as a useful weapon of mass distraction against the urgent need to mothball fossil fuels, regulate corporations, slow production and consumption, achieve a just economic transformation and ensure greater attention to a more equitable distribution of wealth. Increased reliance on mechanisation due to its lower costs eliminated many unskilled labour roles, generating household scarcity at a time when austerity was depleting macro-systemic abilities to respond to growing health and education needs.

Governing the modern 'democratic' State

It is in this mix of circumstances that minorities face their most direct threat from populism, as 'democracy' is increasingly becoming a game of mobilising numbers at the cost of minorities (Chotiner, 2019). For most post-colonial countries, erected on the basis of departing colonial rulers' interests, national boundaries divide communities constructing majority and minority groups based on proximity to power. 'Nation-building' (Deutsch and Foltz, 1973) to unite communities under common 'national unity' rubrics have dimmed and virulent, exclusivist forms of 'nationalism' linked to contested readings of ethnicity and religion flourish (Al-Rasheed, 2013), breeding intense strife and fragmentation. 'Scapegoat politics' is the most recent driver for raising threat levels—specific nationalist narratives are promoted to germinate hate against 'others' deemed 'anti-national'. The danger of historically flawed narratives, when propagated through promoted politically motivated social media and educational materials draw adverse attention to minority communities, fragmenting societies and generating vectors towards conflict. The rise in threat and persistence of ethnic conflict, ethnic cleansing, crimes against humanity, war crimes and genocide is palpable not only in places like Myanmar, where the Rohingya face direct and systematic threats aimed at eliminating them and in Israel's sustained effort at eliminating Palestinians from Gaza. The rise in Islamophobia in India stoked through majoritarian politics is destroying the democratic compact of that State, while a fear of 'splittists' has forced China to abandon its previous attempts to unite the various nations of the Chinese family into a coherent polity (Castellino, 2020). Modalities of twenty-first-century life, not least in the reach of social media, can amplify negative messaging to ratchet up action resulting in atrocities that spill over international boundaries (Karim, 2020).

The situation is not restricted to the developing world. In wealthy countries identity politics is used as a tool to connect with latent xenophobia altering political landscapes in polarising and fragmenting society (Li and Xi, 2022). The rise in hate speech and identity-based attacks clearly signpost this trend. The accepted counter-call for structural change driven by the #BlackLivesMatter movement reflects these concerns, with its spread showing its global salience (Jones, 2019). Further elements exacerbate tension for minorities: (1) population intermixing caused by long-term global migrations leading to complicated layering and confluences of identities; and (2) political 'races to the bottom' where identity-oriented politics, manifesting as exclusivist nationalisms, is increasing. This sets minorities, defined as those of different race/ethnicity, religion or language—in one country, with kin across a national border—to mobilise across frontiers as threats grow. When kin States react to well-founded (or ill-founded) minority grievances in a neighbouring State (Thakur et al., 2011) the threat to international peace and security is perilous indeed (Castellino, 2022) as we see in Ukraine.

This contemporary and continuing threat to minorities that has arisen from scarcity can be captured in six trends:

1. Narrow 'nationalist' identities that enhance fragmentation and reduce participation fuel marginalisation, discrimination and inequality of opportunity, generating grievances around which communities may mobilise;
2. A socially constructed fabricated scarcity that is built on scapegoating minorities in a bid to generate an artificial majority with the specific aim of eliminating minorities from the social space, thereby generating greater capacity for claiming the share that may otherwise be claimed by those minorities;
3. Failures to combat dissemination of hate and disinformation through social media that exacerbate insecurity breeding pre-conditions for conflict;
4. Neighbouring State rivalries that generate threats to kin populations of those States, instrumentalising kin minorities to excuse aggression;
5. Biased socio-historical narratives that promote legacies that compromise prospects of inter-community peace, weaken cohesion, trust and communication within and between countries;
6. Failures to adopt international response-oriented measures that support peace and security undermine legitimacy of international actors and the rule of law.

The irresponsible criticism of human rights has undermined its utility in the fight against tackling injustice, leaving a specific tool designed to be used for accountability to be blunted despite its strong anchors in legal systems of States. The legal guarantees themselves are unravelling as a consequence in the face of the hollowing out of democratic institutions. With human rights laws written in elitist language beyond comprehension of most of society, the battles over minutiae in courts of law and legislative assemblies are lost in translation to the general public, with the communities that dominate the media space in prime position to 'interpret' these battles as providing rights to people who are portrayed as undeserving, carefully picking enemies that are sufficiently different, to orchestrate mass hatred by consensus. Meanwhile, restrictions in the civic space and deliberate attempts to curtail protest and dissent create a caustic atmosphere as scarcities bite harder.

Finally, the prevalence itself of the ambience of real and perceived scarcity in terms of access to natural resources, finance and land, driven by the climate emergency atop the collapse of speculation-based financial systems, has provided significant thrust in competition for the limited resources. Policy choices are often presented as zero-sum games where a limited pie is distributed among ever more people, some with claims deemed 'legitimate' and others whose claims are questioned. The idea has become entrenched in the public discourse of many countries that providing specific rights to one group must come at the cost of others. This deliberate ploy to mobilise majorities through scapegoating is contrary to evidence showing how recognising greater society-wide human rights protections prove beneficial to all. Galvanising a political movement on this basis has proven easy through social media, with data collected through overreliance on web-based services considerably augmenting its impact.

Recalibrating the future

Despite articulations of narrow nationalism in States in nearly every sub-region of the world, the populations of these States are increasingly diverse due to historical and contemporary migration; influx of trade, investment and labour; flight from persecution elsewhere; and intermarriages across ethno-religious and ethno-linguistic barriers. Twenty-first-century norms including around gendered identities make the notion of singular, fixed and finite nationalistic narrative dangerous in its ability to polarise and direct stigma towards segments of the population. The rise in historically flawed nationalistic narratives is an attempt to combat diversity while seeking political power. The consequence of such actions may well place significant State machinery, including the ability to make and revoke laws and use the significant policing and military arsenal against those deemed to fall outside the exclusivist narrative. This could ferment continuing tensions with the ability for these to escalate to breakdowns of peace and security at local, national, regional and international levels.

The scapegoating of populations through active and systematic hate dissemination is growing. Fuelled by ease of access and saturation of social media across the socio-economic spectra in society, messages and fake news have the ability to galvanise action in a manner that could approach genocide as already documented in places such as Rwanda and Myanmar. Unwillingness to reign in social media corporations alongside the breadth of personal data available online has made direct targeting for subliminal messaging possible to a level well beyond the reach of radio stations such as the RTLM in the context of the Rwandan genocide (Des Forges, 1999).

The hostility of public messaging has created levels of tolerance towards aggressive speech in the public realm, making it possible for hate-oriented sentiments to be expressed even by heads of State. This has polarised societies with deep fragmenting effects on communities. Anger-fuelled scenarios are a powder keg for violence with the steps from fighting words to action well understood, including in their ability to flare large societal incidents that draw in others in locales far removed from the site of the conflict.

Societal fragmentation has provided significant political opportunities, especially in democracies where new political parties have arisen on minority-hatred grounds. In some instances, more established political parties have bent their own agendas to respond to populist hate in a bid to become/stay electable based on cynical calculations about vote banks. Framed as anti-political narratives at a time of scarcity, austerity and economic stagnation, this has provided access to mainstream vote banks turning hitherto unacceptable values, regulated by strong constitutional provisions, into electable agendas. On seizing power these parties have made significant changes to the basic structure of societies, with institutions in favour of the rule of law and human rights becoming hollowed out and unable to contest actions that are blatantly against the constitutional and international legal values (Lazaridis et al., 2016).

With the agendas of these parties driven and supported by scapegoat politics, it is inevitable that as they form governments the direct threat to minorities grows. Contestation of these trends through domestic institutions is becoming near impossible, with strong repressive measures applied to close civic spaces, pushing societies towards conditions where the threat of violence grows exponentially, forcing communities to accept harassment and oppression that may rain down on them (Dixit, 2022). The scarcity narrative also means that they will be at the back of the queue for any public goods, assuming they are not prevented from joining such a queue in the first place.

The permeation of hate within societies is not merely driven by State institutions. There appears to be significant growth in self-help paramilitaries and 'citizen-action' vigilante groups—both physical and others operating within social media—who, emboldened by governmental messages, claim to act in the name of 'popular values'. These vigilantes rarely face sanction due to tacit acceptance of their actions by police forces and criminal justice mechanisms that implicitly or explicitly share their biases. This rapidly undermines the rule of law, challenges State monopoly of violence and mirrors reactions with potential to escalate threats to peace and security (Chatterjee et al., 2019).

The polarisation within State boundaries is often watched closely by kin communities across borders, where the majority-minority paradigm may well be reversed. In these situations, a government which may have been formed on similar grounds of scapegoating of minorities may feel justified in acting, usually on the basis of pre-existing inter-State rivalries and simmering tension. Before long such actions could become classically inter-State in the manner that led to the devastation that motivated the formation of the United Nations in 1945.

Polarisation within States is also reflected at the international level, with complex allegiances stemming well beyond borders. The interconnected nature of global societies has recently been demonstrated in grave terms with the spread of the pandemic. This interconnection includes the ability to divert funding and influence activities in other sovereign States. Thus, it is now possible for foreign interests to fuel conflict in a different State on the basis of its national interests. This could prolong conflict and poses significant threats to global peace and security (Ohlin, 2020).

The path to rethinking a new security apparatus to address threats to the peace and security that stem from scarcity are beyond the remit of the many confronted with this issue. Obvious power dynamics make such a path near impossible to achieve, not least because of the significant implication of many of the protagonists charged with maintaining the system as it stands, using it when suited, and ignoring it on other occasions.

Intergovernmental organisations like the United Nations and regional organisations like the Organization for Security and Co-operation in Europe, Council of Europe, European Union, African Union, Association of Southeast Asian Nations, Organisation of American States and others were set up precisely to ensure that threats to the peace and security were de-escalated. There remain steps that could be taken within inter-institutional cooperation frameworks to minimise and potentially resolve some of these threats below the radar at which they engage politics on a grand scale.

The first step towards resolution requires an acknowledgement of the extent to which the contemporary and future threat to minorities directly implicate questions at the heart of the United Nations and other intergovernmental mandates. Whether explicitly or implicitly, the value of acceptance of this causal link can play a significant role in galvanising concerted action towards prevention and redressal mechanisms. Such an acknowledgement need not be dramatic since the agendas of every UN agency already posit values that are inherently inclusive, oriented towards peace and security and pay attention to development needs. Yet ensuring that minorities feature explicitly on the agenda of every intergovernmental organisation could direct tailored interventions mindful of the existence of conscious and unconscious bias in the way that structural discrimination operates to marginalise communities that are deliberately kept far from sites of power. This may generate specific data, fine-tuning and bespoke programmes to better address need and generate engagement and consultation with affected and impacted communities.

Data is key to any intelligence and subsequent design of interventions. Despite the call from UN bodies at every level including the urgent need to truly assess the efficacy and progress towards the Sustainable Development Goals, the lack of disaggregated data on minorities remains a significant obstacle. The role of intergovernmental organisations in addressing this lacuna cannot be understated, not least because there are effective surrogates and proxies that provide insight. Sharing information gained in specific circumstances across sectors could provide a concerted basis for the design of more effective implementation and reach of agency work.

State harassment allegedly stamping out dissent is a significant part of the arsenal directed against human rights activists. This has a chilling effect on civil society. While there is no panacea for addressing this issue due to the nature of international politics, explicitly calling attention to State bullying of targeted individuals remains an important marker of the legitimacy of their actions and could serve as an important if permeable shield against the propaganda and subsequent actions against such individuals and their organisations.

At a time of greater acceptance of the role played by bias and privilege it is becoming imperative for all of society, but especially policy-oriented professionals, to be trained to understand the breadth of diversity within societies and the insidious manner in which structural discrimination undermines attempts to build sustainable prosperous societies. Such training needs to be sub-region specific for it to be meaningful and must prominently feature lived experiences of minorities from that region. Equipping its own staff with minority-sensitive understandings of the histories they may have studied would be crucial to ensuring that the quality and substance of their work is effectively geared towards dismantling structural discrimination and the inherent privilege that accrues to those with proximity to power.

In the final analysis, it could be said that the threat to minorities stemming from scarcity could be best ameliorated through eliminating scarcity, whether through a recalibration of global financial systems, change in consumption patterns or better distribution of value across commercial supply chains. Yet even were that possible, it would still leave the underlying structural racism untouched, merely postponing the problem to future points in history where scarcity will likely raise its head. A better medium and long-term solution would be to confront the underpinning cause of the threat to minorities: the deeply flawed ethno-religious, linguistic and cultural superiorities that explicitly and implicitly facilitate the historical and contemporary hierarchical understanding of differentiated values of human communities. This requires mass reorientation in the narration of histories with an emphasis on educating majorities about the nature of their privilege and where it stems from. That potentially longer and more gentle process must be accompanied by bespoke urgent measures to meaningfully safeguard the rule of law and institutions. If controlling democracies remain quests that are akin to popularity contests, they will throw up what we are already witnessing in many democratic countries: individuals and parties emerging with mediocre governance and comprehension skills that may not be linked to their ability to deliver the job. This is not only a threat to minorities, but, as the twinned pandemic and the climate crisis demonstrate amply, comes at a significant price to all of society.

References

Al-Rasheed, M., *A Most Masculine State: Gender, Politics and Religion in Saudi Arabia* (Cambridge: Cambridge University Press, 2013).

Barsh, Russell L., 'Indigenous Peoples in the 1990s: From Object to Subject in International Law?' 7 *Harvard Human Rights Journal* (1994) 33–62.

Castellino, Joshua, 'The Rise of Majorities and Emerging Existential Threats to India & China' 8(3) *Chinese Journal of Comparative Law* (2020) 538–557.

Castellino, Joshua, 'A Four-Fold Path to Mitigating the Environmental Crisis' *MRG Blog*, June 2021.

Castellino, Joshua, 'Pride, Autocrats, Identity, Nationalism: The Anachronistic Follies of War' *Ukraine Opinion*, 2 March 2022, available at https://minorityrights.org/2022/03/02/ukraine-oped/.

Castellino, Joshua, *Calibrating Colonial Crime* (Bristol University Press, 2024).

Chatterjee, Angana P., Blom Hansen, Thomas & Jaffrelot, Christoffe, eds., *Majoritarian State: How Hindu Nationalism Is Changing India* (Oxford: Oxford University Press, 2019).

Chotiner, Isaac, 'Amartya Sen's Hopes and Fears for Indian Democracy' *The New Yorker Magazine*, 6 October 2019.

Constantinides, Aristoteles, 'Minorities, Rights of' in *Elgar Encyclopaedia of Human Rights* [Christina Binder, Manfred Nowak, Jane A. Hofbauer & Philip Janig, eds.] (Elgar, 2022) 494–507.

Das, Pallavi, *Colonialism, Development & the Environment: Railways and Deforestation in British India 1860–1884* (Springer, 2016).

Des Forges, Alison, *Leave None to Tell the Story: Genocide in Rwanda* (New York: Human Rights Watch, 1999).

Diamond, Jared, *Guns, Germs and Steel: A Short History of Everybody for the Lat 13,000 Years* (Vintage, 1998) New Edition.

Dixit, Priya, *Race, Popular Culture and Far-Right Extremism in the United States* (Cham, Switzerland: Palgrave Macmillan, 2022).

Forrester, Katrina, 'Reparations, History and Global Justice' in *Empire, Race & Global Justice* [Duncan Bell, ed.] (Cambridge University Press, 2019).

Grove, Richard, *Ecology, Climate and Empire: Colonialism and Global Environmental History, 1400–1940* (White Horse Press, 1997).

Hamilton, Clive, Gemenne, François & Bonneuil, Christophe, eds., *The Anthropocene & the Global Environmental Crisis Rethinking Modernity in a New Epoch* (Routledge, 2015).

Hoffman, Kira M., Davis, Emma L., Wickham, Sara B., Schang, Kyle, Johnson, Alexandra, Larking, Taylor, Lauriault, Patrick N., Le, Nhu Quynh, Swerdfager, Emily & Trant, Andrew J., 'Conservation of Earth's Biodiversity Is Embedded in Indigenous Fire Stewardship' 118(32) *PNAS* (2021).

ICCA Consortium, *Territories of Life: 2021 Report* (ICCA Consortium Worldwide, 2021), available at: https://report.territoriesoflife.org.

IPCC, *Climate Change 2022: Impacts, Adaptation and Vulnerability: Contribution of Working Group II to the Sixth Assessment Report of the Intergovernmental Panel on Climate Change* [H.-O. Pörtner, D. C. Roberts, M. Tignor, E. S. Poloczanska, K.

Mintenbeck, A. Alegría, M. Craig, S. Langsdorf, S. Löschke, V. Möller, A. Okem & B. Rama, eds.] (Cambridge University Press, 2022) 3056.

Jones, Leslie Kay, '#BlackLivesMatter: An Analysis of the Movement as Social Drama' 44(1) *Humanity & Society* (2019) 92–110.

Karim, M. A., *Genocide & Geopolitics of the Rohingya Crisis* (Nova Science, 2020).

Karl, Deutsch & Foltz, WilliamWilliam, *Nation Building* (New York: Atherton Press, 1973).

Lazaridis, Gabriella, Campani, Giovanna & Benveniste, Annie, eds., *The Rise of the Far Right in Europe: Populist Shifts and 'Othering'* (London: Palgrave Macmillan, 2016).

Li, Yuchen & Xi, Tianyang, 'Trade Shock, Refugee, and the Rise of Right-Wing Populism: Evidence from European Parliament Elections' 2(2) *China Economic Quarterly International* (June 2022) 124–137.

Mayer, Jane, *Dark Money: The Hidden History of the Billionaires Behind the Rise of the Radical Right* (Anchor Books, 2017).

O'Bryan, C. J., Garnett, S. T., Fa, J. E., Leiper, I., Rehbein, J. A., Fernández-Llamazares, Á., Jackson, M. V., Jonas, H. D., Brondizio, E. S., Burgess, N. D., Robinson, C. J., Zander, K. K., Molnár, Z., Venter, O. & Watson, J. E. M., 'The Importance of Indigenous Peoples' Lands for the Conservation of Terrestrial Mammals' 35(3) *Conservation Biology* (2021) 1002–1008.

Ohlin, Jens David, *Election Interference: International Law and the Future of Democracy* (Cambridge: Cambridge University Press, 2020).

Reyes-García, V., Fernández-Llamazares, Á., Aumeeruddy-Thomas, Y., Benyei, P., Bussmann, R. W., Diamond, S. K., García-del-Amo, D., Guadilla-Sáez, S., Hanazaki, N., Kosoy, N. & Lavides, M., 'Recognizing Indigenous Peoples' and Local Communities' Rights and Agency in the Post-2020 Biodiversity Agenda' 51 *Ambio* (2022) 84–92.

Thakur, Ramesh, Vesselin, Popovski & Walter, Kemp, eds., *Blood & Borders: The Responsibility to Protect & the Problem of the Kin-State* (Tokyo: United Nations University, 2011).

5 Beyond the Western idea of scarcity. Contributions to a relational theory of law from indigenous cosmovisions

Silvia Bagni

Introduction

Crises are often moments of disruption, where old systems of beliefs and social structures may collapse; but they correspond also to unpredictable possibilities that emerge within the future scenario. The recent COVID-19 pandemic, for instance, could represent an opportunity for transformative changes, if understood in a broader context, that is not limited to a sanitary emergency. As many commentators have recognized, the global pandemic was embedded into one of the most vital challenges humanity has faced since the dawn of culture: the climate and environmental crisis that our current economic model has produced, menacing the stability of the Earth System (ES) and our survival as a species.

The aim of this chapter is to suggest that indigenous cosmovisions, here assumed as a form of minority's knowledge and epistemology, may provide a fundamental contribution to tackle the ecological crisis, through their holistic way of conceiving the relationship between human beings and other non-human entities. In fact, the current failure of the international community to enforce, and even to reach, the environmental objectives determined in the Sustainable Development Goals and in the final documents of the Climate Conferences of the Parties, can also be explained, on a cultural basis, by a typical Western bias: the dualistic paradigm between humans and nature; the preference given to a highly competitive style of life; and the refusal to accept intra- and inter-species mutual cooperation as a fundamental rule of the complex ES.[1]

My main assumption is that the core problem is not scarcity of resources but lack of a holistic understanding of life, which is instead still practiced by

1 "Life did not take over the globe by struggle, but by establishing interrelations" (Margulis and Sagan, mentioned in Capra and Luisi, 2014); "the way to sustain life is to create and nourish the community" (Capra and Luisi, 2014, p. 562). This is what ecology teaches us, that the principle of collaboration and sustainability is an emerging property of the ES (Odum and Barrett, 2004, p. 8).

DOI: 10.4324/9781032661780-6

indigenous peoples and tribes. Economic and social literature about scarcity has usually focussed on material goods. The holistic cosmovision of indigenous peoples considers that good life (*buen vivir*) can only be achieved through immaterial goods, in particular the care for the (human and natural) relationships in which we are embedded. As a consequence, the concept of scarcity should be updated and referred to "scarcity of empathy" with other living beings and the planet as our common home (*Pacha Mama*).

So, our contribution departs from the idea of scarcity as an economic and development concept (see the introduction to this volume) and embraces a critical perspective, such as that of Bookchin's social ecology (Morris, 2017, p. 229) or that of the environmentalism of the poor, which is based on the incommensurability of values with respect of negative environmental externalities (Martinez-Alier, 2002). Leonardi explains the point very clearly:

> The problem is not scarcity, but the surplus (which reinforces the criticism of the logic of value implicit in contemporary consumerism and puts the desirability of sharing as an expression of the logic of riches—we are entirely on a qualitative ground).
>
> (Leonardi, 2017, p. 171)

As a consequence, our framework of analysis reverts the binomial minorities-scarcity. Indigenous and tribal minorities (who belong to the majority that has been negatively affected by the voracious capitalist model), together with few other examples of ecological societies, such as the Rojava Democratic Confederation (Locchi and Paffarini, 2023), live within a social and economic model based on the recognition of mutual interdependence between humans, non-humans and the environment where they live, so that the maintenance of this balanced relationship is the premise for good life.

The inverted conceptualization of *scarcity* and *abundance* is very well described by Murray Bookchin in his book *Post-Scarcity Anarchism*. Scarcity of resources led humanity along the path of conflicts and to the construction of a dualistic and hierarchical society, based on relationship of dominion: of humans on nature, of men on women, of white on black, of owners over proletarians. On the contrary, the industrial revolutions and capitalism have led us into a "society of abundance", where technology was meant to free us from the obligation of working, allowing humanity to dedicate herself to the pursue of happiness and good life. However, this situation is not at all egalitarian. Instead, it is based on the exploitation of minorities by a majority (see Castellino, Chapter 6) and on the permanent creation of instrumental needs to feed the growth of the market. The concept of abundance has been commodified and deprived of its social and cultural aspects. In the capitalistic society, we live in abundance of material goods, but in scarcity of social, cultural and spiritual relationships. Often, we are not even aware of our condition of subjugation, since we live in a global society that pretends to be free.[2]

Another example of how Western cultural (liberalism) and economic (capitalism) paradigms affect our understanding of the concepts of scarcity and abundance, totally irrespective of our real needs, can be found in the historical research of Graeber and Wengrow. When describing the societies of hunter-gatherers, they note:

> True, a forager might seem extremely poor by our standards—but to apply our standards was obviously ridiculous. "Abundance" is not an absolute measure. It refers to a situation where one has easy access to everything one feels one needs to live a happy and comfortable life. By those standards, Sahlins argued, most known foragers are rich.
>
> (Graeber and Wengrow, 2021, p. 147)

They define these societies as "free societies", where the highest values among their members were liberty and freedom of choice, goals that they enforced refusing any type of coercive hierarchy between them and by rejecting forms of private properties, except those related to religious rituals (Graeber and Wengrow, 2021, p. 174). In the 1960s, Gluckman described how, even among African tribal societies hierarchically organized, where the king was considered owner of the whole land, the ideal of richness was superposed to that of sharing. The monarch redistributed most of the goods he had conquered in tribal conflicts to his people. Moreover, ownership of goods was strictly linked to the definition of social bonds of kinship or quasi-kinship (Gluckman, 1965). This same attitude is reported also by Graeber and Wengrow among neolithic communities of hunter-gatherers in North America. Many of these features can still be detected among indigenous communities.

As a law scholar, I will focus on how indigenous cosmovisions fit within the ecosystem approach predicated in reports by the Intergovernmental Panel on Climate Change and Intergovernmental Science–Policy Platform on Biodiversity and Ecosystem Services, and how and why Western legal paradigms should adopt those premises. I will argue that relationality, which represents the systemic interconnectedness of all ecological subjects, should shift from the periphery to the core of law. I will then investigate how this superposes and integrates with other critical approaches from the Global South, such as (eco)feminism, decolonial law, the ethics of care, Earth Jurisprudence and the Nature's rights movement, which all represent a form of minority thinking, strongly related to indigenous knowledge.

2 Describing how the capitalist model has affected the world's peripheries, Alberto Acosta speaks about the "curse of abundance" (*maldición de la abundancia*) (Acosta, 2009), implicitly referring to Galeano's expression about the "curse of richness" of Latin America (Galeano, 1971).

The contribution of indigenous and tribal peoples to the shift from a cultural paradigm based on scarcity of resources to one based on intra- and inter-species relationality

Life is an endless process of creation of matter and energy, resulting from the co-action of all components of the ecosphere. Therefore, we are not only interdependent in terms of our survival, but also co-creators of the system in which we live. In other words, the ES is characterized by a set of relationships between all its components. On the one hand, these assumptions come from ecological studies, which have been developing since Ernst Haeckel first introduced the word *ecology* in the scientific field (Grober, 2012, p. 106) and have been strengthened in the last century, in particular since James Lovelock and Ann Margulis' publication on the Gaia hypothesis (Lovelock and Margulis, 1974).

However, in the West, this sensibility about interconnectedness of all things remains confined to the academic realm. Descola refers to his thesis as an "ecology of relationships" (Descola, 2013, p. 121), because the focus of his research is on the relationships between natural and non-natural entities. The non-humans are considered "agents that interact with humans in certain situations" and not as resources, illusory representations or commodities.

Animist and totemic ontologies generate particular social structures and specific legal paradigms that tend to almost sterilize conflicts with nature, even if maintaining conflicts of identities in inter-human relations.

Even the indigenous "legal" paradigm is based on the principle of *relationality*. Comparing Andean indigenous perspectives with the Western legal tradition, Maria Elena Attard Bellido imagines a dialogue on legal pluralism between two goddesses: Themis, the Greek goddess of justice, and Mama Ocllo, the female ancestor of the Inca culture. Themis explains to Mama Ocllo the origins of liberal constitutionalism. Mama Ocllo, on the other hand, offers the epistemological tools for an intercultural translation of her legal arguments, based on a plurinational, communitarian and decolonizing perspective (Attard Bellido, 2019, p. 93). This alternative jurisprudence rejects the binary code of legal disputes in favour of solutions that defend harmony and sustain *vivir bien*. Within this understanding of the law, jurists are called on to "feel the reality" before "knowing" or "thinking" it (Attard Bellido, 2019, p. 93).[3] Knowledge is the result of collective experiences and practices, transmitted through generations. The author proposes applying to the analysis of legal conflicts the methodology of the *chakana*, which represents the Andean cosmovision. The *chakana*, as an intercultural interpretative tool, invites the lawyer to consider the legal facts from four dimensions: being (*ser*), knowing (*saber*), doing (*hacer*) and power (*poder*). This

3 "Desde esta ética aymara, el runa/jaqi—el ser humano como parte de la naturaleza—siente la realidad, más que conocerla o pensarla" (Josef Estermann, 2009, cited by Attard Bellido, 2019, p. 93).

multidimensional approach (*sentipensar*, or "thinking our feeling") guarantees the harmony of humankind with its environment and aims at the realization of *vivir bien*. This methodology aims at reaching the *jaqi* (Attard Bellido, 2019, p. 97),[4] a solution that produces a balance between the parties in conflict. The four dimensions of life are interconnected by principles, such as relationality, correspondence, complementarity and reciprocity, which together build a relational logic.

Elizabeth Macpherson has recently defended the idea of Australasian Environmental Constitutionalism as Relational Legal Pluralism (Macpherson, 2022). She has studied the cases of recognition of ecosystem rights in New Zealand and Australia, and she considers that they represent an innovation in the context of environmental constitutionalism, specifically because of their relational function. In fact, the recognition of rights to rivers and other natural ecosystems is a Western way of interpreting indigenous concepts and values about the relationship of interdependence between humans and nature (Macpherson, 2022, p. 182).

Christine J. Winter very clearly shows how Maori and Aboriginal cosmovisions can contribute to build an intercultural theory of intergenerational justice, based on their philosophy of life, which is inspired by relationality and interrelationship (Winter, 2022, p. 14 ff.). Their worldview is ecocentric, which means it does not privilege humans. Instead, "there is an understanding of connectedness between human and nonhuman, and a recognition of interconnectivity between living and non-living elements of the environment" (Winter, 2022, p. 17). The interconnectedness applies synchronically intra- and inter-species, but also diachronically between past, present and future generations. On these premises, Maori and Aborigines recognize an ecological responsibility towards future generations, to whom we owe the same care we owe to the present one, as both constitute our family, together with the natural world (Winter, 2022, p. 108).

For State law, taking into consideration these cultural premises means adapting regulation to a dialogical process of decision-making and to a participatory model of management, based on the recognition of legal pluralism with respect to the management of natural resources. Macpherson indicates that Australasian Environmental Constitutionalism is indeed an example of the " 'relational turn' in socio-legal theory, which departs from static notions of law to a focus on the relational processes of dialogue and negotiation in plural, multicultural legal settings" (Macpherson, 2022, p. 171).

The examples illustrated above underline the contributions of minority indigenous knowledge to an ecological understanding of the ES. They

4 "Propugna una decisión jurisdiccional que tenga la finalidad de consagrar el jaqi, lo que superaría la lógica binaria de las partes ganadoras y perdedoras en un litigio—que, por cierto, en pocas ocasiones contribuye a la paz social en términos de armonía y equilíbrio" (Attard Bellido, 2019, p. 97).

propose to us solutions to the global environmental crisis based on relationality. From a legal point of view, this means (1) changing the *Grundnorm* of each legal system, that is the ultimate rule of recognition of the legitimacy of the legal order (Kelsen, 1967); 2) considering new conflict resolution rules, directly descending from the ecosystem *Grundnorm.*

As the Earth life-system is the precondition for the existence of our species, and humans regulate their intra-species relations through a set of rules called *law* (Tamanaha, 2008), the consequence of this syllogism should be that the law should preserve first and foremost the conditions that guarantee the stability of the ES, from which the life of humans depends.

Following Hans Kelsen's pure theory of law, we could reformulate the previous reasoning by saying that the protection of the stability of the ES should be considered the new *Grundnorm* of our species. In indigenous terms, the new *Grundnorm* preserves the interconnectedness of each human and non-human element of Nature.

Once the final goal is redetermined from an anthropocentric to an ecocentric perspective, we have to understand which principles and rules are governing the relationships between individuals, species, communities and ecosystems. The ecology of Nature must become the ecology of law (Capra and Mattei, 2015; Bookchin, 1971).

This issue implies that in some intra- and inter-species legal relations, the value to defend is not the claim of one individual over the other (adversarial right) but the persistence of the relationship itself (relational right). As stated in the European Economic and Social Committee Report *Towards an EU Charter of the Fundamental Rights of Nature*, "We also need to reframe rights from adversarial to synergistic, moving from 'rights' to 'right relationships', a 'right relationship' being one that supports the wellbeing of the whole" (Carducci et al., 2020, p. 10).

Other minority contributions to the construction of a relational theory of law

From a legal point of view, how can we protect the relationship between the parties instead of focusing only on their individual claims? To answer the question, I will analyse other minority contributions from the Global South to the idea of a "relational theory to law", where indigenous and tribal knowledge has been integrated into other philosophical movements. Even if the concept has mainly been applied to solve intercultural conflicts between humans, its premises can offer meaningful insights into the process of shifting to an ecological legal paradigm. Law is a cultural (and so a human) construct; more than extending the liberal categories by analogy, it is a matter of rethinking them and possibly creating new ones suitable for the legal protection of the interests of ecosystems, to which human beings belong.

The feminist approach and ecofeminism

In the introduction to her seminal book *Law's Relations: A Relational Theory of Self, Autonomy, and Law*, Jennifer Nedelsky states: "The very concept of ecology is relational" (Nedelsky, 2011, p. 12). So, she recognizes an analogy between re-orientating human relations from a feminist perspective and doing the same between human and non-human relationships. By redefining the self from a relational perspective, she supports a new concept of law and a new language for rights that could also fit a new ecological law:[5]

> A relational analysis provides a better framework for identifying what is really at stake in difficult cases and for making judgments about the competing interpretations of rights involved. . . . Both law and rights will then be understood in terms of the relations they structure—and how those relations can foster core values, such as autonomy.
>
> (Nedelsky, 2011, p. 4)

Anglo-American constitutionalism is deeply rooted in a very strong interpretation of liberalism, which conceives rights as a defence from others, especially from the State (Nedelsky, 2011, p. 92). In this framework, one of the main difficulties is to understand *relation* as not being in opposition to *autonomy*. In fact, the more common understanding is that the claim for autonomy is a reaction to the limits and constraints posed to the self by the community in which one lives. Nedelsky points out that "the perverse quality of this conception is clearest when taken to its extreme: the most perfectly autonomous man is the most perfectly isolated" (Nedelsky, 2011, p. 97). On the contrary, the author tries to defend a relational concept of autonomy, which generates from the relationships in which the self is always re-created.[6] This approach can be easily extended to incorporate also the relations one has with nature.

Nedelsky also takes into consideration the consequences that relational autonomy projects onto the paradigm of equality, with respect to non-human entities. In fact, she underlines that the relational approach would foster a redefinition of our relationship with Nature, on a stance of mutual respect, concern, care, interdependence and responsibility.

Conceiving rights in a relational perspective would imply considering that there is a mutual relationship between the rights' bearers, which makes them also reciprocally responsible towards one another (Nedelsky, 2011, p. 248).

5 "My point throughout is that law needs an alternative conceptual framework to do its work optimally, and new concepts need to be given life in the law" (Nedelsky, 2011, p. 4).

6 "Autonomy is made possible by constructive relationships—including intimate, cultural, institutional, national, global, and ecological forms of relationship—all of which interact" (Nedelsky, 2011, p. 118).

Responsibility, accountability and sense of care are the dimensions missing in the liberal theory of rights. This is totally coherent with the idea of intra- and inter-generational responsibilities conceived by indigenous cosmovisions.

In comparing American and South African constitutionalism, Peggy Cooper Davis argues that in the United States, people are no longer able to think relationally, recalling Carol Gilligan's work on the rejection of relational thinking in public spheres. Both authors support their position on a patriarchal interpretation of the history of human development. Besides, what is interesting for our purpose is the explanation of how public issues, such as the environment and climate change, are conceptualized. Reasoning from a position of detachment, fostering individualism and rationalism, affirmative actions can be perceived as investments only if directed to the benefit of the self. Otherwise, they will always be seen as a sacrifice. "But if I share a bond of community with those who benefit from my tax dollars, and if I value our collective well-being, then, once again, I can feel that I have made an investment rather than a sacrifice" (Cooper Davis, 2008, p. 248). Moreover, this framework rejects the total sacrifice of the self. On the contrary, "maintaining the importance of 'I' is necessary to the health of 'we'" (Cooper Davis, 2008, p. 250). This approach totally corresponds to the basic rules of the ES and indigenous cosmovisions and encourages us to take a holistic view of our choices and actions, considering ourselves part of the whole, which is never merely an arithmetic sum of each single individual.

Another important contribution from feminist thinkers to a relational theory of law that embrace both humans and non-humans comes from Catherine Keller. In her book *From a Broken Web. Separation, Sexism, and Self*, referring to Jung, she says that "authentic individuality can be gained only when I experience myself as fundamentally connected to all of life: this is the wisdom of the Jungian outlook. An ego-transcending selfhood is massively relational" (Keller, 1988, p. 114) and radical world-openness. In her book, she shows that a relational self is a characteristic not only of women, but of all beings. She starts her analysis from the myth of Eros and Psyche, so claiming that love is the sublime form of connection. At a certain point, she shifts to environmental science and evolution. The self is intrinsically social as "individuality emerges through a process of interaction between the organism and the environment" (Keller, 1988, p. 179). She introduces the word *empathy* to describe this sensation as feeling the world as part of myself. The other important aspect is that "it is not one over and against the others, but among them, and including them . . . Interconnection and individuality seem to coexist without contradictions, indeed to enhance each other" (Keller, 1988, p. 186). If the self reflects and include all the world within her/him, there is no sense in owning natural resources. As indigenous cosmovisions suggest, in her theory the process of knowing the other "is the feeling of its feelings as it passes into immanence within my own constitution" (Keller, 1988, p. 199).

On the other hand, ecofeminism correlates its critics on the overexploitation of natural resources both to patriarchy and racialization. Eco-feminists build a parallel between violence and domination exercised on women and on Nature by the capitalist patriarchal world system. They consider that both share a past and present of oppression, and suggest to overcome this scenario by rehabilitating ancestral, rural and feminist knowledge, calling in particular for the role of care traditionally exercised by women (Coral Díaz, 2016). Ecofeminism aims at re-creating a new ethics of life, opposed to the biopower and necropolitics of the capitalist model (Braidotti, 2007). This ethics is based on relationality, integrity and interdependence, so that biodiversity is no more conceived as a resource to be exploited but as one of the principles that maintain the equilibrium in the ES, and so preserve life (Santacruz Benavides, 2017, p. 58). For Mies and Shiva:

> An ecofeminist perspective propounds the need for a new cosmology and a new anthropology which recognizes that life in nature (which includes human beings) is maintained by means of co-operation, and mutual care and love. Only in this way can we be enabled to respect and preserve the diversity of all life forms, including their cultural expressions, as true sources of our wellbeing and happiness.
>
> (Mies and Shiva, 2014, p. 6)

Even these authors, as Nedelsky and Keller, claim for the necessity of a different idea of liberty, one "within the realm of necessity", which means respecting the natural limits of our planet (Mies and Shiva, 2014, p. 8). This objective must not be pursued through equalization policies with men (as white feminism seems to imply) but proposing a new relational paradigm between humans and non-humans, inspired by care and responsibility for everyone.

The post-colonial approach and the Caring State

In her studies about Singapore's relational constitutionalism, Li-ann Thio starts from the premise that even among legal scholars the model of contemporary Western liberal constitutionalism is intrinsically considered as hegemonic and taken for granted as a point of departure for every constitutional analysis. Instead, with the aim of pluralising the idea of constitutionalism, she considers the Singapore experience as a valuable and original product of a different cultural and legal sensitivity, based on non-liberal views: "to be is to exist in relation to other beings and relationalism prioritises the longevity or durability of mutually dependent relationships, rather than treating relationships as discrete short-term transactions" (Thio, 2019, p. 233).

Even if the main objective of relational constitutionalism in Singapore is to manage inter-group conflicts and assure religious harmony, its cultural basis and the methods followed to reach its goal can offer food for thought on how to shape the ecological legal paradigm. First of all, relational constitutionalism focuses on the maintenance of a peaceful relationship within and among religious groups:

> A primary goal of relational constitutionalism relates to sustaining healthy, durable, on-going relationships—in this universe, rights co-exist with other-centric responsibilities, reciprocity and the common good . . . The vision of the individual within a relational framework is not the vision of an atomistic rational being asserting rights against the state, which many liberal theorists favour. Instead, individuals are situated in communities, shaped and constituted by the network of relationships they interact with and are fundamentally connected to.
>
> (Thio, 2019, pp. 206–207)

Following Thio's arguments, a constitution that imposes specific values, or better, a particular idea of what is good, such as environmental conservation, must be ascribed to non-liberal constitutions, where the State proactively encourages the formation of a collective identity among citizens, based on selected values. So, depending on the specific ideas that the State puts at the basis of the common identity of the people, different non-liberal forms of State can be classified. We could consider the stability of the ES as the common value at the basis of a sustainable and harmonic society, where people are aware of their vulnerability and interdependency with respect to other non-human lives, and the matter and energy we co-produce by our interactions. As in Singapore's relational constitutionalism, the maintenance of social harmony would not be guaranteed by the judicial protection of atomic individual rights, but by the preference for solidarity and care responsibilities among all the legal subjects of this relation. This idea corresponds to the interpretation we gave of the constitutional architecture of the State designed by the new constitutions of Ecuador and Bolivia in 2008 and 2009, that we have called the Caring State (Bagni, 2023). The Caring State was based on two main pillars: environmental and social justice. These goals are to be understood in the light of a "sympoietic" perspective. In fact, environmental justice should be understood in a broader sense than the international idea of the environment. Its foundations are rooted in the indigenous cosmovisions, which consider the *Pacha Mama* as a subject. Meanwhile, the Caring State, as plurinational and intercultural, embraces a more powerful concept of social justice, giving voice and representation to the most vulnerable members of society, including indigenous and Afro-American peoples.

However, the Caring State has been trapped in liberal structures and legal mechanisms, unable to develop original forms of interaction. A new hope came from the draft Constitution approved by the Chilean Constitutional Convention. For the first time ever, the constitutional draft had recognized a "right to care", meaning that "all people have the right to take care, to be taken care of, and to care for themselves since born to death".[7] Moreover, it had recognized to the domestic work of caring the status of a job, like other type of professions, explicitly accounting for the social and economic value of such activity for the well-being of the whole society.[8] Unfortunately, the draft was rejected by popular vote on 4 September 2022.

Singapore's relational constitutionalism could be helpful in highlighting an original path of implementation for the Caring State.

Relational constitutionalism in Singapore aims to pursue religious harmony through soft constitutional norms, that is, non-binding acts and documents, which suggest common principles of behaviour and call for the responsibility of citizens. When these types of norms are widely accepted, they determine the limits of anti-social behaviour. Disobedience can be pursued by public rebuke and shame, and by temporary exclusion from the community. This same mechanism can be seen in the idea of traditional justice among indigenous peoples, where the goal is to preserve harmony within the community, and forgiveness is a fundamental part of the restoration process. From this perspective we could consider that "soft constitutional law" (as defined by Thio) can be used as an instrument for implementing the ecological paradigm. Of course, we cannot imagine tackling climate change and the environmental crisis only by soft law or nudge. However, the stick accompanies the carrot. As a radical change in our own lifestyles is the indispensable premise of every legal change, we absolutely need to instil a renewed sense of belonging in a community, where everyone gains from mutual care. So, concrete experiences of co-living in harmony with nature, such as the public rituals of reconciliation between the religious chiefs in Singapore or the *buen vivir* pursued in some indigenous communities in Latin America, can help to strengthen this sense of a shared fate, which currently seems lost in the upsurge of State particularism and populism. To this aim, another formulation of relational

7 "275.- Artículo 10.- Derecho al cuidado. Todas las personas tienen derecho a cuidar, a ser cuidadas y a cuidarse desde el nacimiento hasta la muerte. El Estado se obliga a proveer los medios para garantizar que este cuidado sea digno y realizado en condiciones de igualdad y corresponsabilidad. El Estado garantizará este derecho a través de un Sistema Integral de Cuidados y otras normativas y políticas públicas que incorporen el enfoque de derechos humanos, de género y la promoción de la autonomía personal. El Sistema tendrá un carácter estatal, paritario, solidario, universal, con pertinencia cultural y perspectiva de género e interseccionalidad. Su financiamiento será progresivo, suficiente y permanente. El sistema prestará especial atención a lactantes, niños, niñas y adolescentes, personas mayores, personas en situación de discapacidad, personas en situación de dependencia y personas con enfermedades graves o terminales. Asimismo, velará por el resguardo de los derechos de quienes ejercen trabajos de cuidados".

8 "276.- Artículo 11.- Reconocimiento del trabajo doméstico y de cuidados. El Estado reconoce que los trabajos domésticos y de cuidados son trabajos socialmente necesarios e indispensables para la sostenibilidad de la vida y el desarrollo de la sociedad, que son una actividad económica que contribuye a las cuentas nacionales y que deben ser considerados en la formulación y ejecución de las políticas públicas. El Estado promoverá la corresponsabilidad social y de género e implementará mecanismos para la redistribución del trabajo doméstico y de cuidados".

constitutionalism can help building a methodology for enhancing relationships over individual claims.

The Earth Jurisprudence and the rights of nature approach

The founder of Earth Jurisprudence is Thomas Berry. The starting point of his argumentation is that "our human destiny is integral with the destiny of the earth" (Berry, 1990, p. xiv; 2009, pp. 81, 135). He supports the idea that we share a universal coding with the grass, stones, other animals, the Earth, stars and the other planets, expressed in the curvature of the Universe, that possesses an impressive regenerative and creative energy. After denying this primordial nature for centuries, with the arrogance of attempting to prosper alone, humanity must rediscover nature and listen for the guidance of her inner coding. Acting like this can still allow a harmonious life on earth on an egalitarian basis for all humans and non-humans. Indigenous people can be a model, since they have defended their relationship with the Earth, resisting the industrial era.

Cormac Cullinan, Berry's disciple and a South African lawyer, in his best-seller *Wild Law. A Manifesto for Earth Justice* (Cullinan, 2012), speaks of "wild law", in the sense that it should reflect the natural rules that govern "wildness", which is usually considered outside the law. The premise of his argumentation is that Nature must be considered as a whole, and human beings as part of Nature, whereas the actual legal paradigm puts Man above all other creatures and separates him from Nature, as an autonomous and independent subject (Cullinan, 2012, p. 59). This false postulate is the cause of the current social and environmental crisis, which the global legal order is not able to tackle. We need a complete shift in our understanding of what "law" is, and for whom and for which goal law must be implemented, but we also need to rediscover how to communicate, feel empathy and care for Nature and other beings, *sentipensar* with the Earth, in Escobar's words (Escobar, 2014).

The Earth Jurisprudence is among the philosophical basis of the rights of Nature movement, which began to flourish after the recognition, in art. 71 of the 2008 Ecuadorian Constitution, of the legal personhood to Nature/*Pacha Mama*. As Ramiro Ávila points out, "Rights of Nature require another modernity . . . which in the Andean world indigenous people have called sumak kawsay" (Ávila Santamaría, 2022, p. 81). *Sumak kawsay*, or *buen vivir*, has been defined as "a deeper change in knowledge, affectivity, and spirituality, an ontological opening to other forms of understanding the relation between humans and non-humans which do not imply the modern separation between society and nature" (Chuji et al., 2019). It is an expression that recollect the many cosmovisions of Latin America indigenous peoples.

Even if the Ecuadorian example remains the only one at constitutional level (except for some Member States' constitutions in Mexico and, again, the rejected 2022 Chilean constitutional project), the recognition of legal subjectivity to Nature or specific natural elements such as rivers, lakes, *paramos* and forests has spread out in many countries, in particular in Latin America and Asia.[9] There is an evident link between recognition of legal personhood to natural elements (by statutes or jurisprudence) and the existence of indigenous and tribal peoples in the State.

However, the rights of Nature approach has a wider scope of application, not limited to legal subjectivity. This different conceptual framework can be explained both through a deeper understanding of indigenous ontologies and from a Western scientific perspective. As Alberto Acosta reminds us, "When we speak about the Rights of Nature, it is not a question of renouncing the vast and rich scientific legacy" but "to accept that Nature, as a social construction, that is to say as a term conceptualized by human beings, must be reinterpreted and revised in its entirety if we do not want to put at risk human survival on the planet" (Acosta, 2012).[10]

As already mentioned, indigenous peoples recognize that humans are part of a whole system of life, regulated by countless connections of interdependence, and where humans are asked to live in harmony with Nature, as part of the ES.

Following the ecosystem approach, we can translate the spiritual link described above with its scientific definition incorporated as the primary framework for action under the UN 1992 Convention on Biological Diversity:

> An ecosystem approach is based on the application of appropriate scientific methodologies focused on levels of biological organization, which encompass the essential structure, processes, functions and interactions among organisms and their environment. It recognizes that humans, with their cultural diversity, are an integral component of many ecosystems.
>
> (COP 5 decision V/6)[11]

So, indigenous and tribal knowledge and Western modern science converge on a systemic understanding of life on Earth.

Conclusions

In this chapter, we have moved away from literature interested in understanding scarcity as shortage of resources and the interface between scarcity, conflict and tensions (see Topidi, Chapter 1). Our premise, instead, is that the actual ecological crisis is due to the condition of "abundance" of goods and products that capitalism needs to guarantee a "sustained economic growth" (UN

9 For a detailed and actualized map see https://ecojurisprudence.org/.

10 "Cuando se plantean los Derechos de la Naturaleza, no se trata de renunciar al amplio y rico legado científico" but "aceptar que la Naturaleza, en tanto construcción social, es decir en tanto término conceptualizado por los seres humanos, debe ser reinterpretada y revisada íntegramente si no queremos poner en riesgo la vida del ser humano en el planeta".

11 https://www.cbd.int/ecosystem.

General Assembly, 2015). So, from a material point of view, it is the (obviously unequally distributed) existence of abundance, generated by the global system of production, which stands at the basis of the ecological crisis.

We then identified indigenous and tribal peoples as minorities whose cultural repository of knowledge has the potential to contribute in proposing a different path to tackle the ecological crisis. Indigenous and tribal knowledge is based on a monistic relationship between human and nature, which prevent to consider non-humans as objects or resources. So, their critics towards the Western cultural and economic model is based on the necessity of shifting the focus from abundance of material resources and goods to scarcity of relational and spiritual resources, which affects the global society.

Later, we reconstructed the relational foundations of indigenous "ontologies" and broadened our investigation to include other Global South contributions to a relational theory of law, which is fed from minority epistemologies.

From the Western legal tradition, it is certain that a relational theory of law could be criticized both as a dangerous erosion of individual rights and freedoms, as well as utopic.

As for the first critique, the individual is not erased by our proposal but empowered by its relational dimension, which can foster a more inclusive and respectful community. Relationality applied to human-human relations integrates the dogmatic structure of rights, trying not only to solve a conflict but also to advance workable solutions to complex social problems, encouraging social transformation (Nedelsky, 2011, p. 342). On the other hand, relationality between humans and non-humans comes from nature herself, from the rules that govern our ecosystem.

The law and the State can ignore it until mitigation and adaptation to climate change and ecological unbalances will be able to contain damages. But much damage is already irreversible, at least in a temporal dimension significant for our generation and the future ones that will stem from our contemporary society. Relationality requires us to move the focus towards the protection of the interconnections between the different subjects involved, instead of considering which party's interests should prevail. In Braidotti's words:

> The main implication for the practice of a new cosmopolitical sense of planetary interconnection is that the political, scientific and juridical laws need to be retuned according to a view of the subject as a complex singularity, an affective assemblage and a relational vitalist entity.
>
> (Braidotti, 2012, p. 15)

As for the utopian critique, we are strongly convinced that our mental structures produce a strong impact on how we behave. Additionally, our language, as a product of our thinking, shapes our behaviour. So, we absolutely need to create a "habit of relational thinking". This could generate a shift in our epistemological paradigm, from a liberal to a relational/ecological one, to request from humanity a real change in the pattern of consumption and exploitation of our planet and our fellow living beings. As it has been asserted in the 2020/2021 UNU Interconnected Disaster Risk Report, "changing the underlying systems that create disastrous situations can only begin when individuals recognize their part in the larger, whole iceberg, rather than just the tip" (*UNU Interconnected Disaster Risk Report*, 2020/2021, p. 88).

The relational legal paradigm that we have proposed thus finds its basis on the consideration of the human being in an ecosystem perspective, as indigenous and tribal peoples also suggest. While natural selection affects individuals, it is only species that evolve and co-develop. This approach is an invitation to make our societies more democratic, and not to dismiss responsibilities towards other beings. In fact, it is the ambition of ecological democracy "to forge the character of each individual, his autonomy, according to his natural capacities (autopoietics), thanks to a gradual process of reorientation and transformation of preferences in light of the context not only socio-political, but also ecological" (Messina, 2019, p. 150).

References

Acosta, Alberto, *La maldición de la abundancia*. Quito: Swissaid/Abya-Yala, 2009

Acosta, Alberto, 'La Naturaleza con Derechos Una propuesta para un cambio civilizatorio', 2012, https://www.garn.org/wp-content/uploads/2021/09/Acosta_DDN_2012.pdf (accessed 5 October 2023)

Attard Bellido, Maria Elena, 'Entre la diosa Themis y Mama Ocllo: La propuesta de argumentación jurídica plural desde la filosofía intercultural andina de la Chakana', in *Diálogo de Saberes*, no. 50, 2019, pp. 79–100

Ávila Santamaría, Ramiro, 'Rights of Nature vs. Human Rights? An Urgent Shift of Paradigms', in Domenico Amirante and Silvia Bagni (eds), *Environmental Constitutionalism in the Anthropocene. Values, Principles and Actions*. London and New York: Routledge, 2022

Bagni, Silvia, 'Forms of State in Latin America', in Silvia Bagni and Serena Baldin (eds), *Comparative Latin American Constitutionalism*. Trieste: EUT, 2023, pp. 45–70, open access, https://www.openstarts.units.it/server/api/core/bitstreams/4944da4a-e57c-411b-884c-9ffe658aa564/content (accessed 4 October 2023)

Berry, Thomas, *The Dream of the Earth*. San Francisco: Sierra Club Edition, 1990

Berry, Thomas, *The Sacred Universe: Earth, Spirituality, and Religion in the Twenty-First Century*. New York: Columbia University Press, 2009

Bookchin, Murray, *Post-Scarcity Anarchism*. Menlo Park: Ramparts Press, 1971 (trad. it. *L'Anarchismo nell'età dell'abbondanza*. Milano: La Salamandra, 1979)

Braidotti, Rosi, 'Biomacht und nekro-Politik. Uberlegungen zu einer Ethik der Nachhaltigkeit', in *Springerin, Hefte fur Gegenwartskunst*, Band XIII, Heft 2, Fruhjahr 2007, pp. 18–23

Braidotti, Rosi, 'Becoming-World', in Rosi Braidotti, Patrick Hanafin and Bolette Blaagaard (eds), *After Cosmopolitanism*. London and New York: Taylor & Francis Group, 2012

Capra, Fritjof and Luisi, Pier Luigi, *Vita e Natura. Una visione sistemica*. San Sepolcro: Aboca, 2014

Capra, Fritjof and Mattei, UgoUgo, *The Ecology of Law: Toward a Legal System in Tune with Nature and the Community*. Oakland, CA: Berrett-Koehler, 2015

Carducci, Michele et al., *Towards an EU Charter of the Fundamental Rights of Nature, con Study*. Brussels: European Economic and Social Committee, 2020, pp. 1–189, https://www.eesc.europa.eu/en/our-work/publications-other-work/studies ISBN 978-92-830-4971-5

Chuji, Mónica, Rengifo, Grimaldo and Gudynas, Eduardo, 'Buen Vivir', in Ashish Kothari et al. (eds), *Pluriverse: A Post-Development Dictionary*. New Delhi: Tulika Books, 2019, pp. 111–113

Cooper Davis, Peggy, 'Toward a Relational Constitutionalism', in *Acta Juridica*, 2008, pp. 239–253

Coral Díaz, Ana Milena, 'Ecofeminismo: Integrando saberes, explicando la dominación', in Lina Marcela Muñoz Ávila and Leonardo Güiza Suárez (eds), *El Cuidado de La Tierra: Mujer, Ambiente y Cambio Climático*. Bogotá: Editorial Universidad del Rosario, 2016

Cullinan, Cormac, *Wild Law: A Manifesto of Earth Justice*. Cape Town: Siber Ink, 2002 (trad. it. *I diritti della Natura—Wild Law*, Prato: Piano B, 2012)

Descola, Philippe, *L'écologie des autres: L'anthropologie et la question de la nature*. Paris: Éditions Quae, 2011 (Italina translation: *L'ecologia degli altri. L'antropologia e la questione della natura*. Roma: Linaria, 2013)

Escobar, Arturo, *Sentipensar con la tierra: Nuevas lecturas sobre desarrollo, territorio y diferencia*. Medellín: Ediciones UNAULA, 2014

Galeano, Eduardo, *Las venas abiertas de América latina*. Bueno Aires: Siglo XXI Editores, 1971

Gluckman, Max, *Politics, Law and Ritual in Tribal Society*. Chicago: Aldine Publishing Company, Routledge, 1965

Graeber, David, Wengrow, David, *L'alba di tutto. Una nuova storia dell'umanità*. Milano: Rizzoli, 2022 (original title: *The Dawn of Everything. A New History of Humanity*, London: Penguin, 2021)

Grober, Ulrich, *Sustainability: A Cultural History*. Devon: Green Books, 2012

Keller, Catherine, *From a Broken Web: Separation, Sexism, and Self*. Boston: Beacon Press, 1988

Kelsen, Hans, *Pure Theory of Law*. Berkley: UC Berkeley Press, 1967

Leonardi, Emanuele, *Lavoro Natura Valore. André Gorz tra marxismo e decrescita*. Nocera Inferiore: Orthotes, 2017

Locchi, Maria Chiara and Paffarini, Jacopo, 'Una democrazia oltre lo Stato? Il modello confederale del Kurdistan siriano', in *DPCE Online*, vol. 57, no. 1, April 2023, https://www.dpceonline.it/index.php/dpceonline/article/view/1803 (accessed 3 October 2023)

Lovelock, James E. and Margulis, Lynn, 'Atmospheric Homeostasis by and for the Biosphere: The Gaia Hypothesis', in *Tellus*, Series A, vol. 26, no. 1–2, 1974, pp. 2–10

Macpherson, Elizabeth, 'Ecosystem Rights and the Anthropocene in Australia and Aotearoa New Zealand', in Domenico Amirante and Silvia Bagni (eds), *Environmental Constitutionalism in the Anthropocene: Values, Principles and Actions*. London and New York: Routledge, 2022

Martinez-Alier, Joan, *The Environmentalism of the Poor: A Study of Ecological Conflicts and Valuation*. Cheltenham and Northampton: Elgar, 2002

Messina, Sergio, *Eco-democrazia. Per una fondazione ecologica del diritto e della politica*. Napoli: Orthotes Editrice, 2019

Mies, Maria and Shiva, VandanaVandana, *Ecofeminism* [2nd edition]. London and New York: Zed Books, 2014

Morris, Brian, *Pioneers of Ecological Humanism*. Montréal: Black Rose Books, 2017 (accessed 4 October 2023)

Nedelsky, Jennifer, *Law's Relations: a Relational Theory of Self, Autonomy, and Law*. Oxford: Oxford University Press, 2011

Odum, Eugene P. and Barrett, Gary W., *Fundamentals of Ecology* [5th edition]. Stamford: Thomson, 2004

Santacruz Benavides, Lucy, 'Ecofeminismo, espiritualidad, y subjetividad', in *La manzana de la Discordia*, vol. 12, no. 2, 2017

Tamanaha, Brian Z., 'Law', in *Oxford International Encyclopedia of Legal History*. St. John's Legal Studies Research Paper No. 08-0095, 2008. Available at SSRN. https://ssrn.com/abstract=1082436

Thio, Li-Ann, 'Singapore Relational Constitutionalism: The "Living Institution" and the Project of Religious Harmony', in *Singapore Journal of Legal Studies*, 2019, pp. 204–234

UN General Assembly, *Transforming Our World: The 2030 Agenda for Sustainable Development*, Resolution adopted by the General Assembly on 25 September 2015, A/RES/70/1

UNU Interconnected Disaster Risk Report, 2020/2021. Available at https://collections.unu.edu/eserv/UNU:8288/UNU_Interconnected_Disaster_Risks_Report_210908_META.pdf (accessed 4 October 2023)

Winter, Christine J., *Subjects of Intergenerational Justice. Indigenous Philosophy, the Environment and Relationships*. London and New York: Routledge, 2022

6 Vulnerabilities, minoritizing processes and concerted solutions for rural scarcities. Learning lessons and tackling marginalisation in Northern Italy

Roberta Medda-Windischer and Federica Maino

Introduction

For the past 60 years, cities have been the main focus of public policies and decision-making strategies. Cities have been considered the ideal hotspot for innovation and change, the best place to develop and benefit from business, education programs and centralized services. Plans, projects and different kinds of initiatives have been tested and implemented mainly for urban communities. It is a consequence of the socio-economic changes of recent decades, of policies that have mainly favoured the development of urban areas (Mantino 2010), a scarcity of economic resources and political representation for rural areas, including those located in mountain regions, and an absence of adequate multilevel (regional, national and European) unitary policies and strategies (Barca 2009; Omizzolo and Streifeneder 2013), as well as the use of traditional planning tools (Porcellini 2013).

Due to this, there is a risk of rural areas, and even more as mountain territories are concerned, being abandoned or being developed in a way that does not reflect sustainability criteria. The latter is, for example, the case of mountain areas which have been developed as recreational areas for urban communities, with negative impacts on these fragile environments and their communities. Rural and mountain areas are more vulnerable to climate change, land degradation and natural disasters than surrounding territories, but they provide long-term benefits not only to their residents, but to society as a whole. Rural and mountain areas can ensure the hydrogeological protection of the land; they are rich in values and resources, since they are diversity centres, both under the biological and the cultural perspectives. In our analysis, we consider "minoritized" rural communities, including those located in mountain areas, as those subject to various forms—economic, social, and/or political—of scarcity and having strong bonds with their own territory, bonds that are characterized by diversity and resilience. Rural areas are often, though not always, characterized by depopulation, lack of essential services, and topographic and climatic restrictions (Reynaud et al. 2020). Accordingly, when these features are present, they have long been considered "residual" with respect to the

DOI: 10.4324/9781032661780-7

processes of urbanization and modernization, and for this very reason reputed as "marginal" (Andreoli and Tellarini 1998), "fragile" (De Rossi 2018) or "cities optional" when developed to meet the needs of people living in the cities (Corrado and Durbiano 2018).

Rural communities have a strong bond with their territory: they developed the capacity to adapt to their fragile environment over time and have learned to cope with difficult living conditions, such as scarcity (Cantiani et al. 2016; Ianni et al. 2015). In the past they have provided solutions for sustainable management of natural resources—as in the case of the traditional collective use of forests. Thus, the knowledge and the potential coming from rural communities lead us to believe that they could become new leading models of development to imagine new ways of conceiving the future (Maino et al. 2018).

By looking at minoritized and marginalized communities living in rural areas, this chapter aims to explore which lessons can be learnt from them to be transposed and applied in settings characterized by scarcity for the accommodation of linguistic, religious and cultural minorities. The interdisciplinary approach applied in this contribution is thus based on cross-fertilization among linguistic, religious and cultural minorities and marginalized rural communities in terms of both the construction of synergies and sharing of common solutions. This approach is particularly promising as it provides new insights on common issues such as minoritizing processes related to vulnerability and marginalization, multiple and intersectoral grouping and individual belonging, asymmetry in access to power, empowerment and participation. By encompassing different marginalized groups, this chapter aims to turn scarcity into opportunities for change, to promote solution-oriented and need-based decisions, emphasizing concerted processes to support structural changes.

Drawing on research action methodologies, this chapter seeks to explore how a specific type of rural community located in a mountain area may deal with conditions of scarcity. Here, we mainly refer to scarcity both in terms of power dynamics and in a material sense as lack of access to some critical resources, especially goods, job opportunities, infrastructures and services such as public transport, schools, telecommunications, high-speed internet connection, small shops, post offices, pharmacies, elderly care and so on. As a consequence of scarcity, we observe phenomena of depopulation and migration flows, as well as the prominence of global urbanization and modernization processes, all conducive to scenarios of vulnerability and minoritization for rural and mountain communities.

The chapter is structured along five sections. After the introduction, the second part provides some terminological and conceptual clarifications on main terms and notions used to analyse the commonalities among linguistic, religious and cultural minorities, and rural communities within the overarching concepts of scarcity, marginalization and vulnerability. The third part analyses main difficulties that minorities generally face in times of crisis and scarcity and some emblematic policies commonly applied to achieve social cohesion in diverse societies with a focus on special measures. The fourth part discusses the main outputs of the Vital Mountains project (2019–ongoing) that focuses on the development of a marginalized mountain area located in the north-east of the Italian Alps (Trentino region) through the empowerment of the local community. The chapter concludes with some final remarks on the need to develop concerted solutions beyond mere reasonable accommodations with the involvement of local communities, decision makers and academia as a sine qua non approach to combine local interests, needs, global vision, funds and expertise.

Minorities, marginalization and rural vulnerabilities: conceptual and terminological clarifications

The concept of marginality, as well as the notions of scarcity, vulnerability and minorities, is a frequently used concept in social science with varying interpretations and perceptions. It is generally acknowledged that marginality and marginal regions have, at least, two broad interpretations and meanings. The first is a more traditional understanding of marginality as an economic concept, in which a region is deemed marginal when it is distant from markets, depends on primary resources, has a small and sparse population and is not politically or economically autonomous (Cullen and Pretes 2000, 217). A second understanding of marginality is one in which marginalization is viewed as a social construction in which marginality is seen as a power relationship between a group that sees itself as a "centre" viewing all minorities and non-members as marginal or "other" (Cullen and Pretes 2000, 217).

Marginal regions and rural areas, including mountain territories, are closely intertwined, and this aspect emerges very clearly in the recent UN Declaration on the Right of Peasants and other People Working in Rural Areas adopted in 2018 by the UN General Assembly.[1] Among the main foci of the UN Declaration on Rural Areas are the access to resources against scarcity and marginalization and the right to cultural rights to maintain, protect and develop traditional knowledge such as ways of life, methods of productions and traditional cultural expressions.[2]

The adoption of the UN Declaration on Rural Areas was the result of a large mobilization of civil society movements and indicates the importance of

1 The UN Declaration on Rural Areas has been approved by 122 states representing 75 per cent of the global population. Most EU countries abstained, and 8 countries voted against, including the United Kingdom, the United States and Australia.

2 The UN Declaration on Rural Areas includes rights for communities in rural areas to access natural resources, right to food, food security and food sovereignty against industrialized agriculture and process of commodification, control over seeds against the negative pervasive effects of globalization; right to land against the phenomenon of land-grabbing, which is one of the main factors of marginalization; right to cultural rights to maintain, protect and develop traditional knowledge such as ways of life and methods of productions, as well as traditional cultural expressions.

this topic in the international area (Paoloni and Vezzani 2019). In particular, it emphasizes the interdependency between sustainable development, as an important tool against marginalization, and cultural rights, in particular traditions and cultural expressions, both considered crucial elements of the identities of rural communities.

The identity of a collective entity such as linguistic, religious and ethnic minority groups, rural communities and other marginalized groups, can be socially constructed and attributed to designate a group and the people who belong to it (Anderson 1983).[3] Whether such identity exist or not, it is not so relevant: what matters are the effects of such ascription on the lives of the members of the group in various contexts, including the legal, political, social and economic domains (Macioce 2022, 102; Marko and Constantin 2019; Medda-Windischer and Crepaz 2022).[4]

Another relevant aspect common to minorities and rural marginalized communities is the asymmetry concerning the access to power, its exercise, and the control over those who are in power. Linguistic, religious and ethnic minority groups and rural communities are groupings whose possibilities of access to power may be more limited in comparison to the rest of the population (Macioce 2022, 102).

Closely linked to this aspect is the fact that many communities reject the term *minorities*, as this may imply to be considered second-class citizens, and prefer using the term *minoritized groups*, as this term captures the active dynamics that create an asymmetry in the access to power and resources (Wingrove-Haugland and McLeod 2022; Özlem and DiAngelo 2012). The term *minoritized* implies that some individuals and groups are being made into a marginalized status by systemic power dynamics. The usage of this term underlines also how overlapping and intersecting identities relate to power systems and structures of oppression and discrimination.[5]

3 The most quoted definition of minorities is the descriptive definition by Francesco Capotorti, the Special Rapporteur of the UN Sub-Commission on the Prevention of Discrimination and Protection of Minorities: "A group numerically inferior to the rest of the population of a state, in a non-dominant position, whose members—being nationals of the state—possess ethnic, religious or linguistic characteristics differing from those of the rest of the population and show, if only implicitly, a sense of solidarity, directing towards preserving their culture, traditions, religion or language." Francesco Capotorti, *Study on the Rights of Persons Belonging to Ethnic, Religious and Linguistic Minorities*, UN Doc. E/CN.4/Sub.2/384/Rev.1, 1977, para.568.

4 On Brubaker's definition of ethnic groups according to which "[ethnic groups] are collective cultural representation . . . that sustain the vision and division of the special world in racial, ethnic, or national terms" (Brubaker 2004), Marko notes that "whenever people perceive mental concepts (. . .) as if they are real (. . .), the consequences are no less real than the existence of physical objects" (Marko 2019).

5 Iris Marion Young, in her seminal work "Five Faces of Oppression" (1990), identified five distinct typologies of oppression: exploitation, marginalization, powerlessness, cultural domination and violence.

Communities living in rural areas have in common with linguistic, religious and ethnic groups the risk that this condition, i.e. the rural dimension for the communities living in rural areas and the linguistic, religious and cultural characteristic that differ from the rest of the population for minority groups, may translate into a lower availability of material, social and legal resources, and this may determine their vulnerability. It is important that these conditions are not considered fixed and pre-determined situations, but they represent a risk that may result in vulnerability that other individuals and groups do not experience (Macioce 2022, 105).

Accordingly, the use of the concept of vulnerability as linked to linguistic, religious and ethnic minorities as well as to rural communities is not supposed to designate or delimit specific groups.[6] The asymmetric access to resources, goods and services leading to a stratification of inequalities renders some groups vulnerable: this condition, shared by individuals and groups to a varying extent, is thus socially induced rather than innate but is nevertheless real (Baumgärtel 2020, 11).

Vulnerability is, thus, situational and the result of social, political and economic relationship within which individuals happen to find themselves (Fineman 2016; Baumgärtel 2020, 5; Timmer 2016). As Fineman puts it: "Success and failure are socially structured and intricately depended on an individual's interactions within the institutions and political structures society has constructed" (Fineman 2016, 24).

The relevance of the concept of vulnerability for minority groups and rural marginalized communities is also that vulnerability is not a pure negative condition: vulnerability is also generative as it forges bonds between human beings and leads us to create institutions (Fineman 2016; Timmer 2016, 149).[7] In particular, vulnerability theorists argue that this approach forms the basis for a claim that the state must be more responsive to that vulnerability (Fineman 2016, 13). In other terms, vulnerability has the potential to define an obligation for the state to ensure a more robust guarantee of equality (Fineman 2016; Timmer 2016, 149).

In a normative perspective, once vulnerability has been determined, it variably gives rise to a number of distinct legal effects: it may impose a positive

6 Drawing primarily on Fineman's work, the concept of vulnerability emerged as a response to the limitations of non-discrimination and equality law. Martha Fineman's seminal conception of vulnerability is a substantive critique of the limitations of legal and socially formal equality. According to Fineman, much of legal theory has been centred around an illusory "universal human subject" defined by "autonomy, self-sufficiency, and personal responsibility". Fineman's analysis leads her to the conclusion that such a vision is shortsighted and inadequate as it fails to address some of the underlying reasons of inequality (such as disparity in wealth and power) and also because it may ultimately entail adverse consequences such as the curtailing of affirmative action (Fineman 2016). For an analysis of Fineman's work, see Baumgärtel 2020.

7 For some, vulnerability offers an opportunity to re-interrogate the role of human rights as key constraints on State power and catalysts for social change (Timmer et al. 2021, 190–197).

obligation for governments to give "special consideration" or "special protection" to vulnerable individuals and groups, as in the case of Roma and their lifestyle according to the ECtHR (Baumgärtel 2020, 6; Timmer 2016; Arnardóttir 2017; Ippolito and Igleasias Sanchez 2015); it may also impact judicial reasoning by enlarging the protective scope of certain provisions such as norms protecting individuals in detention, and it may contribute to lighten the burden of proof on certain occasions (Baumgärtel 2020, 13; Mowbray 2004; Timmer 2016, 165–166; Ippolito 2020).[8]

However, although in the last decade vulnerability has become an en vogue concept (Besson cited by Baumgärtel 2020), it is also very much criticized, especially when it is used to cluster groups and individuals (Macioce 2022, 8).[9] Vulnerability is indeed a concept that remains largely discretionary, in particular as to which groups are to be considered vulnerable, for what reasons, and on the basis of what threshold such vulnerability is worthy of special consideration (Macioce 2022, 50). In addition, vulnerability has also been criticized as leading to essentialization, stigmatization and paternalism. On the one hand, the risk of essentialism, i.e., of making vulnerability a qualifying condition for a group of people, may strengthen processes of labelling and stigmatization (Macioce 2022, 25; Baumgärtel 2020, 6). On the other hand, vulnerable persons might be perceived as deviant, as the exception to the norm and this may justify an attitude of paternalism, whereby vulnerability is equated with the need for greater protection, not so much empowerment or participation, or even acting as a moral justification for social control and behavioural regulation (Timmer et al. 2021, 190–197; Arnardóttir 2017, citing Fineman 2016).[10]

Taking into account the anti-essentialist critiques, the notion of group vulnerability for minorities and rural marginalized communities should be elaborated in a non-essentialist way: vulnerability should be considered situational and the result of the functioning of power structures, cultural mechanisms, or systems of resource distribution (Fineman 2016; Macioce 2022, 68). In other terms, vulnerability should be considered contingent and socially induced, as found in Fineman's work (Timmer et al. 2021, 190–197).

In this regard, Macioce refers to "positional group vulnerability," which is not necessarily associated with oppressive contexts, but it merely depends on the "common occurrence of certain conditions of vulnerability, which affects people's possibility of action, their capacity to protect against risks, and their capacity to cope with the consequences of these risks" (Macioce 2022, 72).

8 Vulnerability conditions ranges from conditions of material deprivation, situations of dependence, forms of incapacity, contexts of social marginalization, to experiences of exploitation and violence (Fineman 2016; Macioce 2022, 86; Timmer 2016, 161; Arnardóttir 2017).

9 In this regard, Macioce speaks of a "vulnerability turn" in social science (Macioce 2022, 2).

10 Due to the many criticisms, the ECtHR, especially the Grand Chamber, seems very cautious towards adopting a vulnerable groups approach in its reasoning, but when it has, it has clearly emphasized how such vulnerability is socially constructed (Arnardóttir 2017, 169).

Positional or situational vulnerability does not, however, exclude that discrimination, and marginalization can occur to individuals and groups who share certain characteristics such as gender, race, sexual orientation and so on. In her work, Fineman acknowledged this by noting:

> There may be a basis for recognition of harm to social groupings based on *shared characteristics* based on statistically relevant distinctions in a quantitative sense, both on an individual and a groups basis; and negative economic and institutional harms may cluster around members of a *socially or culturally determined grouping* who share certain societal positions or suffered discrimination based on *constructed categories* used to differentiate one class of persons from another, such as race, gender, ethnicity, or religious affiliation.
>
> (Fineman 2016, 21, emphasis added)

In an attempt to combine group-identity and vulnerability approaches, the European Court of Human Rights ties up in its case law the classic group-based approach, through the discrimination grounds listed in Article 14 ECHR, with the vulnerable group approach, emphasizing a social-contextual understanding of group membership (Arnardóttir 2017, 159).[11] Although the ECHR and its non-discrimination clause (article 14 ECHR) are largely based on the protection of individuals and groups defined by common characteristic—socially constructed, imagined or real—the ECtHR's concept of group vulnerability is not related by any essential or innate characteristic of the relevant individuals themselves, but it is social-contextual (Arnardóttir 2017, 164). The approach of the ECtHR combining group-identity and vulnerable approaches is particularly relevant because the ECtHR does not look at the relevant identity marker per se, but focuses instead on how the consequences of being associated with that identity marker are shaped by history and other social forces that create and perpetuate disadvantage, and how the experiences of different individuals within the larger group may not all be the same (Arnardóttir 2017, 164).[12]

11 Within the discrimination ground of ethnic origin/race, the ECtHR has only raised group vulnerability in relation to Roma people (Arnardóttir 2017, 162).

12 Timmer clusters conditions of vulnerability as analyzed by the European Court of Human Rights along the following lines/cases: inherent vulnerability, such as children and persons with mental disabilities; vulnerability due to state control, such as persons in detention; vulnerability due to gender, such as women in domestic violence or precarious reproductive health situations; vulnerability due to a legal power imbalance, such as the case of persons who are accused and persons who lack legal capacity; vulnerability due to espousal of unpopular views such as demonstrators and journalists; vulnerability in the context of migration, as in the case of detention and expulsion of asylum seekers; and vulnerability due to group membership, such as Roma, people with impaired health and (to some extent) asylum seekers (Timmer 2016, 152–161).

In conclusion, the notion of group vulnerability should be considered as socially induced, positional/situational as resulting from the functioning of power structures, cultural mechanisms, or systems of resource distribution, as found in Fineman's work (Timmer et al. 2021, 190–197). As acknowledged by Fineman herself, however, vulnerability conditions may also cluster around members of a socially or culturally determined grouping, such as race, gender, ethnicity, or religious affiliation (Fineman 2016, 21). With this background in mind, referring specifically to rural communities, it would appropriate to speak of "rural vulnerabilities" that affect individuals and groups living in rural areas differently depending on various social-constructed factors and contexts that may expose them to risks and an asymmetric access to resources.

Dilemmas and policies against marginalization in times of scarcity: some general considerations

In contemporary societies, cultural, linguistic and religious diversity has increased and will likely continue to do so in the future. Maintaining the bonds of ethnically diverse societies while protecting the identity and diversity of individuals and groups, affording and guaranteeing equal treatment and protection against discrimination and ensuring their participation in decision-making processes are, however, complex and still unsolved challenges that are at the forefront of the current political and public debate in most contemporary societies: these issues can indeed reinforce or diffuse conflicts, tensions and social unrest between groups; and they can be an instrument of inclusion or exclusion.

It is also generally acknowledged that social, economic and political crises, such as the COVID-19 pandemic, and the global energy and food supply crisis resulting from the war in Ukraine, have a more pervasive negative effect on most vulnerable groups of society, in particular on linguistic, religious and cultural minorities and other marginalized groups, since scarcity and marginalization are often intertwined and interdependent parts of a vicious circle of vulnerability.

In increasingly diverse and troubled societies, especially in settings defined by scarcity, there is an urgent need for policies aimed at reconciling diversity—an important component of individual and group identity and thus of human dignity—while preserving and strengthening prosperity and social cohesion; in other terms, policies that aim to maintain the bonds of ethnically diverse societies, reduce tensions and prevent conflicts while guaranteeing the equitable access to rights and non-discriminatory sharing of resources for all. But how to reconcile the demands of diversity and political unity, i.e. how to create a political community that is both cohesive and stable and satisfies the legitimate aspirations of minority groups? This dilemma has been the subject of considerable discussion ever since the rise of the modern state, and particularly during the past few decades. All policies that seek to reconcile social cohesion, unity and diversity are confronted with a veritable minefield of dilemmas.

Societies need to evolve their own appropriate legal and institutional frameworks suited to their history, traditions, demographic composition, political requirements and unique characteristics, but which principles should guide their decisions? Fostering a sense of common belonging, unity and respect for diversity are important principles, but to what extent can they be achieved and, at the same time, combined? This is a central challenge in modern societies because seeking to accommodate minority claims implies the need to look for a balance between unity and separation, cohesion and respect for diversity. If one opts solely for unity, the risk is assimilation and the disappearance of minorities as distinct groups; if one chooses only diversity, the result can be the cultural "ghettoization" of minority communities with their consequent separation and marginalization from society.

Against the backdrop of increasing scarcity, this contribution aims to explore commonalities and synergies between two different categories of marginalized groups, namely communities living in rural areas and, linguistic, religious and cultural minorities in order to develop new perspectives and innovative solutions to the (still) unsolved questions posed by diversity and unity. By looking at these diverse marginalized groupings, this chapter explores which lessons can be learnt from rural and mountain communities for the accommodation of linguistic, religious and cultural minorities.

As seen earlier, an important aspect that these marginalized groups, i.e. communities living in rural areas and linguistic, religious and cultural minorities, have in common is the asymmetry in their access to power and resources compared to the rest of the population. This lack of access to power can have significant consequences for these groups. For this reason, many prefer to use the term "minoritized groups" rather than "minorities" to emphasize the systemic power dynamics that marginalize them (Wingrove-Haugland and McLeod 2022).

Rural communities and linguistic, religious, and ethnic minority groups also share the risk of having fewer material, social, and legal resources, making them vulnerable, especially in times of scarcity. This vulnerability, however, is not a fixed or predetermined state but rather a result of their specific conditions and circumstances. The concept of vulnerability is thus not meant to categorize or limit specific groups but rather to highlight how asymmetric access to resources and services leads to inequalities, making certain groups more vulnerable. This vulnerability is socially induced rather than innate but is nonetheless real.

In our analysis, the concept of identity among various marginalized groups, including linguistic, religious and ethnic minorities, as well as rural communities is also socially constructed and attributed by society. What matters most thus is not whether these identities objectively exist, but rather the impact of these ascriptions on the lives of group members in different contexts, such as legal, political, social and economic domains.

In times of scarcity, most vulnerable groups, in particular minorities and other marginalized groups, are often victims of more pervasive negative effects in comparison to the rest of the population. The recent COVID-19 pandemic and the emergency measures adopted to counteract it (e.g. lockdown, social distancing, health prescriptions) are a good case in point. While it is undoubtedly true that the COVID-19 virus, as it spread, made no distinctions, it is equally true that the housing, work, education and even existential precariousness to which many destitute, vulnerable minorities, refugees, asylum seekers, migrants, Roma and other minority groups are exposed, deteriorated and worsened their situation.

With this background in mind, the question arises which policies are best suited in times of scarcity to achieve social cohesion and prosperity for all, including minorities and marginalized groups. All policies that seek to reconcile social cohesion are confronted with a veritable minefield of dilemmas. If they privilege unity, there is a risk that they will alienate minorities, provoke resistance and endanger the very unity they seek. If they privilege diversity, they may not be able to accommodate the conflicting demands of their communities and pursue common goals, and would risk disintegration.

If it is certain that fundamental human rights and liberties such as the right to life, freedom of religion and belief, freedom of expression and association must be accorded to all human beings, it is less certain what the specific legal obligations of states are towards minorities and marginalized groups and individuals belonging to these groups. This question is, depending on the ideological positions adopted, hotly contested even within the context of human rights protection.

In this field, two major ideological conceptions confront each other: the politics of sameness and the politics of difference. According to the first approach, the same rule should apply to all individuals and groups regardless of whether they profess and practise a majority or minority religion or belief, speak a majority or minority language or express a majority or minority culture, or live in a peripheral and marginal region or not. The second approach advocates special legal measures intended specifically to guarantee non-discrimination against minorities and marginalized groups. The former approach supports the elimination of any distinction grounded on culture, religion, language and other grounds, while the latter accepts that some differences are upheld, provided they are voluntarily accepted by the members of minority groups. In one case, the accent is placed on the politics of sameness; in the other, on the politics of difference.

This ideological discrepancy does not mean, however, that convergence is impossible at the practical level. Many legal systems, without questioning the principle of equal treatment, accept a certain degree of accommodation to answer the challenge posed by deeply ingrained differences and to defuse potential conflicts. Clearly, it has also to be acknowledged that an approach based on difference rather than sameness implies that individuals are required to find a group to which they could belong based on the personal characteristics that separate them from other groups. And this, as seen earlier, can be problematic, as it may reify diversity and reinforce divisions and groupings while also hindering a thorough analysis of intersectionalities and layers of inequalities.[13]

In this regard, the vulnerability approach discussed in the previous paragraphs is particularly relevant. According to this approach, vulnerability is a situational, contextual and socially induced condition that results from existing power structures, cultural mechanisms or systems of resource distribution, but in which also socially or culturally determined groupings, such as race, gender, ethnicity or religious affiliation, have to play a role in exposing groups and individuals to the risk of marginalization and an asymmetric access to resources. In particular, for communities living in rural areas, we introduced the concept of "rural vulnerabilities" that affect individuals and groups living in these areas differently depending on various social- constructed factors and contexts that may expose them to risks and lower access to resources.

Considering the problems that minorities and marginalized groups face in times of scarcity and the difficulties to identify policies that are best suited to accommodate diversities and achieve social cohesion, in the following sections we will look at a very specific development project concerning rural and mountain communities and their empowerment as a good practice through which some relevant lessons can be drawn for other marginalized and minoritized groups, such as linguistic, religious and ethno-cultural communities.

Local development through the empowerment of a rural marginalized community: the Vital Mountains project

Context

Montagne is a hamlet of the Municipality of Tre Ville in the Autonomous Province of Trento, an entirely mountainous area in the north-east of the Italian Alps. Its territory stretches vertically from 300 to 2000 m above sea level and covers an area of 81.57 km^2, with a population of 1,374 and population density of 16.99 inhabitants/km^2. Tre Ville was established in 2016 through the merger of the Municipalities of Montagne, Preore and Ragoli.

Despite its proximity to Lake Garda, Adamello Brenta UNESCO Dolomites, and Madonna di Campiglio, Tre Ville lies outside the main tourist and economic flows. As a consequence, its community is affected by negative phenomena typical of many other rural and mountain areas, including a decreasing and ageing population, and the lack of employment opportunities and services. Montagne, which is the residential core at the highest altitude of Tre Ville, suffered the worse consequences of these negative trends. In fact, since the 1960s the population of Montagne has been inexorably decreasing,

13 A specific domain in which the complexities of vulnerability and intersectionality become apparent is that of artificial intelligence and its algorithms (Medda-Windischer and Crepaz 2025 forthcoming).

compared to the stable situation or slight population growth in the other two hamlets further downstream.

To date, Montagne counts 223 inhabitants (Tre Ville Municipal Register Office 2021). The offer of public services is lacking. There is a grocery store and a cultural club that serves as a café as well. Once a week a municipal counter is open, and the medical clinic is open with the same rare frequency. There is just one bus per day that can be taken to reach the nearest urban center and travel back. For the entire Municipality of Tre Ville, the most important economic sectors in terms of added value production (about 75 per cent of the local value) and number of employees are those related to tourism (accommodation and catering), the tertiary sector (energy, water and waste) and manufacturing, with 132, 68 and 60 local employees on average, respectively (ISPAT and ISTAT 2017).[14]

The city of Trento, about 40 km away, plays an attractive role for the surrounding territories and leads many inhabitants of the valleys to commute to the city every day to work or access services, mainly related to health, education and centralized bureaucracy (Maino et al. 2021). Although the distribution of services in the valleys is above the national average, and although in the Italian Alps the Province of Trento has guaranteed a general stabilization of the population over time thanks to its state of autonomy, the city attracts around 25,000 to 30,000 individuals every day from outside its territory (Gretter et al. 2018).

Thus, for Montagne too, as for many other rural mountain areas in the Alps, a hierarchical relationship of dependence between the mountains and the city must be highlighted. Furthermore, the perceptual dimension of the negative stereotype attributed to rural mountain areas has fuelled dynamics of rejection to diversity, in some cases of resistance to change, or scepticism towards institutions and scientific knowledge, as stated in interviews conducted within the project Vital Mountains:

> This mistrust is only a house of cards, but it is difficult to break down because it is ingrained even in the youngest people, it passes through a widespread family imprint, and it configures a sort of unconscious inferiority complex of the mountain area towards the city, which makes dialogue and collaboration difficult.
>
> To the city, we always play second fiddle.
>
> I feel so many shortcomings here, which make me hesitant to return. I don't give up, and I'd like things to change.

14 Among the distinctive and attractive elements of the territory are "Montagne Racconta", a festival of storytelling and contemporary theatre now in its 11th edition, and the "Regole di Spinale and Manèz", an agrarian community existing since ancient times, owned by the populations of the former municipalities of Ragoli, Montagne and Preore.

At the same time, all these same dynamics have helped preserve an almost uncontaminated area that still retains age-old knowledge and traditions, together with high environmental and cultural value.

This is the background of the Vital Mountains project, which started in 2019 with the aim of fostering the sustainable socio-economic development of rural mountain communities and improving their quality of life to reach a balanced relationship between rural and urban areas. The most salient research questions of the projects are how to maintain viable communities in rural mountain areas, how to enhance their identity and specificity as a driver for sustainable development, and how to empower rural mountain communities.

The project is the result of an initiative of a few inhabitants of Montagne, aware of the global dynamics that impact rural mountain areas and moved by the desire to cope with the slow decline of their hamlet. They found the trust and financial support of both the Tre Ville municipal administration and the provincial administration, which together launched this experimental project. The project has been led by researchers from Eurac Research and aimed at revitalizing this area and, more generally, identifying innovative strategies to support mountain areas at risk of abandonment.

Methodology

From the methodological point of view, researchers adopted the action research approach (Lewin 1951) to lead a real change in the community through research tools. To foster such a change, researchers followed a specific theory of change, the "U Theory" by Scharmer (2016), which is used to address the most pressing global challenges and to co-project the future. Both these theories are marked by a strongly participatory approach. In particular, as far as participatory processes are concerned, researchers referred to the community-led local development approach (CLLD) (EC 2018) and to the community-led rural development theory (Murray and Dunn 1995).

From the outset the entire local community was involved in a broad participatory process which included several phases that are linked together and consist in different activities: these covered plenary meetings, thematic working tables, workshops on the future, meetings with experts, exploratory walks through the territory, presentations of best practices, and visits to sites of interest. A minimum of 4 and a maximum of 60 people participated in the 25 events held so far.

Following the CLLD approach, the participatory process was marked by the following features:

- Active listening to identify and enhance people's attitude and the endogenous potentials of the area under study, followed by a more operational phase to implement the first concrete actions;

- Empowerment of the local community to foster its self-management skills, to promote long-term strategies and need-based solutions, the ownership of projects, plans and programs;
- Diversity as an added value to create synergies among different territories, as well as the importance given to diversity in enriching the process in terms of different roles and ideas of the participants;
- Process per se, which needs to be set up with clear and concrete goals but also with the flexibility required for its remodulation; this means that the process is open-ended with respect to its final outcomes.

Main results

The researchers led the local development process drawing on a strategic plan developed by the community itself in cooperation with administrators and experts. That is the first output of the project Vital Mountains. Three shared future scenarios were identified by the local community, which resulted in three main topics to be considered as priority themes for this area (culture, hospitality, collective goods). Then they defined 13 strategic guidelines that form the shared framework where several project proposals have been developed. Tre Ville is the first small municipality in Trentino that has voluntarily started a strategic planning process at municipal scale, in synergy with the provincial level and the UN Sustainable Development Goals (SDGs). The added value of a strategic plan at the municipal level is to enhance the local engagement, which thus becomes active in the planning phases, in dialogue with the upper scale and through relationships and connections with other similar territories and with the surrounding urban areas. This allows the creation of a setting where it is possible to manage both internal change and global trends. In other words, it requires the communities to be more sustainable and resilient (Maino et al. 2021).

The second output of the project is the start of the implementation of the first concrete project that regards a scattered hospitality system, a network of existing accommodations with shared services and marketing to promote a new kind of community tourism. Participants named this project "generative hospitality", since it aims to impact the whole local community and enhance different types of activities other than tourism. The implementation of the project was suddenly interrupted by the pandemic.

It ought to be noted that, despite significant attention being paid to involving the local community, from the youngest to the oldest members, few people participated in the process, in comparison to what was expected by researchers. The pandemic made the situation even worse but, at the same time, brought both advantages and disadvantages of rural mountain living into focus and made more significant the results achieved in the process so far.

This led the researchers to reshape the whole participatory process and start the implementation of the "generative hospitality" project by working on the underlying motivations that drive people to decide to invest their energies in such a project. Thus, a core team of highly motivated individuals was formed. Thirteen people from different backgrounds, ages and genders made up the core team. While working together they expressed their interests openly, shared their aims and values, and used all their competences to co-create an original and authentic touristic offer enhancing the local resources. Their contributions laid the foundations for the project, which later motivated another 20 people to get involved. Currently the implementation of the project is ongoing, and the first nucleus of the "generative hospitality" will be ready by 2023.

Conclusions

In times of scarcity, addressing vulnerabilities is an important strategy that most countries should adopt in order to retain an adequate level of social cohesion and prosperity. As Einstein once observed, "The value of achievement lies in the achieving." In other words, in dealing with minorities, minoritized and marginalized groups, a more participative and collaborative approach should take precedence over finding solutions that, even if considered reasonable and pragmatic, are sometimes achieved without the involvement of all actors concerned.[15]

The case study, Vital Mountains, analysed in this chapter advanced the understanding of the complex relationship between scarcity, minoritizing processes, vulnerabilities and marginalization. The concept of scarcity has been considered in its multidimensional perspective: as resource limitations, particularly in services, goods and infrastructures; as related to depopulation and migration patterns; in terms of urbanization and modernization processes in contrast to rural and peripheral patterns; and, especially, as shaped by power dynamics, domination and subjugation. To better reflect this aspect, we used the concept "minoritized groups" rather than "minorities" to emphasize the systemic power dynamics that marginalize them.

Within the context of increasing scarcities, this chapter explored commonalities and synergies between two categories of marginalized and minoritized groups, i.e. rural communities on the one hand and linguistic, religious and cultural minorities on the other. The objective was to develop new perspectives and innovative solutions to address the persistent challenges posed by diversity and unity. By examining these diverse marginalized groupings, this chapter investigated the potential lessons that could be drawn from rural and

15 The concept of reasonable accommodation was first developed by the American and Canadian legal doctrine and foreseen also in EU legislation for workers with disabilities (Art. 5 of the EC Council Directive 2000/78/EC establishing a general framework for equal treatment in employment and occupation, OJ 2000 L303/16. <https://eur-lex.europa.eu/legal-content/EN/TXT/?uri=celex%3A32000L0078> accessed 18 March 2021). Among the vast literature, see Bouchard and Taylor 2008; Modood and Sealy 2021; Bowers 2021. Specifically, on the EU Directive on equal treatment in employment and reasonable accommodation, see Jackson-Preece 2010.

mountain communities for accommodating linguistic, religious and cultural minorities. Our analysis underlined the importance of the local community involvement to turn traditional top-down policies upside down. Over the last 20 years, the application of the principles underlying CLLD have spread across Europe and all the European programs. However, it is not sufficient to foster participation. This case study proves how important it is to adopt appropriate policies and tools to proactively overcome the specific disadvantages of mountainous environments and support real change.

The Vital Mountains project showed how difficult it is to involve people in long-term projects for the community, to motivate them to take their destiny into their own hands and imagine a different future. In embarking on such a path identities, values, behaviours, and long-established roles are challenged, bringing fears and resistance to the surface. To cope with these inertias, it is first and foremost necessary to raise awareness in the local community about the importance of these processes and to explain the need of profound changes. To do that is essential, as a first step, to favour the change in perspective and mindset: to re-connect the people to their deepest values, interests, and motivations, to turn weaknesses into opportunities. The active listening phase was essential to identify the real needs, to foster the problem setting and the comprehension from different standpoints—but without action, there is no transformation. Knowing things but not acting does not yield any results. Mountain communities, resilient and hardworking, have always stood out for their concreteness, industriousness and know-how (Salsa 2019). For the community of Tre Ville, proof of this was the ability to develop a strategic plan. This tool was able to turn the community needs into a realistic action plan, funding application and the implementation of the first concrete project.

Furthermore, Vital Mountains project has highlighted the importance of the process rather than the results. Vital Mountains is a long-term project which requires an implementation period much longer than the support phase during which the researchers are active. It's fundamental to activate participants and to provide a working method easy to replicate autonomously. A key dimension of the process was the learning phase, to grow the local community and foster its self-management skills. It has been a learning journey in which everyone contributed with their specific skills and experimented with practical tools. By comparing best practices from nearby and faraway areas, participants were inspired and motivated to take on the challenges posed by the Vital Mountains project. Finally, diversity should be acknowledged as an important value both inside the community, in order to enrich the project, and outside of the community, in order to foster well-balanced relationships between urban and rural areas and enhance their own peculiarities.

In conclusion, actors involved in minority-related issues—in particular local communities, decision makers and academics—should be encouraged to play an active role as promoters of mediation and dialogue through concerted solutions aimed at achieving a fair balance of the interests at stake. This approach, in line with SDGs 16, 11 and 5 on peaceful and inclusive societies, with a particular focus on women and girls, would clearly be beneficial for societies as a whole, as it would provide opportunities for positive dialogue, mutual respect and understanding and for furthering prosperity and economic well-being for society as a whole. This approach should be coupled with the political and social willingness, expressed by decision makers, political elites and society at large, to consider diversity and different groups as integral part of society—the collectivity and those who belong to it—so that minorities, minoritized and other marginalized groups are perceived as allies rather than enemies. Clearly this approach is not without difficulties. Some groups might not be open and experimental, and others might jealously guard their inherited identities. At the heart of any successful model lies, in the end, a sincere willingness on all sides for continuous interaction, mutual adjustments and accommodation.

References

Anderson, B 1983, *Imagined Communities: Reflections on the Origin and Spread of Nationalism*, Verso, London/New York.

Andreoli, M & Tellarini, V 1998, 'Marginality and Development in Italy: A Study Review' in H Jussila, W Leimgruber & R Majoral (eds.), *Perceptions of Marginality: Theoretical Issues and Regional Perceptions of Marginality in Geographical Space* (1st ed.), Routledge, doi: 10.4324/9780429447457

Arnardóttir, OM 2017, 'Vulnerability Under Article 14 of the European Convention on Human Rights', *Oslo Law Review*, vol. 4, no. 3, pp. 150–171.

Barca, F 2009, 'An Agenda for a Reformed Cohesion Policy: A Place-Based Approach to Meeting European Union Challenges and Expectations', *European Commission*, https://www.europarl.europa.eu/meetdocs/2009_2014/documents/regi/dv/barca_report_/barca_report_en.pdf [accessed 06/07/2023].

Baumgärtel, M 2020, 'Facing the Challenge of Migratory Vulnerability in the European Court of Human Rights', *Netherlands Quarterly of Human Rights*, pp. 1–18.

Bouchard, G & Taylor, C (eds.) 2008, *Building the Future: A Time for Reconciliation, Consultation Commission on Accommodation Practices Related to Cultural Differences*, Gouvernement du Québec.

Bowers, J 2021, 'Accommodating Difference: How Is Religious Freedom Protected When It Clashes with Other Rights? Is Reasonable Accommodation the Key to Levelling the Field?' *Oxford Journal of Law and Religion*, pp. 1–23, doi: 10.1093/ojlr/rwab008.

Brubaker, R 2004, *Ethnicity Without Groups*, Harvard University Press, Cambridge.

Cantiani, MG, Geitner, C, Haida, C, Maino, F, Tattoni, C, Vettorato, D & Ciolli, M 2016, 'Balancing Economic Development and Environmental Conservation for a New Governance of Alpine Areas', *Sustainability*, vol. 8, no. 8, pp. 802–820, doi: 10.3390/su8080802

Capotorti, F 1977, *Study on the Rights of Persons Belonging to Ethnic, Religious and Linguistic Minorities*, UN Doc. E/CN.4/Sub.2/384/Rev.1.

Corrado, F & Durbiano, E 2018, 'The "Metropolitan City" in Italy: New Spaces for Dialogue and Interaction Between the City and the Mountain', *Journal of Alpine Research*, Revue de géographie alpine, vol. 106, no. 2, doi:10.4000/rga.4275

Cullen, BT & Pretes, M 2000, 'The Meaning of Marginality: Interpretations and Perceptions in Social Science', *The Social Science Journal*, vol. 37, no. 2, pp. 215–229.

De Rossi, A (ed.) 2018, *Riabitare l'Italia: Le aree interne tra abbandoni e riconquiste*, Donzelli Editore. ISBN: 978-8868438494

European Commission (EC) 2018, 'Guidance for Local Actors on Community-Led Local Development', https://ead.gr/wp-content/uploads/2018/10/EGESIF_18-0034-00_CLLD_for_local_actors_post_Omnibus.pdf [accessed 07/12/2022].

Fineman, MA 2016, 'Equality, Autonomy, and the Vulnerable Subject in Law and Politics', in MA Fineman & A Grear (eds.), *Vulnerability: Reflections on a New Ethical Foundation for Law and Politics*, Routledge, London/New York, pp. 13–27.

Gretter, A, Ciolli, M & Scolozzi, R 2018, 'Governing Mountain Landscapes Collectively: Local Responses to Emerging Challenges Within a Systems Thinking Perspective', *Landscape Research*, vol. 43, no. 8, pp. 1117–1130, doi: 10.1080/01426397.2018.1503239

Ianni, E, Geneletti, D & Ciolli, M 2015, 'Revitalizing Traditional Ecological Knowledge: A Study in an Alpine Rural Community', *Environmental Management*, vol. 56, pp. 144–156, doi: 10.1007/s00267-015-0479-z

Ippolito, F 2020, *Understanding Vulnerability in International Human Rights Law*, Editoriale Scientifica, Napoli.

Ippolito, F & Igleasias Sanchez, S (eds) 2015, *Protecting Vulnerably Groups: The European Human Rights Framework*, Bloomsbury Publishing, London.

ISPAT and ISTAT 2017, *Annual Italian Statistical Report 2017*, Istituto Nazionale di Statistica, Roma.

Jackson-Preece, J 2010, 'Positive Measures and the EU Equality Directives: Closing the Protection Gap Between "New" and "Old" Minorities Through the Reasonable Accommodation of Religion?' *European Yearbook on Minority Issues*, vol. 9.

Lewin, K 1951, *Field Theory and Social Science*, Harper & Brothers, New York.

Macioce, F 2022, The Politics of Vulnerable Groups. Implications for Philosophy, Law, and Political Theory, Palgrave Macmillan, London.

Maino, F, Cutello, G & Ravazzoli, E 2021, 'Le relazioni città-montagna all'interno del Progetto "Montagne Vitali" in Trentino', in F Corrado (ed.) *Urbano montano: Verso nuove configurazioni e progetti di territorio*, Franco Angeli.

Maino, F, Omizzolo, A & Streifeneder, T 2018, 'Marginal Mountainous Areas: Starting Over from Smart Communities The Case Study of Seren del Grappa' in A Bisello, D Vettorato, P Laconte & S Costa (eds.) *Smart and Sustainable Planning for Cities and Regions*. SSPCR 2017, Green Energy and Technology, pp. 649–660. Cham: Springer, doi: 10.1007/978-3-319-75774-2_44

Mantino, F 2010, *Innovazione nella crisi economica: Strategie e fabbisogni di politiche nelle aree montane italiane*. CNEL, Roma.

Marko, J 2019, 'The Interrelationship between Law, Sociology and Political Science' in J Marko & S Constantin (eds.), *Human and Minority Rights Protection by Multiple Diversity Governance: History, Law, Ideology and Politics in European Perspective*, Routledge, Abingdon/New York.

Marko, J & Constantin, S (eds.) 2019, *Human and Minority Rights Protection by Multiple Diversity Governance: History, Law, Ideology and Politics in European Perspective*, Routledge, Abingdon/New York.

Medda-Windischer, R & Crepaz, K 2022, 'Fundamental Rights and Non-EU Minorities: From an Ambiguous Concept to an Integrated Society?' in TH Malloy & B Vizi (eds.), *Research Handbook on Minority Politics in the European Union*, Edward Elgar Publishing, Cheltenham.

Medda-Windischer, R & Crepaz, K 2025 (forthcoming), 'Intersectionality, Artificial Intelligence and Algorithmic Fairness: An Oxymoron or a Reality?' in A Budabin, J Metcalfe & S Pandey (eds.), *Minority Women, Rights, and Intersectionality: Agency, Power, and Participation*, Routledge, Abington/New York.

Modood, T & Sealy, T 2021, 'Freedom of Religion and the Accommodation of Religious Diversity: Multiculturalising Secularism', *Religions*, vol. 12, no. 10, p. 868, doi: 10.3390/rel12100868.

Mowbray, A 2004, *The Development of Positive Obligations Under the European Convention on Human Rights by the European Court of Human Rights*, Hart Publishing, Oxford.

Murray, M & Dunn, L 1995, 'Capacity Building for Rural Development in the United States', *Journal of Rural Studies*, vol. 11, no. 1, pp. 89–97.

Omizzolo, A & Streifeneder, T 2013, 'Institutional Involvement in Studies on Italian Mountains'', in *Mountain Dossier: New Perspectives of Alpine Research*, pp. 14–17, ISSN 2039-5442, Dislivelli (Torino), n. 1/February 2013.

Özlem, S & DiAngelo, R 2012, *Is Everyone Really Equal? An Introduction to Key Concepts in Social Justice Education*, Teacher's College Press, New York.

Paoloni, L & Vezzani, S 2019, 'La dichiarazione ONU sui diritti dei contadini e delle altre persone che lavorano nelle aree rurali: Prime riflessioni', *federalismi.it/Rivista di diritto pubblico italiano, comparato, Europeo, Focus Human Rights*, pp. 1–33, ISSN 1826-3534.

Porcellini, S 2013, *Aree Marginali Italia—Laboratorio di opportunità*, Edizioni del Faro, Trento.

Reynaud, C, Miccoli, S, Benassi, F, Naccarato, A & Salvati, L 2020, Unravelling a Demographic 'Mosaic': Spatial Patterns and Contextual Factors of Depopulation in Italian Municipalities, 1981–2011, *Ecological Indicators*, vol. 115.

Salsa, A 2019, *I paesaggi delle Alpi. Un viaggio nelle terre alte tra filosofia, natura e storia, Saggine n. 325*, Donzelli Editore, Roma.

Scharmer, CO 2016, *Theory U: Leading from the Future as It Emerges*, 2nd ed., Berrett-Koehler, Oakland.

Timmer, A 2016, 'A Quiet Revolution: Vulnerability in the European Court of Human Rights', in M. A. Fineman & A. Grear (eds.), *Vulnerability: Reflections on a New Ethical Foundation for Law and Politics*, Routledge, London/New York, pp. 147–170.

Timmer, A, Baumgärtel, M, Kotzé, L & Slingenberg, L 2021, 'The Potential and Pitfalls of the Vulnerability Concept for Human Rights', *Netherlands Quarterly of Human Rights*, vol. 39, no. 3, pp. 190–197.

Tre Ville Municipal Register Office 2021, *Population of the Municipality and by Hamlet*, Tre Ville, Italy.

UN General Assembly 2018, *UN Declaration on the Right of Peasants and Other People Working in Rural Areas*, Resolution of the UN General Assembly, 17 December.

Wingrove-Haugland, E & McLeod, J 2022, 'Not "Minority" but "Minoritized"', *Teaching Ethics*, 8 January, doi: 10.5840/tej20221799, https://www.pdcnet.org/tej/content/tej_2022_0999_1_7_99?file_type=pdf [accessed 12/10/2023].

Young, IM 1990, 'Five Faces of Oppressions', in *Justice and the Politics of Difference*, Princeton University Press, Princeton, NJ.

7 Emotional scarcity and well-being among international students at times of crisis in South Africa during the COVID-19 pandemic

Faith Mkwananzi, Patience Mukwambo, Matome Winter Seshoka, and Nomzingisi Notenga

Introduction

Over the years, south-north and south-south mobility has been rapidly increasing, making global student mobility in pursuit of higher education (HE) a subject of interest to scholars and researchers worldwide. According to the Global Migration Data Portal (n.d.), the number of international students increased from 2 million in 2000 to over 6.3 million in 2020. Student mobility is an important subset of the internationalisation of HE that has shaped developments in that field, as well as studies in comparative and international education. We draw on Snow's (2021) definition of student mobility as the process of enrolling at an academic institution across a national border for a part of or all of one's education.

International students are those who received their prior education in another country and are not residents of their current country of study (OECD, 2023). They typically hold non-resident or student visas. This is in line with UNESCO's (2024, n.d.) view that students who are internationally mobile are "those who have physically crossed an international border between two countries for the purpose of attending educational activities in a destination country, which is different from the country from which they are originally from". While the students in this study had initially moved to South Africa to attend university, because of the COVID-19 lockdown, some returned home while others remained in South Africa. Therefore, while they were not all physically in South Africa, they were registered and studying in South African universities. Thus, students in this chapter fit into two categories: Internationalisation Abroad (IA) which includes students who moved across national borders; and Internationalisation at a Distance (IaD), where knowledge and ideas are internationally mobile with the support of technologies, rather than the students themselves (Steyn and Gunter, 2021).

While there has been comparatively more literature examining international student mobility from the Global South to the Global North, relatively less has been written on migration flows within the Global South (Bartlett, 2011; França and Cairns, 2020). This gives the impression that international migration flows from the east and south to the west, rather than also south-south,

DOI: 10.4324/9781032661780-8

thus negating the importance of this migration stream (Brooks and Waters, 2022). Because of this neglect, south-south migration is therefore an important field of study. This is especially because of its effect on progress toward achieving broader education goals such as Education for All (Bartlett, 2011) and the UN Sustainable Development Goals, and how these shape the futures of migrants and those left behind.

International students are a desirable global constituency that raise a university's profile and provide funding in addition to bringing skills and knowledge to university life; they also diversify and complexify the HE landscapes (Hudzik, 2011; Pandit, 2013). In Africa, South Africa is one of the leading destinations for international students (Ratshilaya, 2021). Among countries in the Organisation for Economic Co-operation and Development and partner countries, students from African countries constitute the majority (84 per cent) of international students (OECD, 2023, p. 249). According to the DHET (2020), there were 67,435 foreign students (all non-South African citizens) enrolled in public universities in 2017, most of them from Southern African Development Community (SADC) countries. Tagliabue (2022, p. 6) observes that SADC students are treated as home students in terms of fees and accommodation as specified by the SADC Protocol on Education and Training, and live "in a relatively economically and culturally integrated region dominated by South African influence". It thus makes an examination of these students' experience crucial to understanding not just educational arrangements but also broader socio-political relations. According to Pandit (2013), international students are key to the university's undertaking to ready students to live and work in a diverse and intercultural environment. However, literature on internationalisation reveals it to be a convoluted space (Pandit, 2013; Chen and Lo, 2013; Knight, 2014). For instance, Knight (2014, p. 76) traces the development of internationalisation and admits that it has "become a catch-all phrase used to describe anything and everything remotely linked to the global, intercultural or international dimensions of higher education". This leaves it open to diverse interpretations and abuse for economic gain.

To contribute to these ongoing debates in the fields of student mobility and internationalisation of education, the chapter examines the experiences of international HE students at two South African universities during the COVID-19 pandemic. These two study sites offer a window into the general practices of HE institutions, especially in response to the pandemic. Although international students are diverse and include those from privileged backgrounds, they are positioned as a minority group, or a group in a temporally bounded minoritised state in this chapter for two reasons. First, there has been a growing anti-foreigner sentiment in South Africa culminating in microaggressions and xenophobic tendencies towards migrants, including international students (Sehoole, 2015). Second, ordinarily, international students are more prone to mental challenges such as depression and loneliness (Sehoole, 2015) and are less inclined to seek psychological service than their domestic peers (Alharbi and Smith, 2018). The COVID-19 pandemic and consequent reactions by universities placed them in "a more isolated position abroad with less access to public resources due to monetary, informational, language, or cultural barriers" (Chen et al., 2020). Their specific needs, such as accommodation, access to safe return to their home countries, and exposure to the pandemic, were overlooked by their host countries (Chen et al., 2020; Sahu, 2020). These two reasons make a case for the minoritisation of international students.

To shed some light on the interface between the socio-economic and emotional experiences of international students, we draw on the concept of scarcity. Through Mehta (2010), we understand scarcity not as a natural and given condition arising from limited resources but a political construct that perpetuates exclusions. Mehta (2010, p. 2) contends that while scarcity exists, "The 'scare' of scarcity' has resulted in its emergence and endurance as a strategy for powerful groups who then provide simple and usually ill-fitting solutions that cause and perpetrate exclusions" of those without power. Mehta (2010) contends that scarcity transcends material constraints and extends into the realm of emotions and intangible resources, profoundly influencing individual well-being. This lens encourages scholars and policymakers to explore the underlying power dynamics that influence resource distribution and to question the narratives that frame scarcity within societal contexts.

Different authors have examined the concept of scarcity in diverse ways. For example, Fraser (2009) addresses the concept of scarcity and its implications for well-being through the lens of social justice and economic inequalities. Fraser's work highlights the interconnectedness of justice, recognition, and redistribution in addressing scarcity and its impact on individuals and communities. In her earlier work, she underscores the importance of addressing not only the material dimensions of scarcity but also the symbolic and cultural aspects that impact how individuals experience well-being within a given social and economic context (Fraser, 1998). In exploring the dynamics of justice, Fraser contends that scarcity is not merely an inherent feature of resource distribution but a socially constructed phenomenon shaped by power imbalances. Economic scarcity, according to Fraser, results from systemic injustices embedded in social structures, where certain groups are disproportionately disadvantaged, leading to an uneven distribution of resources and opportunities. Similarly, Young (1990) contends that societal structures often perpetuate inequalities, impacting marginalised groups' ability to access resources and opportunities.

Like Fraser and Young, Amartya Sen's (1992) Capabilities Approach (CA) broadens the scope of scarcity to encompass the deprivation of essential human capabilities, including emotional and psychological elements crucial for a flourishing life. Emotional flourishing is integral to overall well-being and emphasises the need for emotional support in discussions of human development. This lens is important when considering the experiences of students during the COVID-19 pandemic and how it exacerbated existing social and economic disparities, affecting international students disproportionately.

While the COVID-19 pandemic created and or exacerbated genuine conditions of material scarcity, universities' responses also created a specific kind of scarcity that affected students' well-being. As this chapter will highlight, the two case study universities implemented a one-size-fits-all response to the pandemic that was directed at supporting local students, with little or no contextual understanding of international students' circumstances. Thus, to better understand students' experiences, it becomes important to go beyond a resource-oriented understanding of scarcity to include other non-economic but equally important categories, such as emotional scarcity, which affect students' well-being.

The chapter adds to the work that problematises and operationalises scarcity beyond the common material resources–based approaches dominating the field of scarcity by looking at students' emotional well-being. In the next section, we provide a brief landscape on HE and internationalisation, which is our launchpad to the discussion on internationalisation, the CA, and scarcity. We then turn to the data collection process, which is followed by a report on the findings. Before we conclude the chapter, we provide a capability-informed discussion on how the challenges experienced by international students led to different forms of scarcity, especially emotional scarcity, and what this means for international HE.

Higher education and internationalisation

Higher education is regarded as pivotal in enhancing national competitiveness and as a profitable service that can be bought in the global marketplace. This understanding has increased the commodification and marketisation of HE, as well as the competition between universities, where students are located as consumers (Naidoo, 2003; Chen and Lo, 2013). According to Banya (2008), the language of globalisation emphasising outputs and outcomes has led to knowledge becoming a commodity that moves between countries. This has led to institutions of HE strategically aligning their policies to link knowledge to global competitiveness (Naidoo, 2011), which has led to "internationalisation" becoming one of the buzzwords in the twenty-first-century academy. In the same vein, Chen and Lo (2013) have argued that internationalisation has therefore become part of the commodification and marketisation of HE, which should ideally teach knowledge and foster values such as tolerance, democracy, intercultural and self-understanding, as well as how to live in the world. However, contrary to this expansive understanding of internationalisation which advocates for an all-inclusive approach incorporating teaching, research, and service, it sometimes ends up as discrete activities, including studying abroad and international student recruitment (Hudzik, 2011). This illustrates a "gap between idealism and reality" (Chen and Lo, 2013, p. 34), where the focus is on marketing campaigns aimed at attracting the best students and academics to supply the "brain power" for innovative research agendas (Knight, 2014).

While the chapter's focus is on emotional scarcity, it is in this landscape that we deduce whether international student experiences are commensurate with what universities claim to provide. For us, it raises concerns about balancing costs, quality, and access and therefore leads one to question whether international students get the immersive international experience they "crossed the border" for. It is within this already contested terrain that the COVID-19 pandemic broke out. Most literature on the effects of the pandemic reveals that in general, access and HE participation were negatively affected (Luescher et al., 2021). This chapter, therefore, examines the existence of different forms of scarcity and how they shaped international HE students' experiences of learning during the pandemic. Student narratives inform the understanding of scarcity and what universities can do to provide a more comprehensive internationalisation HE experience that fosters human development and well-being, particularly emotional well-being.

In Kahneman and Deaton's (2010, p. 6489) definition, emotional well-being refers to the emotional quality of one's everyday experiences, including feelings of joy, fascination, anxiety, sadness, anger, and affections that make one's life pleasant or unpleasant. Ronnie et al. (2022) are of the view that emotional well-being is a useful lens for examining experiences, especially of academics, during the COVID-19 pandemic because it highlights how day-to-day events affect individuals. As noted earlier, the current dominant conceptualisation of HE emphasises neoliberal and market-based approaches which disregard the role, process, and content of education. This emphasis overlooks the value of understanding "what it means lead a valuable life" (Buckler, 2015, pp. 43–44) for international students by sidelining key elements that enable or constrain their capability to be educated. The impact on "how" (procedural experiences) they become educated then has an implication on their conceptualisation of what it means to be educated (functioning), such as the advancement of their emotional well-being. Barry et al. (2017) argue that emotional well-being can be promoted in educational environments, yet during COVID-19, this capability was constrained. Such emotional scarcity may lead to mental health challenges among students, and this, according to UNICEF (2022), influences academic, social, and economic outcomes across one's lifespan. This construct is particularly relevant in understanding the experiences of international students. Their lives were full of uncertainty while in a foreign land, and they could not plan their lives beyond the pandemic. Studies that reported on student experiences during COVID-19 highlighted the multilevel distress that students experienced. For example, an evaluation of 152 online learning students in Brazil found that most students experienced emotional impact, followed by learning impact, financial impact, social impact, and technological impact. In the next section, we draw on the capability approach to unpack our conceptualisation of scarcity.

Capabilities in the context of internationalisation and scarcity

Founded on Xenos's (1989) and Mehta's (2010) problematisation of the notion of scarcity, this chapter's conceptual framing is informed by Amartya

Sen's CA to extend the understanding of scarcity to the field of HE and internationalisation. Mehta (2010) raises the need to be aware of the "politics of allocation and the ways in which scarcity is politicized, especially to suit the interests of powerful players" (p. 2). For Mehta, scarcity results from exclusionary practices and unequal gender, social, and power relations that validate and perpetuate uneven access to, and use of resources. In the field of international HE, one would then ask: "To what extent do international students have access to quality education that supports their academic and non-academic well-being beyond a tokenistic international experience?" and "To what extent did the COVID-19 pandemic influence conceptualisations of scarcity in HE spaces, and did these affect international students?" Answering these questions requires an examination of internationalisation, educational arrangements, and student well-being in general, and specifically within the context of the COVID-19 pandemic as a step towards reducing inequalities for international students and achieving more social justice.

The CA, as a normative framework, enables an evaluation of individual well-being and social arrangements, policy design, and suggestions about social change (Robeyns, 2005). The approach stresses the existence or absence of freedoms that enable individuals to make choices that they have reason to value. Examining international students' capabilities (opportunities) and functionings (what they are subsequently able to do) is important because, despite HE being a resource that can lead to the expansion of other opportunities (employment, socio-political participation, critical thinking), it might be restricted by the wider socio-political environment or HE policy arrangements, which the CA considers (Robeyns, 2005). The frameworks' tenets guiding our chapter are capabilities, functionings, and well-being and are explained next.

Capabilities

Capabilities constitute the freedoms that enable what people can effectively do and be. As freedoms, they imply the existence of "valuable alternatives, in the sense of opportunities that do not exist only formally or legally but are also effectively available to the agent" (Crocker and Robeyns, 2012, p. 70). For international students, examining their capabilities would importantly illustrate the range of possible options from which they can choose, for example, having the choice to go home or remain in the host country during lockdown. In the chapter, the various capability deprivations we present, before we focus on emotional scarcity, highlight the lack of freedoms experienced by the students who participated in our project and how these shape their experiences.

Functionings

Functionings are "the various things a person may value doing or being" (Sen, 1999, p. 75) and range from simple achievements, including being well nourished and having shelter, to more complicated ones, such as being well educated, being respected and participating in discussions (Walker, 2006).

The difference between functionings and capabilities is between achievements and freedoms, or valuable options one can choose from. In the context of this chapter, an examination of international students' functionings will be associated with what they are able to do and be based on the opportunities available to them (Mkwananzi, 2019). For example, emotional support of students would lead to them being confident.

Well-being

Well-being is the aim of development and constitutes more than an individual's economic position or contribution. The CA advocates for an expansive notion of well-being as being multidimensional and incorporating "material, mental, and social well-being, or to the economic, social, political, and cultural dimensions of life" (Crocker and Robeyns, 2012, p. 65). For example, if we are to evaluate education policies according to their effect on students' capabilities and their actual functionings, in this context, it means looking at how international students experience HE with an emphasis on the differences between policy and practice. In addition to the opportunity to study in another country, this means asking if students "have access to a high-quality educational system, to real political participation, and to community activities that support them, and enable them to cope with struggles in daily life and that foster real friendships" (Crocker and Robeyns, 2012, p. 64).

Methods

Methodologically, data from this chapter was drawn from a research project that proposed a fresh and contextual understanding of HE, both empirically and theoretically. The project provided features of emotional scarcity amongst international students across multiple universities located in three different provinces, between rural and urban universities, consisting of University A, University B, and University C. However, this chapter was informed by data from only two of the universities. We sensitively considered the challenges posed by the shift to online education and documented how African international students in these institutions experienced emotional scarcity while learning in and outside the universities. All participants were above the consent age (18 years) as they were registered university students. In this case, informed consent was sought from the participants after giving them detailed information on the study. Although the participating students came from different linguistic backgrounds, there was no language barrier. All three participating institutions (University A, University B, and University C) use English as a medium of instruction.

Qualitative research methods were adopted and relevant for the project because the aim was to learn more about a certain subject from the viewpoints of participants (Rosenthal, 2016). Specifically, in-depth individual interviews were conducted with 15 international students studying different degrees from the three sampled universities. In-depth interviews were adopted because researchers sought to elicit specific information that clarified international students' experiences and feelings related to emotional scarcity. The data collection process took two months across the three institutions. In this chapter, findings from two institutions, University A and University C, are reported (see students' profiles in Table 7.1).

The interviews were transcribed verbatim, and thematic analysis was adopted to make sense of the collected data. Open coding was done line by line to explore the emotional scarcity factors that affected the learning experiences of African international students at the two South African universities between 2020 and 2022. Following that, conceptual categories were created out of the ideas the raw data presented. As researchers, we independently conducted constant comparisons for the purpose of establishing themes and looking for data that did not fit into each theme. No fresh data was derived at the end of this procedure, and the repetition of data across all categories was considered. To observe the axiological requirements in empirical research, all the collection and storage of original research material was subjected to a rigorous ethical approval process at each of the three institutions. In addition, all participating international students were assigned pseudonyms when reporting findings. The main objective guiding this study was to examine if and how any factors affected the learning experiences of African international students

Table 7.1 Student Profiles

*Name**	*Programme of Study*	*Country of Origin*	*Name of University*
Homes	BA Integrated Communication Science	Lesotho	University A
Jemmy	Honors Governance and Political Transformation	Namibia	University A
Kate	BA Integrated Communication Science	Lesotho	University A
Shami	BA Law	Zimbabwe	University A
Kourt	BA Governance and Political Transformation	Zimbabwe	University A
Honan	B.Sc. Honors Forensic Genetics	Ghana	University A
Konstan	BA Social Work	Zimbabwe	University A
Esther	MSc Agriculture (Animal Production)	Kenya	University C
Ibu	Bachelor of Laws	Nigeria	University C
Ralph	B Com Economics	Zimbabwe	University C
Ntshayi	Bachelor of Laws	Eswatini	University C

* The students' names are pseudonyms.

in the three South African universities between 2020 and 2022, and if these led to emotional scarcity.

Findings

This section presents findings that contribute to emotional scarcity as extracted from the interviews with international students. From the interviews, students shared how the change in the learning format and moving countries affected their emotional well-being. Students explained that they were isolated, away from their homes and families, which compounded the challenge of learning. Furthermore, lack of institutional support, language barriers, and cultural differences made it challenging for some students to socialise and seek help from others, contributing to their sense of isolation. The transition to online learning transition required them to adapt and learn in a way they were not accustomed to. These findings are not further from O'Shea's (2020) assertion that the decision for institutions to move to online learning during COVID-19 impacted the diverse students that universities serve. Many found themselves in a position of academic, logistical, financial, and personal disadvantage. The students' varied experiences of working from their home countries and within South Africa are shared below.

Lack of institutional support

Some students felt unsupported by their specific institution, which exacerbated their anxiety and affected their overall emotional stability. Students mention a lack of adequate support and resources by the institution. This absence of institutional support left international students feeling isolated and abandoned during challenging times. The extracts also highlight issues with the registration process, which international students found stressful and inequitable. One student from Lesotho mentions how ill-treated she felt and how anxious she became during the registration period, because despite getting the same time to register as local students, she was required to complete more paperwork. This sense of inequality and the additional demands placed on international students portray bureaucratic requirements and documentation hurdles during registration, which can be a source of stress. While the registration process has always been challenging, the COVID-19 pandemic and everything moving online, including registration, meant that there was no one to ask if one faced challenges.

> During that time, I felt isolated, like I was just alone, yes, we were all going through the same thing. As an international student, registration is crazy. It's not fair. The fact that international students and non-international students are given the same time to complete registration. Meanwhile, international students, there's more we're required to present more documents, and some of these documents take longer to

> get them. This stresses me every time, for the past three years I am always anxious during this period, there are so many things to produce.
>
> (Homes, University A)

> I mostly remember towards 2021, as an international student, you had to have your papers ready and valid. So, by the time you get your things together, already universities have opened, unlike a citizen who just registered online, and then it's done. For us, you must go through these million processes, and even if you submit your documents, they take ages to reply. No one cared.
>
> (Esther, University C)

Another student highlighted how the university's practice of giving students laptops was exclusionary. It was more supportive of learning for local students. Subsequently, he had to use his phone to attend classes online.

> Although the university had come up with a programme that allowed students to collect laptops, only students with bursaries were allowed. Those laptops would be paid for by the bursaries they were having. But for international students, like me, I could not since I did not have a bursary. It was not advisable for me to collect a laptop from the university because, at the end of the day, it would, uh, add up to my fees, which I would not be able to pay. So, imagine if the number keeps going up, you know. Instead, I use my phone mostly.
>
> (Ibu, University C)

Financial distress

While it is assumed that international students are all from financially stable backgrounds, some of the international students indicated that they faced financial challenges. A lack of finance meant that students were not able to buy data. While the case study universities provided data for students to use, it was only available for use in South Africa, so those out of the country had no access to it. In some of their home countries, data was overpriced, and even though students could be with their families during COVID-19, they could not study remotely online.

> It was, it was going to be effective as international students if we were catered, because basically, we were forced to go back home as in our countries where we come from. And data was only provided for African students or for people who were in South Africa. When you are at your home country, you did not have data. No one had to provide data for you. So, you had to make sacrifices so that you can be able to attend classes like other students.
>
> (Ralph, University C)

> In eSwatini, it was a whole different stuff because we were given data by the university. Right. So, when I'm home, I have data on the sim card, but it did not work. I had to buy my own data that side because I can't use the same network that side.
>
> (Ntshayi, University C)

> So, and assessments, let's say maybe if I had network issues, because in other countries, especially in my country, it is very difficult with the network and the data is so expensive. So, like whatever that happened through, uh, writing an exam or it says your data depleted or if your Blackboard froze, it's up to you. Like, I literally had to repeat one of my modules because I couldn't finish a test, due to network issues and so forth. So, and they would be like, there's nothing that they can do. So, it was just a one-way street thing. You had no choice but to adhere to whatever they said. I was always under stress and pressure because, um, I always had to stress about where I would get the money to buy data for tomorrow's class. Uh, sometimes, if I don't have data, what if the lecturer doesn't record the lesson? How will I study? How will I get clarity? So, I always had stress.
>
> (Ralph, University C)

In addition, Honan from Ghana mentions that he relied on his mother's income and the pandemic had disrupted his family's financial stability, leading to increased anxiety and uncertainty.

> I could say the biggest strain for me during that time was the financial aspect although mentally I was okay, because I made friends in SA, they are my ride or die. My mom is a hairdresser, therefore when the lockdown happened, she had to close. This impacted the financial stream, there was a lot of stress around that. I had to rely on my own drive to get beyond.
>
> (Honan, University A)

Social exclusion

Some students felt that the universities did not care about their well-being as they were forced to leave their university residences without being given further support to continue with their studies remotely. In other countries, such as Eswatini, the social exclusion of students was exacerbated by political instability. Consequently, this made students feel isolated and unsupported as they had to devise means of continuing with their studies whilst in their home countries.

> There was no support given to me by the institution; we were on our own. We had to like to push ourselves on our own and because of that,

> I somehow got anxiety. My health was at a detrimental point; it was starting to go down.
>
> (Kate, University A)

> I was away from my family when COVID hit, I was alone. And at some point, I had to be isolated even from other housemates that I was staying with because everybody was just in fear mode. Everyone was scared. This whole COVID thing—we don't know who it can take, you're just hearing death cases. So, I was always alone. So, this thing didn't help me mentally to cope. And to be able to just navigate and push the role to pass my modules.
>
> (Shami, University A)

> There was a time wherein the government would just shut down the network for whatever reason, political or whatever. So that would also affect things because you'd find that they might close the NetApp for the whole day because they're trying to control the situation. People were striking. So, then the government would close the internet so that people don't really communicate. I don't know why. It was just political and all that.
>
> (Ntshayi, University C)

Language barriers

Students from Nigeria and Zimbabwe mentioned the difficulty in interacting with others because they spoke a different language. One mentions the challenge of being the only international student in their classrooms, making it hard to find someone who shared similar experiences. Students also mentioned being unable to socialise or ask for help due to language differences, resulting in feelings of isolation and frustration. Additionally, their reluctance to ask for assistance from people they did not know personally and their reluctance or inability to seek help or connect with others due to emotional barriers worsened their circumstances. This accentuates Sehoole's (2015) claim that while students from the region come to study in South Africa, there is a "dark side" to their experiences where they face discrimination, xenophobia, fear, and loneliness.

> Mentally it was hard because I am used to physical interactions with people. So, I am a very outspoken person. I am a very outgoing person. So now I had to shrink myself in and not interact as much. So that forced me to restrict myself a lot more. My international status for sure did make it challenging, because as an international student sometimes you do get lonely in terms of having to speak another language and not your home language. whereas you are in a space where now you cannot even try and find someone else that comes from the same country as you.

> Within my residence space or even in my class when we were asked if there were international students, I was the only international student in our classroom. So, it does make some interactions a bit difficult because we do not relate in the same manner.
>
> (Kourt, University A)

> I did suffer internal issues as an international student because, not even being able to socialize, maybe with the people that I am staying with, because of the language barrier they are speaking to us. I speak English and I didn't understand any other local languages. So then to converse, to socialize with others, to ask help from others, it's just difficult because also as a person that comes from my culture, asking things from people, especially people you don't know personally, is very difficult. So, I think I had it hard.
>
> (Konstan, University A)

Isolation, anxiety, and abandonment

Students also underscored the lack of emotional connections and resources that would typically be accessible on campus. Students reported that they did not have access to a strong support system, leading to emotional challenges and a sense of loneliness.

> I think I am feeling strained. Online learning does put a strain in the sense that you are more confined to your house or wherever you're studying from. So, I think with the online, it does sort of make you feel a bit excluded. And I think that that did have sort of an impact on mental health as well.
>
> (Jemmy, University A)

> Leaving home was one of the challenges that affected me, because even though we were learning online, I was here in Bloem, and I was not at home. So, I didn't know anyone and had no one to ask, when everything was happening, I was just alone at the time. And at home they're doing their part, like sending you to school and stuff, and they don't even understand these things so you end up with no one who will understand.
>
> (Konstan, University A)

Lack of motivation and family support

Residing in a new country away from the family home added to students' emotional challenges. The separation from the family support system and the uncertainty of being in an unfamiliar place was detrimental to students' emotional well-being. This situation made students feel alone and unable to connect with their family, who could not fully understand the challenges they were facing as international students learning online. When asked about their experiences, one aspect they highlighted was being physically distant from family and facing uncertainty and fear in a foreign country. This significantly contributes to emotional scarcity. The isolation, combined with the anxiety generated by the pandemic's impact, influenced mental well-being. These emotional challenges hindered students' ability to cope effectively with their academic responsibilities and personal life.

> When I got here, it was quite difficult because I was struggling with accommodation, and I was struggling with my finances. I was struggling with almost everything financially, and mentally, I was not okay. I didn't know anyone at the residences. Well, I didn't know how things work in the residence because I've always stayed at home with my mom doing everything. Now I'm all alone, and I'm expected to be an adult and look after myself. There's no one out there in South Africa with me. There was a point where I stopped eating. The pressure regarding my academics made things worse. I arrived in SA late because of study visa technicalities, and classes were already on-going, I had to pace myself.
>
> (Shami, University A)

> The beginning of the e-learning phase was quite difficult because I was not motivated to wake up and attend class. It's just waking up, attending class from your bed, and the information you have it on you. So that whole motivation of waking up to learn something new was not there. So, I think at first it was just difficult, and this had an emotional toll on me, but as I went into it, it became easier.
>
> (Konstan, University A)

Discussion

We refer to Mehta's (2010) point that discussions of scarcity should address fundamental issues such as resource allocation, access, and social justice rather than simplistic and universalist notions of scarcity. As part of our research, we apply a capability lens to understand how students' experiences of capability deprivation led to emotional scarcity, which impacts their emotional well-being. The extracts presented in this chapter are in line with literature that shows that most solutions to the learning challenges provided by universities during the COVID-19 pandemic were mostly in support of local students and did not regard the contexts of international students. While all students (local and international) were anxious about the unknown future, international students at home and in South Africa also worried about their particular circumstances. As illustrated in Table 7.2, international students suffered a range of capability deprivations that led to emotional scarcity. Some capability

Table 7.2 Capability Deprivations Leading to Emotional Scarcity

	In-Country International Students[1] *Internationalisation at a Distance (IaD)*	*Out-of-Country International Students*[2] *Internalisation Abroad (IA)*
Form of Capability Deprivation	Lack of access to data provided by the university	Financial distress
	Lack of access to online learning material/resources	Isolation away from family
	Feelings of anxiety about missing online lessons	Language barriers
	Feelings of anxiety about the future	Social exclusion
	Limited family support	Feelings of anxiety about the future
	Lack of motivation	Lack of family support
		Lack of motivation
	Emotional scarcity	

deprivations were specific to students in IaD, while others affected those in IA, or both groups.

Some students who remained in South Africa also suffered financial distress. For many, this had major implications for whether they could return home before the lockdown was effected. As many of the students were not able to return home, they were secluded as isolation on campus was on an individual basis with restricted contact with fellow students. As Bauman (2019) notes, many international students already had low self-esteem and felt uncomfortable in a foreign land because of the language barrier. Such language barriers in times of isolation where students are excluded from relations that they value tend to cause emotional scarcity and a deterioration in mental health (Hossain et al., 2022). Furthermore, limited family support because of being far away and the costs associated with frequent communication between students and their family members sometimes resulted in a lack of motivation to continue learning even though classes were online. Even though students staying on campus might have had unlimited access to Wi-Fi, it cannot be taken for granted that their families had access.

While students who returned to their home countries were with their families, they faced their own set of challenges. For example, although data for online learning was provided by universities, it was accessible to students residing in South Africa and not those in IaD. This was because service providers were based in South Africa and there were no similar arrangements made with other international broadband providers. Not being able to easily attend lectures because of lack of data and connectivity, compounded by the

1 Students who went back home during lockdown.

2 Students who stayed in the host country during lockdown.

lockdown-induced economic challenges, added to these students' anxiety and emotional scarcity.

Also, because of the economic precarity induced by the pandemic, some parents and guardians could not afford data for their children, as well as laptops. This illustrates the digital divide among students in HE institutions in Africa (Pather et al., 2020; Naidoo and Naidoo, 2021). In countries that experience load shedding (power cuts), even with access to the internet, participation in online class activities was constrained. While the literature on the digital divide during the COVID-19 pandemic mainly focuses on differentiating between the experiences of students in historically marginalised and privileged universities (Mtshweni, 2022; Azionya and Nhedzi, 2021), this research reveals that it was also experienced by international students in different universities. Thus, Moonasamy and Naidoo (2022) underscore the need to highlight that digital transformation is one of the ways to improve international students' well-being. The online challenges caused anxiety about missing online classes with the fear and reality of having to repeat different modules. Missing the online classes would be time and money invested into learning but without the expected or desired outcomes. Like IA students, IaD students also experienced limited family support as families were generally struggling with dealing with anxiety.

According to Sen (1999), such capability deprivation constrains the individual freedoms of international students. While internationalisation is ideally meant to enable students to experience different cultures, learning environments, and resources (Knight, 2014), the existence of the scarcity explained above highlights gaps in the experience. Students end up having limited opportunities to convert, for example, the basic capability of access to international HE into desired functionings, such as being able to create and maintain relationships and friendships with others, being able to fully participate in learning, and being able to access resources in order to achieve emotional well-being, as indicated in Figure 7.1.

Sen (1992) indicates that capabilities are important for achieving well-being. Therefore, addressing capability deprivation has the potential to enhance opportunities that can improve students' lives. Improved lives mean valued functionings and emotional well-being for the students and their communities.

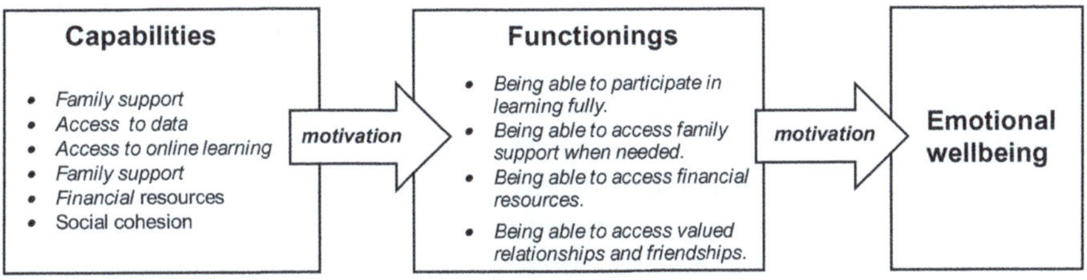

Figure 7.1 Addressing emotional scarcity through a capability lens.

Conclusion

As internationalisation in HE continues to evolve, student experiences and their impact on well-being should be foregrounded. Research findings, such as those presented in this chapter, highlight the need for more strategic conversations and approaches to scaling the internationalisation of HE. The chapter has attempted to critically engage with scarcity, focusing on international students' emotional well-being. The aim is to contribute to broader ongoing discussions on the internationalisation of HE with the intention to influence current and future practices, definitions, and conceptualisations in the field. The chapter has shown that the focus of challenges within HE and its internationalisation processes should move beyond the common, such as lack of funding, to more nuanced and expansive ideas that depict the realities of international students from within the locality, in this case, Africa. In this chapter, South Africa provides an important example of south-south student migration processes. As a regional and educational hub in sub-Saharan Africa, countries on the continent look to South Africa in terms of HE provision. While the two case study universities' response to the pandemic generally mirrors that of institutions internationally, within the sub-Saharan region it highlights the intricate relationship between HE, knowledge production, and the socio-economic and political context. For example, the SADC Protocol on Education and Training (Southern African Development Community, 1997) highlights that while each Member State sets its own educational policies, there is a need for cooperation and mutual assistance in achieving goals such as equitable access to relevant and quality education. The area of internationalisation provides one of those unique spaces where economic and cultural integration is fostered through education.

Drawing on the COVID-19 pandemic and subsequent experiences, we have shown how a global crisis can lead to new ways of thinking about the meaning and everyday applications of macro-level concepts to students' everyday life experiences. For example, because of emerging conditions of material scarcity, an equally harmful emotional scarcity ensued for international students. While the COVID-19 pandemic did induce different forms of scarcity, to some extent, it also highlighted universities' limited understanding of the experiences and needs of international students. Understanding such experiences and needs might limit universities' risk of homogenising students without considering their specific needs. A supportive learning environment, therefore, needs to be created to facilitate the holistic well-being of diverse students considering differing positions of power and privilege organised around academic, logistical, financial, and personal opportunities. In thinking sustainably about the future of international student migration, further research exploring the link between forms of scarcity and students' well-being and future possibilities for students and institutions of HE is necessary. Universities need additional data addressing international students' future teaching and learning needs but with implications for national students, funding bodies, and practitioners interested in improving HE for international and national students. Such considerations will go a long way in not reinforcing forms of exclusion but enabling international students to have an immersive learning experience as promised.

Acknowledgements

The authors acknowledge funding from the Faculty of Economic and Management Sciences at the University of the Free State in South Africa (2022–2023). The authors also extend their gratitude to the students and staff from the University of Free State, the University of Pretoria, and the University of Limpopo who participated in the study. Special appreciation is also given to Mr. Crespen Ndlovu and Ms. Nomvula Makhubu at the University of the Free State's Centre for Development Support for their invaluable support throughout the project.

References

Alharbi, E. S., and Smith, A. P. (2018) 'Review of the literature on stress and wellbeing of international students in English-speaking countries', *International Education Studies*, 11(6), 22–44.

Azionya, C., and Nhedzi, A. (2021) 'The digital divide and higher education challenges with emergency online learning: An analysis of tweets in the wake of the Covid-19 Lockdown', *Turkish Online Journal of Distance Education*, 22(4), 164–182. Available at: https://dergipark.org.tr/en/download/article-file/200256.

Banya, K. (2008) 'Globalization, knowledge economy, and the emergence of private universities in sub-Saharan Africa', *Research and Praxis*, 6(1), 231–259.

Barry, M. M., Clarke, A. M., and Dowling, K. (2017) 'Promoting social and emotional well-being in schools', *Health Education*, 117(5), 434–451.

Bartlett, L. (2011) 'South-South migration and education: The case of people of Haitian descent born in the Dominican Republic', *Compare: A Journal of Comparative and International Education*. Available at: https://www.researchgate.net/publication/254238810_South-south_migration_and_education_The_case_of_people_of_Haitian_descent_born_in_the_Dominican_Republic (Accessed 17 October 2023).

Bauman, D. (2019) 'Tips for overcoming language barriers for international students'. Available: https://blogs.iu.edu/dbauman/2019/01/10/tips-for-overcoming-language-barriers-for-internationalstudents/#:~:text=Due%20to%20language%20difficulties%2C%20the,also%20affects%20their%20academic%20performance (Accessed 17 October 2023).

Brooks, R., and Waters, J. (2022) 'Partial, hierarchical, and stratified space? Understanding "the international" in studies of international student mobility', *Oxford Review of Education*, 48(4), 518–535.

Buckler, A. (2015) *Quality Teaching and the Capability Approach: Evaluating the Work and Governance of Women Teachers in Rural Sub-Saharan Africa*. London and New York: Routledge.

Chen, D. I., and Lo, W. Y. W. (2013) 'Internationalization or commodification? A case study of internationalization practices in Taiwan's higher education', *Asia Pacific Education Review*, 14, 33–41.

Chen, J. H., Li, Y., Wu, A. M. S., and Tong, K. K. (2020) 'The overlooked minority: Mental health of International students worldwide under the COVID-19 pandemic and beyond', *Asian Journal of Psychiatry*, 54.

Crocker, D. A., and Robeyns, I. (2012) 'Capability and agency,' in C. W. Morris (ed.) *Amartya Sen*. Cambridge: Cambridge University Press, pp. 60–90.

Department of Higher Education and Training (DHET). (2020) 'Fact sheet on foreign students in postschool education and training institutions in South Africa'. Available at: https://www.dhet.gov.za/Planning%20Monitoring%20and%20Evaluation%20Coordination/Factsheet%20on%20Foreign%20Students.pdf (Accessed 17 October 2023).

França, T., and Cairns, D. (2020) 'South-South student migration: Socially integrating students from Portuguese-speaking Africa at UNILAB, Brazil', *Globalisation, Societies and Education*, 18(5), 578–588.

Fraser, N. (1998) 'Social justice in the age of identity politics: Redistribution, recognition, participation'. Available at: https://www.econstor.eu/bitstream/10419/44061/1/269802959.pdf

Fraser, N. (2009) *Scales of Justice: Reimagining Political Space in a Globalizing World*. New York: Columbia University Press.

Global Migration Data Portal. (n.d.) 'The bigger picture', *International Students*. Available at: https://www.migrationdataportal.org/international-data (Accessed 17 October 2023).

Hudzik, J. (2011) *Comprehensive Internationalization: From Concept to Action*. Washington, DC: NAFSA.

Hossain, B., Nagargoje, V. P., Sk, M. I. K., and Das, J. (2022) 'Social exclusion and mental health among older adults: Cross-sectional evidence from a population-based survey in India', *BMC Psychiatry*, 8(22). Doi: 10.1186/s12888-022-04064-1.

Kahneman, D., and Deaton, A. (2010) 'High income improves evaluation of life but not emotional well-being', *Proceedings of the National Academy of Sciences of the United States of America*, 107, 6489–6493. Doi: 10.1073/pnas.1011492107.

Knight, J. (2014) 'Is Internationalisation of higher education having an identity crisis?' in A. Maldonado-Maldonado and R. Bassett (eds.) *The Forefront of International Higher Education*. Higher Education Dynamics (Vol. 42). Dordrecht: Springer, pp. 75–87.

Luescher, T. M., Schreiber, B., Moja, T., Mandew, M., Wahl, W. P., and Ayele, B. (2021) 'The impact of Covid19 on student affairs and higher education in Africa', *Journal of Student Affairs in Africa*, 9(1), v–xiii. Available at: https://upjournals.up.ac.za/index.php/jsaa/article/view/1721 (Accessed 19 October 2023).

Mehta, L. (ed). (2010) *The Limits to Scarcity: Contesting the Politics of Allocation*. New York: Taylor and Francis.

Mkwananzi, F. (2019) *Higher Education, Youth and Migration in Contexts of Disadvantage: Understanding Aspirations and Capabilities*. London: Palgrave Macmillan.

Moonasamy, A. A., and Naidoo, G. M. (2022) 'Digital learning: Challenges experienced by South African university students' during the COVID-19 pandemic', *The Independent Journal of Teaching and Learning*, 17(2), 76–90. Available at: http://www.scielo.org.za/scielo.php?script=sci_arttext&pid=S2519-56702022000200005&lng=en&tlng=en (Accessed 17 October 2023).

Mtshweni, B. V. (2022) 'Covid-19: Exposing unmatched historical disparities in the South African institutions of higher learning', *South African Journal of Higher Education*, 36(1), 234–250.

Naidoo, G. M., and Naidoo, M. K. (2021) 'Digital communication: Overcoming digital teaching and learning barriers during the COVID-19 lockdown', in M. Montebello (ed.) *Digital Pedagogies and the Transformation of Language Education*. IGI Global, pp. 183–203.

Naidoo, R. (2003) 'Repositioning higher education as a global commodity: Opportunities and challenges for future sociology of education work', *British Journal of Sociology of Education*, 24(2), 249–259.

Naidoo, R. (2011) 'Rethinking development: Higher education and the new imperialism', in R. King, S. Marginson, and R. Naidoo (eds.) *Handbook on Globalisation and Higher Education*. Cheltenham and Northampton: Edward Elgar Publishing, pp. 40–58.

OECD. (2023) *Education at a Glance 2023: OECD Indicators*. Paris: OECD Publishing. Available at: https://www.oecd.org/en/publications/2023/09/education-at-a-glance-2023_581c9602.html (Accessed 17 October 2023).

O'Shea, N. (2020) 'Forecasting needs and risks in the UK'. Available at: https://www.centreformentalhealth.org.uk/publications/covid-19-and-nations-mental-health-october-2020/ (Accessed 3 November 2023).

Pandit, K. (2013) 'International students and diversity', in H. C. Alberts and H. D. Hazen (eds.) *International Students and Scholars in the United States*. New York: Palgrave Macmillan.

Pather, S., Booi, E., and Pather, S. (2020) 'An assessment of student resource readiness for online learning during COVID-19: A South African case study', *Proceedings of ICERI2020 Conference*. Doi: 10.21125/iceri.2020.2186.

Ratshilaya, A. J. (2021) 'International students' academic integration experiences in South Africa', in C. T. Sehoole and J. J. Lee (eds.) *Intra-Africa Student Mobility in Higher Education*. Cham, Switzerland: Palgrave Studies in Global Higher Education, pp. 137–156.

Robeyns, I. (2005) 'The capability approach: A theoretical survey', *Journal of Human Development*, 6(1), 93–117.

Ronnie, L., Bam, A., and Walters, C. (2022) 'Emotional wellbeing: The impact of the COVID-19 pandemic on women academics in South Africa', *Frontiers in Education*, 7.

Rosenthal, M. (2016). 'Qualitative research methods: Why, when, and how to conduct interviews and focus groups in pharmacy research', *Currents in Pharmacy Teaching and Learning*, 8, 509–516. https://doi.org/10.1016/j.cptl.2016.03.021.

Sahu, P. (2020) 'Closure of universities due to Coronavirus disease 2019 (COVID-19): Impact on education and mental health of students and academic staff', *Cureus*, 12(4).

Sehoole, C. (2015) 'International students love South Africa, but xenophobia could be a heartbreaker', *The Conversation*. Available at: https://theconversation.com/international-students-love-south-africa-but-xenophobia-could-be-a-heartbreaker-41707.

Sen, A. (1999) *Development as Freedom*. Oxford: Oxford University Press.

Sen, A. K. (1992) *Inequality Reexamined*. Oxford: Clarendon Press.

Snow, N. (2021) 'Student mobility and its relevance to international relations theory'. Available at: https://www.e-ir.info/2021/12/05/student-mobility-and-its-relevance-to-international-relations-theory/.

SouthernAfrican Development Community. (1997) 'Protocol on education and training in the Southern African development community (SADC)'. Available at: https://www.sadc.int/document/protocol-education-training-1997.

Steyn, C., and Gunter, A. (2021) 'When an international student stays at home: Defining an international student in distance education', *Journal of Geography in Higher Education* 47(3), 1–15.

Tagliabue, V. V. (2022) 'Too rich to care? Southern African (SADC) international students navigating transnationalism and class at South African universities', *Journal of Southern African Studies*, 48(1), 5–21.

UNESCO. (2024) *Internationally Mobile Students*. Internationally Mobile Students | UNESCO UIS.

UNICEF. (2022) *Five Essential Pillars for Promoting and Protecting Mental Health and Psychosocial Well-Being in Schools and Learning Environments: A Briefing Note for National Governments*. UNICEF.

Walker, M. (2006) *Higher Education Pedagogies.* Society for Research into Higher Education and Open University Press.
Xenos, N. (1989) *Scarcity and Modernity.* London: Routledge.
Young, I. M. (1990) *Justice and the Politics of Difference.* REV-Revised. *JSTOR*. Princeton University Press. Available at: https://doi.org/10.2307/j.ctvcm4g4q (Accessed 29 March 2025).

8 A people without a land

Scarcity, biopolitics, and Romani people in the Middle East

Arpan Roy

Introduction

Much of the discussion around scarcity in the social sciences literature revolves around a materiality of resources and is therefore often economic, geopolitical, and legal in nature. "Resource grabbing," for instance—the appropriation of land, minerals and other goods by powerful financial and political actors resulting in the impoverishment of native or local communities—is an economic practice widely denounced by scholars and practitioners. Less attention, though, has been devoted to examining how the lack of some key material resources, such as land, may shape cultural practices for ethnic or minority groups. However, any logical precondition for a discussion of minorities rests upon—perhaps obviously—the viability of the category of "minority" in historical and epistemological contexts outside of Europe. In this chapter, I discuss the case of Romani groups in the Middle East who are, on the one hand, not recognized as minorities in a region in which the concept of minority does not correspond to liberal politics of recognition in which *x* group is the majority and *y* and *z* groups are distinguished on linguistic or ethnic grounds (see Mahmood, 2015),[1] and also whose economic life is a complex interaction between structural barriers—sometimes cultural—and biopolitical instability. More specifically, I examine in this chapter this interaction as it pertains to difficulties inflicting Romani groups in the region in acquiring property and being able to capitalize on land and resources.

In theorizing the labor practices of Romani groups around the world, one long-standing position in the field of Romani studies has been consistent with the Marxist etiology for the emergence of a lumpenproletariat with the dawn of industrial capitalism. With traditional agriculture and village economies decimated by industry, as Marx famously held, peasants flocked to cities in search of a better life but found only partial and occasional employment in the competitive capitalist labor market. In this new urban milieu, it was labor

1 An exception to this is religious minorities, but the complexity of the matter cannot be accommodated in this chapter.

DOI: 10.4324/9781032661780-9

scarcity that drove these populations "in massive quantities into beggars, robbers and vagabonds, partly from inclination, in most cases under the force of circumstances" (Marx, 1976, p. 896). It has been a version of this thesis that scholars studying the Romani peoples of the world have adapted into a framework that they call "foraging"—a striking metaphor that audaciously draws a continuity between prehistoric hunter-gatherers and contemporary Romanies and related peoples in the liberal world order, a more extreme version of the continuity that Marx had drawn between precapitalist villagers and the urban poor. In a classic book on the topic, Sophie Day et al. (1999, p. 7) refer to this process as the

> incorporation or domination within pre-modern, colonial, and, now, nation states, where hunter-gatherers live in enclaves because they do not participate in the ways of life practiced by more powerful neighbors—they do not till the land, breed animals, pay taxes, honor the dead, build houses, and so on.

Foraging, in contrast to the prescribed practices of a liberal market economy, is an ethos of "living in the present," with no economic or ethical foresight that allows for a social safety net and is the basis for the often antisocial behavior popularly associated with Romani groups; however imagined or real, particularly in Europe.

This chapter takes these arguments as the basis for a discussion of two groups of Romani people in the Arab Levant—Doms and Aptal Turkmen—but I also distance myself from the positions briefly sketched above. Although I accept a Marxist political economic framework for partially explaining contemporary social phenomena, I complicate the anachronism of the Romani studies scholars with two supplemental factors to consider: (1) property as a base for social action and (2) *capacity* to maintain fidelity to a form of life in the midst of various state, economic, and social pressures. The two factors are interrelated. As I will discuss in detail shortly, Romani people are singularly unique in the Levant region for being a people historically without having owned property. Yet, they are also a people who have at various points in recent history nearly acquired property—"*nearly* acquired," that is, because various attempts by Romanies to acquire property have been thwarted by the tumultuous political climate of a region that has for several decades been characterized by war, colonialism and imperialist projects, religious militancy, and economic scarcity. I place these impediments under the rubric of "biopolitics," in that it is the biological body that is the site into which abstract economic and political events are inscribed and, later, reproduced through kinship.

The importance of property ownership in rendering a given people politically viable has been a consistent current in European thought, as argued masterfully by Hannah Arendt (1958), evident in thinkers as diametrically opposed as liberals like Locke and no less of an anarchist than Proudhon. I have recently discussed these matters elsewhere (see Roy, 2023), so I will be brief in my overview of these arguments here. The point is that in the European philosophical tradition, property ownership is the means by which to have mastery over one's own life, and therefore have the basis to "enter the world all have in common" (Arendt, 1958, p. 65). Not only is it a prerequisite for politics, as is in Athenian democracy, in which property ownership was a requirement for participation—a resolutely reduced concept of a *demos*—but it is also a safeguard against tyranny in the public sphere; and a kind of refuge, a place for speech and action in which the public sphere cannot have sway over the private lives of its citizens (p. 29). Without having this "sacred" boundary (Arendt, 1958), "man could not participate in the affairs of the world because he had no location in it which was properly his own."

In the Arab/Islamic tradition, however, property has been theorized not necessarily as a base for social action but, rather, as the basis for what is permissible or impermissible in society. In classical Arab/Islamic scholarship, the private sphere is valued as the site where otherwise intolerable social tendencies like sexuality immorality and religious deviation can be tolerated, lest it be out of view of society (see Alshech, 2004). It is perhaps because of the irrelevance of property to politics in this tradition that Ibn Khaldun, the towering fourteenth-century figure of Arab/Islamic thought, did not consider the implications of property ownership in his famous division of Arab society into three categories: *fellaheen* "peasants"; pastoral Bedouin; and the urban society of merchants, government functionaries, artisans, religious leaders, and so on.[2] Yet, a close perusal of Ibn Khaldun's typology reveals that these categorical divisions are not spatial or exactly conceived through modes of production, such as the town/country premise for premodern Britain as proposed by Raymond Williams (1973), but, rather, the categories are ultimately conceived through property ownership: the collective land ownership institution known as *musha'*, by which peasants in many parts of the Arab world (especially in the Arab Levant) were not landless serfs like in European feudalism; livestock for the Bedouin, as well as informal tribal alliances in designating land; and businesses and other enterprises for the urban population. Given the knowledge that Romani people have been present in the region since at least the eighth century (see Richardson, 2020, 2017), I find their exclusion from Ibn Khaldun's typology to be a glaring omission.

Again, I have written about these topics elsewhere, so I do not wish to enter into technical details in this particular line of argumentation here. The crux of the matter is that Romanies being outside of property relations, in my view, is at least partly the reason why Ibn Khaldun was unable to "see" them. Here I am making a case for the universality of the centrality of property in determining political viability, in spite of the intellectual relativity between European and Arab/Islamic thought. Romani people in the Arab world have

2 Ibn Khaldun does, in fact, discuss property rights elsewhere, but in the context of economic prosperity (see Khalil, 2007).

historically been a people without property, and it is this crucial point that, as I will discuss with ethnographic case examples later in this chapter, continues to perpetuate a specific form of life into the present. You might call this a political economic "inheritance" that one is born with, a kind of deck of cards that one is dealt at birth, an argument that is often made of displaced and colonized people, or descendants of slaves, but rarely of Romanies.

This is the first point. My second point challenges the prevailing view in Romani studies that Romanies are "anti-economic" (Day et al., 1999), meaning that Romanies resist the logic of rational choice economics by which the acquisition of property is based on cost-benefit analysis and long-term security is a sovereign "choice." In other words, it is implied here that Romani labor is a question of *consciousness*. Here, again, the line taken by these scholars is implicitly a Marxist one, in that it was Marx who took a metaphysical stance regarding the advent of private property, and often derided his contemporaries for a vulgar economic reductionism in theorizing the human condition. I will return to this point in my conclusion, but I flag here that it is certainly not my intention to negate the importance of individual (and collective) desire, communal pressures, and traditional knowledge in determining Romani labor, but my ethnographic discussion will show that any rational choice is nonetheless conditioned by biopolitical factors that, in the case of Romanies of the Arab world, include war, labor scarcity, displacement, political conflict, and more. In my first case example, I will discuss the continuing unfolding of the Palestinian tragedy as a direct inhibiting factor for Dom Romanies who have been unable to settle a given territory and, in the second example, how labor scarcity in Jordan drives Aptal (Turkmen) Romanies away from newly developing ethnic enclaves in Amman where Romanies have acquired property in recent years. In both cases, the acquisition of property emerges as a question of *capacity* more than rational choice. Consider it to be like following the "rules" of grammar or of society, in which the ethical choices that one makes is determined by one's skill, circumstances, and aptitude to fulfilling a given ideal. Here, again, I defer to a separate article on this matter for a more detailed discussion (see Roy, 2023).

If property is the base for social action in the European philosophical tradition, and the basis for recognition as in Ibn Khaldun's puzzling exclusion, then the question of *capacity* to acquire property has serious political and social consequences. For instance, if the argument for a topic so critical in our contemporary world like reparations is based on a historical injustice that has permanently inflicted an economic handicap on a given people, a fundamental inequality in the economic trajectory of Romanies raises interesting questions. The Romani case for reparations has largely been a European issue and has been based on historic crimes against Romani groups in Europe, namely the Holocaust (see Von dem Knesebeck, 2011). The story of the Romani peoples of the Arab world, however, presents new problematics. To be clear, my aim in this chapter is not to make an argument for or against reparations for Romanies—far from it—but, rather, to highlight the immense possible stakes in discussing a people without land in a region in which the land has become a point of utmost geopolitical importance. Here, the capacity to acquire land and property, the basis for permanent settlement, is an instance of constructed scarcity; a politically manufactured situation injuring the trajectory of a particular group in a way perhaps not experienced by the landed elites of the same society.

I turn now to two cases from my ethnographic research with Romani people in Palestine, Jordan, and (to a lesser extent) Egypt to highlight biopolitics as the agent that interacts with consciousness and political economy in shaping Romani ethics. As a final introductory note, as frustrating as it may be for the reader, I resist restricting "biopolitics" to concrete discursive limits; not even to those established by Michel Foucault, the father of biopolitics. Rather, I hope that a picture of biopolitics comes into focus through the crevices of the cases that I describe. Scarcity and political violence, as it will be clear, are two central aspects of this biopolitics.

Settling and unsettling Gaza

Doms are the largest Romani group in the Middle East, although, like many other Romani groups, distinctions between subgroups, tribes, clans, and families do not adhere to rigid classificatory practices but, rather, are a generally ambiguous affair (see Roy, 2024). Certainly, none of these levels of classification corresponds to the notion of "minority," which, as mentioned earlier, does not appear in Arab/Middle Eastern contexts in the way that it does in a liberal politics of recognition in Europe and elsewhere. Because of the certainty of Domari language's relation to Romani, the family of languages spoken by various Romani groups in Europe, Doms belong to what the Romani studies scholar Yaron Matras (2017) refers to (unfortunately) as "Gypsy 2"; meaning groups that have an ancestral connection, mostly determined by linguistic data, to a historic Romani migration from the Indian subcontinent. Known in literary Arabic as *ghajar* and locally in the Arab Levant as *nawar*, Doms continue to constitute an unmissable presence in the entirety of the region in question, with the notable exception of Palestine. Reasons for this will be discussed shortly. Romanies elude a comprehensive historical record—precisely, in part, because property is the basis for recognition in society—and, thus, the only alternative to making any generalizations about Romani history and culture is through careful, close-to-the-field ethnographic work. Because this work has largely not been done, it is imprudent to speculate about Romani settlement history beyond my own long-term sites of field research: Palestine and Jordan.

Prior to the catastrophic events of 1948, when around 800,000 Palestinians were expelled by Zionist militias to facilitate the founding of Israel, seasonally nomadic Dom tribes had a notable presence throughout historic Palestine—a crucial node in trade and pilgrimage routes, and, in the late nineteenth and early twentieth centuries, a hub of energetic economic activity for a confluence of factors including renewed Ottoman investment in the territory, Jewish settlement from Europe, and, after World War I, British colonial interest. However, with the expulsions of 1948, Doms largely fled Palestine to surrounding countries like Lebanon and Jordan, leaving behind significant populations only in the cities of Jerusalem and Gaza. The difference between these two Dom communities, today still marked by differing labor practices, religious rituals, and more, can be explained in part by settlement history and property. Doms who remained in Jerusalem after 1948 were, with some exceptions, already present in the Jerusalem area prior to the expulsions. After the war, these Doms began a process of settling into permanent housing in the city's walled medina that was complete only in the late 1960s, after another major rupture—the 1967 Six Day War during which Israel captured the remaining Palestinian territories not captured in 1948, including the entirety of Jerusalem. As a result, those that we now call "Jerusalem Doms" are more or less integrated into the Palestinian labor economy.

By contrast, Gaza was not the site of a Romani presence comparable to Jerusalem before 1948, and most Doms who ended up becoming "Gaza Doms" were refugees from the economically prosperous Palestinian central-coastal region, particularly the cities of Jaffa, Lydd, and Ramla. After 1948, a minority of Doms in Gaza did, in fact, purchase property, but only to lose this property in 1967, when a new wave of approximately 300,000 Palestinian refugees fled mostly to Jordan. There are more details to the story that cannot be told here, but the point is that the Dom experience with property in Palestine in the twentieth century has been directly in correlation with the overall narrative arc of the Palestinian tragedy.

This narrative correlation continues today. Gaza Doms, in particular, having had their social structure assaulted by the two displacements of 1948 and 1967, continue to feel the repercussions of the fate of Gaza. Remaining semi-nomadic even after being made refugees in Gaza in 1948, Doms in the region continued to move between Gaza and Egypt, which fell under single regimes successively between 1948 and 1982—first Egyptian and then Israeli—and did not begin settling into permanent housing on a large scale until the 1980s, when movement became severely restricted by the increasing militarization of both Israel and Egypt. Having survived the two Palestinian intifadas of 1987–1993 and 2000–2005, yet another Dom migration has emerged as a response to circumstances generated by a later chapter in the Palestinian tragedy: the aerial, naval, terrestrial, and diplomatic blockade of Gaza beginning in 2007. Having quickly become one of the most isolated and destitute regions in the world, Gaza, since the implementation of the blockade, saw the emigration of thousands of Doms to the West Bank, the economically more preferable of the two nominally Palestinian-administered territories. Such a migration is highly implausible given the spartan restrictions on movement in Gaza, but Doms rely on a traditional knowledge of subverting borders and devising long-term strategies for migration to make this implausible migration somehow possible. Those who stayed in Gaza, also several thousands, later became victims to Israel's genocidal campaign in the territory beginning October 2023—still unfolding at the time of writing—and which I am unable to address in this chapter. This unprecedented humanitarian catastrophe stifles any kind of rational analysis. Focusing instead on the Gaza-to-West Bank migrations that had been occurring prior to the genocide, we can see that Gaza Doms had already again become a people without property in their new environments.

Troubles, however, do not end there. Take the case of a man who I will call Abu Sami. Born in Gaza, Abu Sami fled his natal region with his wife and some of his children in 2015, shortly after the devastating Israeli bombing campaign on the territory the previous year. Moving several times in the first few years after arriving in the West Bank, he had by the time I first met him in 2017 established a kind of family compound in a working-class area in the conurbation between Jerusalem and Ramallah, where he and his extended family settled in rented apartments. This compound has since then fragmented, as Abu Sami's household has moved to another locality in the same area to be nearer to his wife's brother—a constant movement along kinship lines, and facilitated by not being bound to property, that gives amorphous shape to Dom geography. Registered as a Gaza resident under the Israeli-devised ID system, Abu Sami is undocumented in the West Bank, thus living the perilous and absurd life of an illegal immigrant in his own country, always cautious that he is not discovered by Israeli authorities and deported to the misery of blockaded Gaza. Partly because of not having many options for legal work, and partly for other reasons including knowledge of the craft, Abu Sami and a few other members of his family earn a living by begging—a highly organized and generations-old labor for Doms that here perpetuates into the present under these most exceptional conditions. In the Romani studies literature, this would be considered "foraging," but, if taking the *longue durée* of Dom relation with property into account, especially the following paragraph, it would not be entirely correct to say that begging as labor is incompatible with long-term planning. Rather, it is the biopolitical interruptions that trap Doms into a life cycle that is all too easily shorthanded as "culture."

In late 2019, upon making one of my regular visits to Abu Sami, I was surprised to learn that he had purchased a flat in a nearby area. When he took me to see it, I found a squat, humble four-story building under construction, on a quiet street in an otherwise chaotic and traffic-jammed suburb in the Jerusalem/Ramallah peripheries. Abu Sami told me that he had bargained a great deal. The flat only cost him $25,000 USD, he told me, with a $5,000 down payment and then what would be monthly installments of $1,000. This struck me as unbelievably low, but because the flat was *adam* "unfinished" and Abu Sami would be paying for the electrical work, tiles, and so on, and because the area is a generally lawless zone abandoned by both Israel and the Palestinian Authority, it was a somehow possible price. It turned out that the developer who was erecting the building was of Gazan origin but born in the Qalandia refugee camp near Ramallah. Some of his relatives had known Abu

Sami's relatives in Gaza, so they were tied, as it were, by the bond of belonging to a shared geography. He was also courting Abu Sami's eldest daughter for marriage, a courtship that she ultimately resisted. It soon emerged that the developer was swindling those who had bought flats in his constructions, and he was swiftly sent to prison. He had been erecting several unfinished buildings in the Ramallah area for which he had accepted down payments but had no intention of finishing. Abu Sami's home would probably have been among these abandoned projects. Without the binding of a legal contract, and without residency rights in the West Bank, Abu Sami had no way of recovering the $5,000 that he had advanced to the developer, nor the amounts he had paid in monthly installments in the course of the unfolding of these events. Abu Sami, thus, remains a man without property.

Pity the nations

Scholarly attention has evaded the Turkmen Romanies, who are among the Turkic-speaking people of the Arab world, but with indeterminate origins and a nomadic lifestyle still into the twenty-first century. Reasons for this, as we will see, are in large part conditioned by biopolitics. Comparative linguistic research, still the prevailing scholarly measure by which to determine the genealogies of Romani groups, has not been done on Turkmençi, the Turkmen Romani language. A self-published memoir written by an evangelical missionary (OddChild, 2014) working with Turkmen in Syria, Lebanon, and Jordan identifies loan vocabulary in Turkmençi from Persian, Kurdish, and Russian, throwing open a wide array of genealogical possibilities. Nonetheless, Turkmen Romanies belong to Matras's (again, unfortunate) "Gypsy 1" classification, meaning people with close lifestyle similarities and affinity with other Romani groups, regardless of the shared ethnic or linguistic genealogies that constitute his "Gypsy 2" category. Indeed, Turkmen in Jordan tend to coinhabit spaces with Doms, forming parallel communities in what to outsiders seem like homogenous Romani ethnic enclaves. This was also the case in many localities in Palestine prior to the radical reordering of the social order with the founding of Israel. I have been researching with the Aptal, the largest Turkmen Romani tribe in Jordan, since 2019—a relatively short period by ethnographic standards. Because of this, I will limit my discussion here to a specific situation of land, property, and labor.

The Aptal in Jordan began acquiring property only in the last two decades. A man who I will call Abu Kemal was born in Nablus, Palestine, where a Turkmen population lived in ambulant commercial communities in the outskirts of the city until 1967, when they fled during the violence of the Six Day War. The Aptal fled first to Jordan and then to Baghdad, Iraq, where they joined an already populous Romani population in what was then Iraq's prosperous oil boom years. There, Abu Kemal eventually purchased a small plot of land on which he had planned to build a home—a plan that would remain unrealized. Iraq's unfortunate turn shortly thereafter is well-known: a decade-long war with Iran, a botched annexation of Kuwait, war with the United States in 1991, ten years of crippling sanctions by the American-led world order, the American invasion in 2003 and the regime change, counter-insurgencies, and sectarian warfare that followed. Nowhere on earth is a better case study for biopolitics in the contemporary world than Iraq, the pitiful nation that the anthropologist Laura Adwan calls *homeland sacer* (2011), a play on Giorgio Agamben's well-known figure from Roman law that can be killed but not sacrificed.

It was during the sanctions period, a time of immense economic scarcity and hardship in which it is estimated that 500,000 Iraqi children died of malnourishment, that the Aptal, like many Iraqis, fled to Jordan. A new polity in an antique land, Jordan had not been a significant destination for Romani tribes until recent biopolitical events contributed to massive influxes of populations: the two Palestinian expulsions of 1948 and 1967, Iraq's tragic chronology, and, later, economic scarcity in Egypt and the violence of the Syrian War. The numerous Turkmen settlements that are found in Jordanian cities today are thus narratively linked to two major biopolitical zones of abandonment of our time: Palestine and Iraq. These settlements are often tent cities, characterized by wooden-framed tent structures known as *barakiyat*, but increasingly the tents are being swapped for multi-story villas—elegant houses that the Turkmen (and Doms) build over several months and sometimes years, whenever there is enough surplus money to buy materials. In a neighborhood in the industrial outskirts of Amman that I call Wadi al-Timsah, where I have been doing fieldwork the last several years, Turkmen and Doms both bought the properties where their tents and houses presently stand in a process that began in the 1990s and is today complete. Wadi al-Timsah, thus, is a mostly Romani-owned neighborhood and, despite its peripheral location, a rather lovely place to live.

Most recently, however, a new Turkmen migration is occurring; one that defies the laws of capital: to economically poorer Egypt, from where an otherwise reverse flow of labor migration is occurring to Jordan. The reason for this seemingly illogical move is that the Turkmen, still ambulant salesmen selling clothes, watches, and other accessories, are increasingly harassed by the Jordanian police who in recent years have become stricter about enforcing a long-standing ban on peddling. In a derelict residential hotel in Old Cairo, I visit Abu Kemal's nephew. He, along with many Aptal Turkmen families from Wadi al-Timsah, are living in cramped, unhygienic quarters that shock even the laconic anthropologist who has seen it all. They are in debt, owing large sums to their creditors who supply the capital necessary to purchase wholesale goods to be sold. Unable to earn enough of a profit to pay back the creditors in Egypt's crisis economy, and meanwhile developing new amphetamine addictions so as to be able to work around the clock, the Turkmen are in bad shape. It is entirely possible that, in a previous era not burdened by property, the Aptal tribes would splinter; some would leave Egypt and move on to more hospitable terrain, while some would return to their homes in Jordan.

But bounded by their newly acquired property in Jordan yet unable to work there, and miserable in Egypt, the Turkmen are in a historical terra incognita. Again, we see here that it is not that the Turkmen are "anti-economic," but, if anything, it is the economy that is antithetical to human welfare, and that it is property—acquiring it, losing it, acquiring it again, losing it again—that is the nexus of a particular kind of social action.[3]

Conclusion

I would like to close my discussion of the inadequacies of treating Romani labor and property relations in the Arab world through Marxist political economy and related "cultural" concepts like "foraging" and "anti-economic" activity. I do this, ironically, by turning to Marx. Namely, it is the important and often overlooked Marxist position that rejoins political economy with individual consciousness and—in my view—biopolitics. In an inverse position of the gross popular misrepresentation of Marxist thought being vulgar economic determinism, Marx consistently discouraged an objection to private property conceived solely on grounds of political economy. In his early work *The Holy Family*, Marx defended the anarchist Proudhon as being misinterpreted by critics who held that the classic formula of "property is theft" grossly reduces private property to merely a condition of some people "having" and others "not having." Rather, forecasting his later theory of alienation, Marx encouraged a position on abolishing private property based on the "practically estranged relation of man to his objective essence and the economic expression of human self-estrangement" (Marx, 1975, p. 43). He wrote:

> Not having is the most despairing *spiritualism*, a complete unreality of the human being, a complete reality of the dehumanized being, a very positive having, a having of hunger, of cold, of disease, of crime, of debasement, of hebetude, of all inhumanity and abnormity. But every object which for the first time is made the object of thought with full consciousness of its importance is the *highest object of thought*.
>
> (Marx, 1975, p. 43)

What is Marx's "dehumanized being" here if not the being of biopolitics? It is the being of hunger, cold, disease, and so forth on the basis of the incapacity (at best) or indifference (at worst) of the state to provide for its subjects. For Marx, being without property is closely discursively linked to this dehumanized being. It is thus indeed curious that the Romani studies position that contrasts the Marxist etiology for the emergence of a lumpenproletariat with a

3 Since first drafting this chapter, the locus of Aptal deterritorialized labour has shifted from Egypt to Oman; a move motivated primarily by the collapse of the Egyptian pound in March 2023. Here, again, the argument of scarcity holds determining mobilities and settlement holds.

cultural consciousness that resists integration into the liberal world order has not recognized the intrinsic relation between a Marxist political economy and biopolitics.

Moreover, I have shown how political economy interacts with biopolitics to give shape to a specific form of life for Romanies that is too often simplified to culturalist explanations. True, culture is a legitimate factor—no anthropologist would deny this—but this factor is greatly shaped by biopolitical circumstances that, in the stories of Romanies from the Arab world that I have shared, include economic scarcity, war, displacement, and political violence; nowhere more vivid or striking than in (but not only) Gaza, crushed and flattened under the leviathan of biopolitics. In the *longue durée* of these communities, the long-term consequences of such structures of dispossession become inscribed in the Romani consciousness, and with each generation model Romani forms of life and ethics that reproduce the material conditions of scarcity.

References

Adwan, Laura. 2011. "Homeland Sacer: A Nation to Be Killed." *Review of Women's Studies: Institute of Women's Studies, Birzeit University* 1: 35–51.

Alshech, Eli. 2004. "'Do Not Enter Houses Other Than Your Own': The Evolution of the Notion of a Private Domestic Sphere in Early Sunni Islamic Thought." *Islamic Law and Society* 11(3): 291–332.

Arendt, Hannah. 1958. *The Human Condition*. University of Chicago Press.

Day, Sophie, Evthymios Papataxiarchis, and Michael Stewart (Eds.). 1999. *Lilies of the Field: Marginal People Who Live for the Moment*. Westview Press.

Khalil, Elias. 2007. "Ibn Khaldun on Property Rights, The Muqaddimah: An Introduction to History." *Journal of Institutional Economics* 3(2): 227–238.

Mahmood, S. 2015. *Religious Difference in a Secular Age: A Minority Report*. Princeton University Press.

Marx, Karl. 1975. *The Collected Works of Marx and Engels, Volume Four: 1844–1845*. International Publishers.

Marx, Karl. 1976 [1876]. *Capital: A Critique of Political Economy, Volume One*. Penguin.

Matras, Yaron. 2017. "The Role of Language in Mystifying and Demystifying Gypsy Identity." In *The Role of the Romanies: Images and Counter Images of 'Gypsies'/Romanies in European Cultures*. Edited by Yaron Matras. Liverpool University Press, 53–78.

OddChild, Johnny. 2014. *Turkmania: Evangelism to the Turkmen of Syria*. Self-Published on Amazon.com.

Richardson, Kristina. 2020. "Invisible Strangers, or Romani History Reconsidered." *History of the Present* 10(2): 187–207.

Richardson, Kristina. 2017. "Tracing a Gypsy Mixed Language Through Medieval and Early Modern Arabic and Persian Literature." *Der Islam* 94(1): 115–157.

Roy, Arpan. 2023. "A Space of Appearance: Romani Publics and Privates in the Middle East." *Anthropological Theory* 24(2): 175–200.

Roy, Arpan. 2024. *Relative Strangers: Romani Kinship and Palestinian Difference*. University of Toronto Press.

Von dem Knesebeck, Julia. 2011. *The Roma Struggle for Compensation in Post-War Germany*. University of Hertfordshire Press.

Williams, Raymond. 1973. *The Country and the City*. Oxford University Press.

9 Epistemic violence from silencing to "scarcity of empathy"

The experience of Indigenous scholars in Brazil

Camila Ferreira Marinelli

Géssica is Guarani Ñandeva, an Indigenous people located in the south, southeast, and midwest regions of Brazil. She comes from the community *Reserva Indígena Pinhalzinho*, situated in the state of Paraná in the south of the country. Paraná is popularly known for its European migrants, festivals, and cuisine. Indigenous peoples in this region are rarely mentioned in school curricula or are referred to as the "people who were here before Iberian colonisation". The Indigenous people of Brazil are often treated as part of the past, as though they only existed during the colonial period. In these terms, colonisation was "successful" in silencing the country's diversity and variety of Indigenous protagonism. Géssica is very aware of this and carries the weight of historical silence in her words and most heavily in her body.

I began following Géssica's work on Instagram during my PhD fieldwork in Brazil in 2021. Her content caught my attention because of its emotional depth, which focused on her own experiences at university. She describes her Instagram account *@universidadeterritórioindígena* (lit. "university is an Indigenous territory") as a place to "potentialise the Indigenous presence in higher education". Géssica posts about what it means for an "Indigenous body" to be present at the university, from being an act of resistance and pride to being silenced by "centuries of colonial strategies". Through her posts and videos, Géssica shares that being in the university means "demarcating" the space as an Indigenous territory and not allowing the continuous silencing of Indigenous knowledges and peoples. This notion of university as an Indigenous territory is not only about recognising their presence but recognising knowledges and knowers and demarcating the institution on their own terms and with a relevant meaning for the Indigenous peoples. The idea is to "demarcate the university's territory" with Brazil's diverse Indigenous histories, collective knowledges, references, technologies, and intellectuals; reclaiming and re-existing beyond the walls of modern science[1] that have diminished

1 Modern science and its conceptual methodologies and institutional foundations are considered to still guide higher education and are dominant in modern universities, which are based on the idea of knowledge driven by a defined epistemology, by its specificity, specialisation, and universality.

DOI: 10.4324/9781032661780-10

the Indigenous to objects of research, and asserting themselves as authors of their own research, capable of exchanging knowledges and considering the university as their territory as well. Overall, Géssica calls for action to not allow the university from continuing "to silence Indigenous knowledges", asserting that the university is Indigenous by right,[2] and that Indigenous peoples should be part of it, on their terms.

In August 2021, Géssica shared reflections on her Instagram account, inspired by her reading of Grada Kilomba's book *Plantation Memories.* The first post reads: "You silence an Indigenous person when . . .", followed by an arrow pointing to the next image. Beneath the arrow was the text: "Academia is not a neutral place; it is a 'white' space, where the right to speak has been denied to the Indigenous peoples". The second post continued the phrase, "You silence an Indigenous person when . . . you position my discourse on the margins, as deviating knowledge, whilst your knowledge remains at the centre".

When I had the opportunity to speak with Géssica in 2021, she proudly introduced herself as Guarani Ñandeva, a mother of three Guarani children and a teacher at a Guarani Ñandeva school.[3] Yet, I had the feeling that this had not always been the case. During our conversation, it became clear that her pride brewed from pain, not just her own, but the "pain of so many" and of a body that has carried the "experience of violence since childhood", "suffering", and "misery". Entering higher education was no different. She experienced "silencing of Indigenous knowledge, racism, situations of humiliation and illness of the spirit", to the point where giving up seemed the only option. However, as she proudly states, she "resisted, (re)existed[4] and finished" her degree in Portuguese literature and went on to do a postgraduate course.

> I speak with great pride about my trajectory because it was not easy . . . when I remember my time in academia, I see how painful it was . . . yet this pain mobilises my work. I want to share my experience . . . so other

2 The Affirmative Action Law of 2012, known as *Lei de Cotas*, reserves 50 per cent of university and federal institutes' vacancies for students from public high schools. Ethnic-racial criteria are also applied, guaranteeing that in all federal universities in Brazil, a "minimum percentage corresponding to the sum of blacks, browns, and Indigenous students in the state" (Brasil, 2012) is guaranteed.

3 As a result of the Guidelines for the National Policy of Indigenous School Education from 1993, Indigenous communities have the legal right to establish schools on their territory, with the legal expectation of "socio-economic-cultural autonomy of each people, contextualised in the recovery of their historical memory, the reaffirmation of their ethnic identity, and the study and appreciation of their own languages and sciences" (Brasil, 1993, p. 178).

4 The ability "to resist" among Indigenous people—who are questioned on their identity and "Indigenous purity" by non-Indigenous individuals—exists because they have expanded their subjectivity, refusing the imaginary notion "that Indians are all the same" (Krenak, 2020, p. 20). Resistance has been a 500-year-long practice. Indigenous peoples have been existing in the process of "re-existence" as an "insurgent practice that seeks to break with coloniality in the search to make possible other ways of acting, being, knowing and thinking, existing, feeling, co-existing and living-with" (Walsh, 2013, p. 19).

> Indigenous people see themselves represented and find the courage to take this pain seriously, . . . the main purpose is the wellbeing of the Indigenous individuals and a greater sensitivity towards the Indigenous body in the university.
>
> (Nunes, 2021)

Scarcity is mainly understood as and related to a lack of access to material resources. Little to no attention, however, has been given to exploring its emotional, symbolic, and representational dimensions. Indigenous peoples in Brazil are no strangers to material scarcity, from limited access to basic resources, healthcare, and schooling. In this chapter, I will focus, however, on the idea of "scarcity of empathy", which I understand as both an effect of racial and ethnic hierarchies, as an emotional resource and how this specific form of scarcity affects and dehumanises Indigenous academic experiences in Brazilian universities.

The story of Géssica and other Indigenous academics will illustrate how the scarcity of empathy intersects with epistemic violence and the ways in which Indigenous peoples experience its effects. I argue that epistemic violence leads not only to epistemicide,[5] silencing, and the continuity of sovereignty of a hegemonic epistemology but also to scarcity of empathy. Even though in higher education an abundance of diversity of knowledges can exist, there is, nevertheless, an emotional scarcity; through the authentic and painful experiences of Indigenous academics, the damages of epistemic violence are observed. Throughout this chapter, I propose an analytical, critical, and emotional exercise around the struggles faced by Indigenous people in Brazilian universities.

First, I will analyse how coloniality remains present and is felt in the Indigenous academic's experiences, as a process of silencing and the imposition of universal knowledge. Then, through the historical schooling process, I will present the contradictory national imaginary of what it is to "be Indigenous" and the violent repercussions of this imaginary. Next, I will highlight the abundance of diversity of knowledges as a healing process to coloniality and epistemic violence. Finally, I will expand on the notion of scarcity of empathy and how it is carried by the dehumanisation of a collective through epistemic violence.

The university is colonial

When talking to Indigenous academics such as Géssica, it became apparent that many of the challenges they encountered in universities across the country

5 Here, IIT is not being affirmed here that universities directly support genocide; however, universities have a central role in epistemic violence. The argument is that epistemic violence allows for its continuationity to happen under modern science's premise. Even though genocide may seem a strong extreme stance, ignoring it is a way of continuing perpetuating the silence of the Indigenous peoples and what is being said/experienced by them. This is an uncomfortable affirmation statement; I imagine it is much more uncomfortable for those who have to live it.

were directly related to what they referred to as "colonialism", "colonialist mentality", "imperialism", and "eurocentrism". They underline that there is no way to consider the social dynamics of Indigenous peoples from any standpoint without taking into account their relationships with non-Indigenous societies and the historically established conceptions formed throughout the colonial process and their socio-cultural diversity: language, identities, cultural practices, demography, social organisation, economy and politics, history, and knowledge production, among other aspects. As Linda T. Smith (2008) states, the Indigenous experience is framed by imperialism. It is difficult to discuss this experience "without understanding the complex ways in which the pursuit of knowledge is deeply embedded in the multiple layers of imperial and colonial practices" (Smith, 2008, p. 2). There is a direct connection between the invisibility of Indigenous knowledge and coloniality imposing a regime of knowledge, i.e. imposing a dominant worldview that silences any alternative ways of knowing and being.

Based on Quijano's (2007) conceptualisation of coloniality, not to be confused with the "colonial period", this relation is still present in many modern institutions, such as universities, as "in spite of the fact that political colonialism has been eliminated, the relationship between the European . . . culture, and the others, continues to be one of colonial domination" (Quijano, 2007, p. 169). Mignolo (2000, 2021) expands on this notion of the coloniality of knowledge, which implies the hegemony of Eurocentrism as an epistemological perspective as the main framework for domination in the world for the past 500 years. Coloniality has affected both "epistemology (the principles and assumptions that regulate knowing) and aesthetics (the principles and assumptions that regulate taste and subjectivity)" (2021, pp. x–xi), thus regulating both *knowing* and *sensing*.

For Géssica, "the settled imperialism [in universities] is unwilling to recognise or take responsibility for what has happened to us". In her experience, these educational institutions' power relations are unbalanced. The established

> colonial system and project needs to be deconstructed; [the Indigenous peoples] must access these spaces, develop spiritual strategies to ally with people inside higher education, and assert that we are here not to take anything away, but to exist as subjects of knowledge and not merely as objects of study.

The purpose becomes to use new tools, be it the written word or the academic degree, to make their voices heard, assuring that they will not be continuously silenced, erased, and killed. There is an awareness that being in university, having access to the written word, and holding a title create opportunities for dialogue; however, it is an effort that has to be done collectively; otherwise, there is a risk of being continuously "colonised" by the educational structure's rigidity, the annulment of diversity, and the disregard of peoples as collectives with different ways of life and ways of knowing.

Célia Xakriabá, a PhD candidate in anthropology and politician from the Xakriabá people, affirms[6] that there is still resistance within the university towards transformation because the "fight" of the Indigenous people is not only to be included but also to transform, produce knowledge, and challenge the university. However, the university "does not support our presence . . . and the decolonisation of the thought". This can be a very isolating and violent process, as Indigenous people are not only fighting for their rights but, above all, negotiating their "right to life and to live" according to their ways of knowing and being. Célia shares that she was the first Indigenous student to complete a master's degree at the University of Brasília (UnB). She is now the first Indigenous woman to begin a PhD at the Federal University of Minas Gerais (UFMG). However, she does not deem this a fact that makes her "more relevant and/or important". It instead leads her to question, "Why, in the 21st century, was it only in 2019 that the first Indigenous woman started a doctoral degree at the university, and why is there still no Indigenous faculty member within the university?" In her research,[7] she also asks if "when our bodies are made present in universities, are our ideas also being recognised?" This connects to the struggle to affirm themselves in the university's territory and the "territory of knowledge". It is not enough to consider Indigenous people in academia without recognising their potential in creating knowledge: "There is no process that does not generate knowledge. At this moment, too, we need to reclaim the university, the territory of thinking".

This "uniqueness" of being the only Indigenous person in a university, programme, or classroom does not place them in a position of relevance or importance, as we have seen Célia and Géssica testify. However, it isolates them, reinforcing racism, as they do not escape being seen as tokens. Indigenous peoples must be visible and be seen as "makers of knowledges". Even though Indigenous knowledges have played a crucial role in scientific foundations (Alcantara-Rodriguez, Françozo and Andel, 2019), they are rarely mentioned (Smith, 2008), and their knowers are historically erased. What is being brought to the forefront is the overall diversity of the country, more specifically of the Indigenous peoples that live in Brazil, and that this diversity is not reflected in universities, not only with their presence but also through their knowledges, histories, identities, spirituality, sensing, and emotioning, emphasising that the ongoing (historical) violence towards this minority has maintained them in a state of invisibility as peoples.

For Indigenous peoples, the expression of colonialism is not a historical and abstract concept; it is the annulment of their history and existence; it is

6 This was extracted from an online event celebrating the ten-year anniversary of the Master's programme in Sustainability with Traditional Peoples and Territories (MESPT) at the University of Brasília. The event, titled "Waters of Knowledge: Displacements and Confluences Between the Traditional and the Academic," was held on 25 March 2021 on the MESPT UnB YouTube channel.

7 Master's dissertation (Correa, 2018).

felt in their bodies, territories, and their right to live. In addition to its constant reforming, coloniality continues to destroy and spread its legacy of suffering and destruction (Smith, 2008). It is the power relation established in Brazilian society and with all its institutions (e.g., government, universities). Lima and Barroso (2018) highlight how much this relationship still defines the Indigenous demands and their relation to institutionalised education, where the colonial heritage is still present. Despite significant achievements in laws and policies, these have not untangled the effects of colonialism on the national imaginary or the lived experience within higher education. I was told by Indigenous academics[8] that universities should be places of diversity and must be prepared to accept it. Accepting their admission without considering what it means for their experience is not enough. The university must transform and recognise the knowledge diversity that exists in the country, as well as the authors of these knowledges (the "knowers"). The university is also an Indigenous territory and should be considered epistemically plural, where the contributions of Indigenous peoples can transform the violent relationship between the Brazilian nation and its Indigenous peoples.

The university can be violent

Until the 1970s, an explicit and pragmatic project guided Indigenous education in Brazil: catechesis and socialisation aimed at assimilating Indigenous peoples into Brazilian society. The state had never bothered to implement a specific education policy for Indigenous peoples that was not integration-oriented (Kahn and Franchetto, 1994). Since the colonial period, schools aimed to "civilise" through transmitting the knowledge and values of the "dominant society". With Indigenous peoples being seen as "incapable beings" and "savages" (Kawakami, 2019; Ramos, 1998), the nationalist project always aimed at overcoming social diversity and ethnic identity. Indigenous peoples were condemned "to spontaneous acculturation so that their socioeconomic evolution proceeds safely from sudden changes" (Brasil, 1967).

The perspective of Indigenous schooling as a "civilising" project for integrating Indigenous populations began to change subtly in the 1970s in Brazil, when Indigenous movements achieved the implementation of a proposal centred on their educational needs, respecting their culture and knowledges (Pérez, 2007, p. 232). The Indigenous mobilisation was founded on their right to be different and attempts to break with the integrationist tradition, seeking to overcome the traditional practice of paternalistic[9] tutelage that

8 Whom I had contacted during my PhD fieldwork from 2021 to 2022 in Brazil.

9 "Always treated in Brazilian legislation as a residual category, Indians were inserted in the 1916 civil code as objects of guardianship to last until they became adapted to national society" (Ramos, 1998, p. 18). Referred to commonly as the term *child*, the indigenous peoples were/are seen as relatively incapable and "need protection because they are ill equipped to live in modern society" (Ramos, 1998, p. 18).

had always marked the state's relationship with Indigenous peoples in Brazil. However, during the mid-1970s and early 1980s, political opening began to take effect, and popular actions intensified through the unification of social groups from diverse origins, with varied proposals and demands, all fighting against the authoritarian state. The Indigenous movement was among those that organised themselves for local, regional, and national efforts and strategies articulated between communities, peoples, and Indigenous organisations around a common agenda and interests (Baniwa, 2007), one of them being education.

The 1980s brought a turnaround in dealing with the Indigenous issue. The articulated Indigenous movement, supported by allies and motivated by the path built by civil organisations supporting Indigenous rights, managed to approve the rights of Indigenous peoples in the Federal Constitution of 1988 (Kahn and Franchetto, 1994; Grupioni, 2006; Rockwell and Gomes, 2009). The Constitution defined and guaranteed the Indigenous peoples' rights to maintain and reproduce their cultures and languages and to develop their school education under their principles, values, and forms of organisation and reproduction of knowledge (Menezes, 2005). However, the legislation itself often creates great contradictions since it idealises, at the same time, the complete recovery, affirmation, and reproduction of various Indigenous cultures and proposes to relate these with the language, values, and knowledge of the broader national society (Brasil, 1991; Grupioni, 2003; Menezes, 2005). As Ramos (1998) argues, the Constitution grants Indigenous peoples the "right to remain Indians"; however, it specifies them as a "special status", and such "status will eventually be suspended". The idea was, and still is, that inevitably the Indigenous cultures would/will eventually disappear (Kahn and Franchetto 1994), "the Indians will 'adapt' to Brazilian civilisation and hence stop being Indians" (Ramos, 1998, p. 19). If the rights guaranteed by law, such as those of Indigenous peoples in the 1988 Constitution, are not recognised by all members of society, the "deprivation of rights" or "social exclusion" leads to the form of disrespect that corresponds to the non-recognition of these peoples as equals in social interaction (Honneth, 2003). This circumstance tends to categorise individuals and collectives as morally and socially inferior, creating paths for establishing structural violence.

Over time, higher education became one of Indigenous peoples' demands at a national level; however, if the scenario of demands for Indigenous schooling led the Brazilian state to focus on policies for "differentiated education", the same did not happen with the access of Indigenous students to higher education. By disregarding the specific and differentiated trajectories of the Indigenous peoples, policies such as affirmative action could eventually erase their varied modes of existence, conserving the notion of civilising the Indigenous peoples—seen as deprived of knowledges and references—while maintaining an epistemic hierarchy that perpetuates oppression and allows epistemic violence to continue.

Epistemic violence is a structural mechanism through which a knowledge self-perceived as more accurate and valuable, asserts superiority over another, which it deems inferior and uncertain. It can be understood as a form of symbolic power exercise of an individual, group, or nation over another through a dominant knowledge to make this "other" invisible (Spivak, 2010), establishing a specific worldview to impose itself on others, where the alternative knowledges become "peripheral" and often considered the object of study within modern science or to complement modern scientific arguments. As Martins-Baniwa (2012, p. 123) argues, Indigenous productions in universities often serve "to trigger reflections or to motivate interpretive possibilities but lack value for the academy . . . Indigenous knowledges circulate in academic spaces, which are worthwhile [for academia] to stimulate reflections but have no scientific value".

Being active online after completing her undergraduate was a way for Géssica to navigate the painful feelings that had once silenced her within the university. She recalls that she often remained quite because she "didn't want to be inconvenient", and the silencing of "people like us" within academic spaces, she explains, allows for fear and pain to perpetuate. According to her, keeping the "colonial imagination" alive reaffirms the belief that Indigenous knowledge is not valid, that "what we have to say is considered wrong, while Western knowledge is right".[10] She reflects on how power is still centralised in a singular way of knowing the world, leaving "minorities like us" excluded from these spaces. "Because with us in the university, we will say things that many people don't want to hear".

The "colonial imagination" reflects the analyses of anthropologist Alcida Ramos (1998) in the term *Indigenism*[11] as a notion that is sprawled in the nation's fabric and that leads to silencing of any other way of being and knowing, shaping both education and institutionalised academic knowledge. The national imaginary of *Indigenism* takes many forms, one being the notion of "child" as referencing the Indigenous peoples and their knowledge as "infantile", naïve, sensorial, and bodily. The narrative is that children depend on adults to obtain knowledge, so the "adults"—those in positions of academic

10 The use of Western and/or Eurocentric knowledge responds to the specific characteristics of the consolidation of academic institutions in Brazil, which were based on the European scientific and educational modern institutions, reproducing exclusively the Eurocentric model of knowledge developed in the West in the modern period (De Carvalho and Flórez-Flórez, 2014).

11 *Indigenism* is a concept that Alcida Ramos conceives as "the result of many overlapping factors that history has compounded" to explain "the vast realm of both popular and learned imaginary among the national population onto which are carved the many faces of the Indian" (Ramos, 1998, p. 5), a set of ideas and ideals that feeds the minds of Brazilians as a result "of the contradiction between certain pride in the countries multiethnicity and the aspiration for national homogeneity" (Ramos, 1998, p. 3).

authority—see no relevance in the latter's knowledge (Ramos, 1998). Because the Indigenous peoples are referenced as innocent and incomplete, it brings them closer to the usual idea one has of Western children. However, once Indigenous individuals engage in Western knowledge, there is "a certain widespread common understanding says they are no longer Indians" (Ramos, 1998, p. 23). As Ramos (1998) states, from "this point of view Indians as Indians are by definition in a permanent state of ignorance, in need of learning from civilised teachers" (Ramos, 1998, p. 23), but if they access Western knowledge they are considered no longer "Indians", which puts them in a category that is forever invisible to the national society.

"Being Indigenous" in Brazil under this tension between Indigenous existence and the national imaginary of modernity has many challenges which, unfortunately, categorise the Indigenous peoples in an impossible status of temporality and identity. In praxis, these categories take away the many layers of their experiences that are violently intertwined to form a controlled image of what is to be Indigenous under the national quest for development, civility, and progress. The Indigenous peoples are violently controlled in the quest for Brazil to become a civilised nation with its "primitives" silenced, eliminated, or assimilated. However, what Géssica and other Indigenous academics emphasise is that this interweaving is pulled to such tension that it not only breaks under pressure but is painfully maintained and entertained for the national desire to be, in fact, a modern nation, reflecting European models, including having Eurocentric universities. That is why silencing, negating, and erasing the existence of Indigenous peoples, for example, in a state such as Paraná, elevates its European proximity and history to the forefront, alleviating the anxiety among Brazil's elite about being the developed country that was promised in the 1950s.[12] The Indigenous people's existence, challenges, and pain are referred to as a distant past and distances them from peoples of the present that, in fact, carry rights, emotions, knowledges, and cultures.

Illness of the spirit

Laura is Parintintin, from an Indigenous people located in the state of Amazonas. Laura left her village at a young age to continue her studies. When she moved to Porto Velho (the capital of Rondônia state), she struggled with racism and prejudice, encountering violence towards Indigenous peoples for the first time. As a result, Laura sought a city with low unemployment, a low

12 The 1950s in Brazil was a period in which the discourse around national development was placed on the agenda, especially in the second half of the decade. The idea that fuelled the national imaginary reinforced the notion that progress required a transformation of the present to build an alternative future (more developed). The narrative and the meanings associated with this idea represent "an imaginary solution to the tensions, conflicts and contradictions" (Chauí, 2003) faced by Brazilian society in relation to the dilemmas and challenges of economic, political, and institutional modernisation.

illiteracy rate, and high quality of life to escape the poverty and violence that Indigenous people commonly encounter in large urban centres. In Florianópolis, the state capital of Santa Catarina, she began her undergraduate studies in Social Sciences at the Federal University of Santa Catarina (UFSC) in the south of the country.

At the beginning of her degree, Laura was so excited to be in the university that it felt "surreal"; she had never imagined reaching this position. When she recounted this to me, Laura was overwhelmed with emotions of happiness and pride, just remembering the moment she saw her name on the approval list. However, like a "shock" of reality, a "cultural, structural, socioeconomic shock", during her first semester, Laura felt "stupid"; it was like the teachers were not speaking the same language as her. When she went on to read the assigned texts, nothing made sense, and she failed all her classes. There was no support system for Indigenous students; "today there is some support, and we try to help each other", she told me. Laura was also experienced discrimination in class, both from colleagues and staff. A professor once told her that the way she spoke "had to be changed because now you are in academia, in the university you cannot speak that way". From that moment onwards, she has never participated in another group activity: "I always did it alone". When I asked if this continues now that more Indigenous students were entering the university each year, she said that nothing had changed: "we now have 230 Indigenous students,[13] and they share the same stories".

For Laura, affirmative action in universities is a policy people in the universities never truly wanted. The "elite did not want it; they were opposed to it . . . our presence was not in their interest, the Indigenous, the blacks, and the poor". Although it is a law, universities are not concerned with "adapting to these new realities". The policy does not align with minorities' realities, as they need to adapt to the university, rather than the other way around. They are "left behind again" and denied their particularities of being, living, and knowing. As Laura explains, it is by their own efforts the Indigenous students collectively organise to achieve something that guarantees a better university experience. Still, it feels like a never-ending battle for access to food, accommodation, and transport, just to name a few. Besides dealing with racism and constant "delegitimisation of our ethnic identity", Laura says that as Indigenous, they constantly hear people saying they are no longer "Indians" because now they live in the cities and speak Portuguese. She refers to it as "the same old stereotype". It is, she says, "extremely tiring" to have to constantly reaffirm their ethnic identity and deal with the constant questioning of their presence at university.

These battles take a toll on these academics, their bodies, and their spirits. As Lidiane Kariri, a postgraduate in social anthropology from the Kariri people

13 The number of Indigenous students who matriculated in the Federal University of Santa Catarina, at the time we spoke, in May 2022.

located in the northeast region of the country, shares during an online event.[14] Racism and the violent colonial process cause a feeling of "illness of the spirit" and overall illness. She says that one way of continuing her degree was by "going back home to strengthen spiritually. I needed to do this constantly during my master's and PhD". Lidiane explains that one way of dealing with "racism daily" is by supporting other Indigenous colleagues, as it is common to see many getting ill along the way. She still considers that there is a long way for the university to become a democratic space; it is not enough to have "inclusion", but mostly that the diversity of Indigenous knowledge and knowers is recognised.

The university can be diverse

Edgar is Xakriabá, a people from the north of Minas Gerais, a state in the country's southeast region. Minas Gerais is known in Brazil for its colonial architecture, arts, and historical cities from when the Portuguese crown explored gold. The Indigenous are once again left to the confinements of historical past. However, Edgar comes from a Xakriabá lineage of strong identity, and he is sensitive to the vitality of the Indigenous in the country today, as well as in the past. Also Edgar is from a generation of Xakriabá children who attended Xakriabá schools and had Xakriabá teachers, only moving to Belo Horizonte (the state capital) when he started his undergraduate degree in Social Sciences at the Federal University of Minas Gerais (UFMG). Edgar completed his degree through a programme called *Licenciatura Intercultural Indígena* (Indigenous Intercultural Degree)[15] at UFMG, a course focused on training Indigenous teachers, with a combination of classes offered at the university and the Indigenous community. Edgar tells me he knows of the importance of this programme and that, "fortunately", he entered university through it, which was "already thinking of ways to break the structural barriers of the university".

It is a programme that has a "differentiated approach to education" as a way of "slowly breaking the barriers of the rigid university structure, which is not an easy task". He notes that it "is a pioneer programme, in applying the courses to the many knowledges fields", and values and recognises the importance of

14 A roundtable on "Ancestral Dialogues: The Importance of Including Other Knowledge Within the University" was promoted by the Federal University of Cariri in the state of Ceará on 1 June 2021. It had the participation of other Indigenous academics from different regions of the country, where they discussed the dialogue between the knowledge produced in academia and that produced in Indigenous territories.

15 The course aims to promote the training of Indigenous teachers with practical, theoretical, and methodological preparation to work in schools in Indigenous communities. The course varies from one university to another, respecting the different ethnic groups and their particularities, such as language, culture, knowledges, and so on. What is similar is the pedagogical framework: the course lasts four years, with Indigenous students spending some time in the community and some time at the university.

"variety of knowledge", a variety that can only exist with the presence of Indigenous people (and other minorities) in the university. During our conversation in 2021, Edgar told me that the Xakriabá value their presence in the universities not only because they "gain by being in the university, but the university gains from Indigenous presence". Their presence carries their territories[16] and knowledges, and this abundance in the university can potentially "provoke" the university as an institution and the people at these universities "who are prejudiced and often racist against Indigenous people". To exemplify the importance of exposure to diversity in the university, Célia Xakriabá (who is Edgar's sister) uses the image of a colourful meal: "many people say a healthy meal is a colourful one, but the same is not said about knowledge and society". In Brazil, it is customary to say a good meal is varied in colour, meaning it is healthy and made up of all the necessary nutrients. Célia uses this example to convey the importance of diversity not only in a meal but in thought, where colourful systems of knowledge are much healthier than a monochromatic system. She presents the idea of monoculture as "social blindness, a monocular vision". She continues by saying that "all monoculture kills, such as the monoculture of the mind. All monoculture kills; it kills the thought and bodies; it tries to colonise our lands, ways of thinking, and territories".

The effort seems to be about the Indigenous gaining recognition of their knowledges and epistemologies, and the diversity that this entails. Edgar states, however, that the Indigenous "do not want one knowledge system to overcome another; that is already what Western knowledge does to ours; we want dialogue between worlds". There must be "dialogue across the boundaries of oppositions" (Smith, 2008, p. 39), not a rejection of Western knowledge; it means "affirmation, validation, valorisation and promotion of indigenous knowledge" (Baniwa, 2019). The recognition of Indigenous knowledges is crucial to the process of dehegemonisation, in their own terms, by relying on their epistemic framework and not exclusively on the colonisers. There must be epistemological independence beyond political independence to construct knowledge outside "Anglo-European frameworks" (Gegeo, 2001, p. 182). For Bergamaschi, Doebber and Brito (2018), thus, the Indigenous presence in higher education precisely offers possibilities for self-reflection about the pedagogic practices of the higher education institution and its social role.

Their presence can provoke a reflection on "alternative knowledge systems" in the academy and destabilise the "Eurocentric matrix of knowledge production, validation and circulation" (Kawakami, 2019, p. 12), a knowledge system that assumes an individual and homogeneous society faces the challenge of dealing with the concept of peoples, that is, with "collectives that wish to remain culturally differentiated" (Lima, 2007, p. 268). The Indigenous

16 The cosmology of their territories is carried by their bodies wherever they are present. It goes beyond the geographical aspect and represents their ways of being, living, knowing, and relating to nature, spirituality, and the non-human world.

academics, representatives of peoples with differentiated social and historical knowledge, who now enter spaces historically identified with the interests of colonial elites and, therefore, anti-Indigenous in their conception, may have different impacts on the university scenario (Brand and Nascimento, 2010). The tendency with the entry of more Indigenous students, according to Baniwa (2018), is to force a revision of classic epistemological and methodological paradigms to account for these new academics who have "other epistemological, philosophical, cosmological, sociocultural, and spiritual references" (Baniwa, 2018, p. 182).

Edgar perceives history continues to be "told through the white people, the Western and Eurocentric perspective, . . . killing, in fact, a diversity of peoples and knowledges" while universities "lack this diversity". This diversity can be a healing process to "colonial wounds" inflicted in all areas of lived experience. A healing process that can not only heal the pain endured by the Indigenous peoples but also the wounds of all that fall ill emotionally and spiritually due to the mono-epistemic approach of knowledge. Knowledge should not create illness or kill; on the contrary, it should be attributed to life and a healthy coexistence.

Scarcity of empathy and the experience of Indigenous scholars in Brazil

Violence manifests in many forms. One form that is not disconnected from other forms of violence is epistemic violence inflicted epistemically (based on knowing, knowledge), although its effects can transform peoples sensing, believing, and emotioning (Mignolo, 2021). I tried to direct a critical reflection through the experience of Indigenous academics in Brazil, where epistemic violence is still present in some forms and felt by Indigenous academics. In part, the colonial process led to the establishment of epistemic violence, to the point where it is not even considered a violent act, meaning the consequences are not seen as harsh by outsiders, those that do not have to deal with and feel it. These are what Mignolo (2021) named as "colonial wounds" that can be "inflicted in a wide array of harm beyond the physical and emotional pain" epistemically. Another harm of epistemic violence, which not only an individual can experience but also collectives, is epistemic dehumanisation, which justifies "violence and physical wounds. . . If you are labelled a terrorist, an epistemic/aesthesic wound is inflicted on you, opening the gates to all kinds of physical violence by this name" (Mignolo, 2021, pp. 9–10). That is, those who are not recognised as fully humans. With that, the permission for violence towards a group perceived as inferior, primitive, and savage is much greater.

This chapter focused more specifically on violence towards Indigenous knowledges and peoples in universities. Epistemic violence that imposes on ways of knowing, sensing, emotioning, and believing, in a clear manifestation of epistemic inequality, where Indigenous knowledge is undermined for its alleged lack of scientific rigour or punished for being superstitious/spiritual and for being regarded as an object of Western science, but not recognised in the same value. This violence, perpetrated through education, science, technology, and development projects, has had multiple consequences, one of them being what I called in the title of this chapter "silencing" in universities in Brazil, which in turn perpetuates pain and illness.

The result of the long process of epistemic violence maintained by coloniality is what I tried to illustrate by sharing the Indigenous academic experience. This is continuously granted because of what I named scarcity of empathy, a dehumanisation towards a collective that affects people's experiences individually. Whether it be through racism, silencing, or epistemicide, all of them clearly have visible and tangible effects. Through coloniality that still perpetuates in all sectors of societies, specifically in Brazil, a notion of a hegemonic epistemology painfully forces its tentacles, exterminating and silencing experiences and knowledges that diverge from the "Eurocentric knowledge". It leads to "both genocide and epistemicide, thus configuring epistemic violence . . . And this denial of one part of humanity is sacrificial, insofar as it constitutes the condition for the other part of humanity to assert itself as universal" (Santos, 2007, p. 76). Be it called universal, civilised, or developed, it permits the annulment of any "other humanity" that diverges from the so-called universal. Thus, the imaginary created during colonialism/modernity results in epistemological mutilation from the hegemonic domination of Eurocentric thought, progressively restricting the diversity of knowledge and establishing "abyssal lines between them" (Santos and Meneses, 2010). This allows for an inability to access/recognise the abundance of diversity of ways of knowing and the diversity of ways of being.

Célia Xakriabá, I think, sums up perfectly when she says that this imposed control/violence disguised by the discourse of state protection becomes a contradictory one, as it ends up revealing the absence of action by the Brazilian state on what really matters to the Indigenous peoples, especially when it comes to access of their rights, such as access to their own territory and public policies. The political structure of control violates the right to, as Célia puts it, "our own territories, but also our minds, ancestral expressions, and identity", resulting in silencing and leading to the "illness of the spirit". She adds that once you remove their right to express their identities and ways of life, you take away their community life, and "community life is like food for us. When we are denied land, it is like a weapon that exterminates our people. Culture feeds the soul, agriculture feeds the body, community feeds the well-lived life".

Part of the emotional exercise that I proposed through the experience of the Indigenous academics is to connect the still present epistemic violence to the emotional consequences it has on both the Indigenous and the non-Indigenous people of the country. One emotional consequence is that of scarcity of empathy. Scarcity generally refers to limited human and non-human resources, and in economics, it is related to something quantifiable, where demand for a good exceeds its supply. To align empathy to a resource is quite a leap, on the one hand, because empathy is hardly quantifiable. On the other hand, empathy has had a range of definitions since it was coined more than a century ago (Cuff et al., 2016).

Interestingly, when first introduced, empathy "constituted a modality of knowledge *sui generis*", being in part "knowledge of others" (Zahavi, 2017, p. 34). Even though there is still no well-defined notion of empathy, more specifically in the field of psychology, Cuff et al. (2016) list more than 40 definitions, where the recurring aspect in all of them being a variation of the experience of an other/another individual emotional state. Regardless of the scientific definition that is agreed upon, empathy is directed precisely towards other experiences that are recognised to have emotions and feelings. Suppose a group and/or individual is not regarded as equally human and has been destitute of humanity, no number of definitions or academic agreement will relieve the experience of those suffering from scarcity of empathy.

For the purpose of expanding the notion of scarcity and empathy, I present this provocation as a challenge to consider scarcity not as a concept that signifies a general condition but as a temporal characteristic of scarcity or lack of immaterial resources. As for empathy, even though there is no firm agreement on its definition, it is generally understood as an emotional experience directed towards the other/another. While empathy is hard to quantify, it is qualifiable through the words and experiences of those on the margin of such emotion, such as academics like Géssica, Edgar, Laura, Lidiane, and Célia, to name a few. As a collective, they have been historically diminished, erased, and silenced, feeling and living with the effects of scarcity of a resource that is not cultivated towards them. This has real and tangible consequences for their lives.

References

Alcantara-Rodriguez, M., Françozo, M. and Andel, T. V. (2019). Plant Knowledge in the Historia Naturalis Brasiliae (1648): Retentions of Seventeenth-Century Plant Use in Brazil. *Economic Botany*, XX(X), pp. 1–15.

Baniwa, G. L. (2007). Movimentos e políticas indígenas no Brasil contemporâneo. *Tellus*, 7(12), pp. 127–146.

Baniwa, G. L. (2018). Educação superior e as contribuições do Projeto Trilhas de Conhecimento. In: A. C. S. Lima and M. M. Barroso, eds., *O projeto trilhas de conhecimentos e o ensino superior de indígenas no Brasil: Uma experiência de fomento e investigação para ações afirmativas*. Rio de Janeiro: E-Papers.

Baniwa, G. L. (2019). Antropologia colonial no caminho da Antropologia Indígena. *Revista do PPGCS—UFRB—Novos Olhares Sociais*, 2(1), pp. 22–40.

Bergamaschi, M. A., Doebber, M. B. and Brito, P. O. (2018). Estudantes indígenas em universidades brasileiras: Um estudo das políticas de acesso e permanência. *Revista Brasileira Estudos Pedagógicos*, 99(251), pp. 37–53.

Brand, A. J. and Nascimento, A. C. (2010). La construcción escolar de la educación intercultural: Desde la educación infantil hasta la educación superior. In: *Anales*. Congreso Internacional en la Red sobre Interculturalidad y Educación. Cidade do México: Editora da Universidad Autónoma Metropolitana—Iztapalapa, pp. 1–15.

Brasil. (1967). *Lei n. 5.371/1967*. Brasília: Presidência da República.
Brasil. Ministério da Educação. (1993). Diretrizes para a política nacional de educação escolar indígena. *Em Aberto*, 14(63), pp. 176–187.
Brasil. (1991). *Lei n. 8.213/1991*. Brasília: Presidência da República.
Brasil. (2012). *Lei n. 12.711/2012*. Brasília: Presidência da República.
Carvalho, J. J. D. and Flórez-Flórez, J. (2014). The Meeting of Knowledges: A Project for the Decolonization of Universities in Latin America. *Postcolonial Studies*, 17(2), pp. 122–139. https://doi.org/10.1080/13688790.2014.966411.
Chauí, M. (2003). A universidade pública sob nova perspectiva. *Revista Brasileira de Educação*, [online] 24, pp. 5–15. https://doi.org/10.1590/s1413-24782003000300002.
Correa, C. N. (2018). *O barro, o genipapo e o giz no fazer epistemológico de autoria Xakriabá: Reativação da Memória por uma educação territorializada*. Master Lever. Universidade de Brasília.
Cuff, B., Brown, S. J., Taylor, L. and Howat, D. (2016). Empathy: A Review of the Concept. *Emotion Review*, [online] 8(2). https://doi.org/10.1177/1754073914558466.
Gegeo, D. W. (2001). (Re)visioning Knowledge Transformation in the Pacific: A Response to Subramani's 'The Oceanic Imaginary'. *The Contemporary Pacific*, 13(1), pp. 123–198.
Grupioni, L. D. B. (2003). Experiências e Desafios na Formação de Professores Indígenas no Brasil. *Em aberto*, 20(76), pp. 13–18.
Grupioni, L. D. B. (2006). *Formação de professores indígenas: Repensando trajetórias*. Brasília: Ministério da Educação, Secretaria de Educação Continuada, Alfabetização e Diversidade.
Honneth, A. (2003). *Luta por Reconhecimento: A gramática moral dos conflitos sociais*. São Paulo: Ed. 34.
Kahn, M. and Franchetto, B. (1994). Educação Indígena no Brasil: Conquistas e desafios. *Em Aberto*, 14(63), pp. 5–9.
Kawakami, É. A. (2019). Currículo, ruídos e contestações: Os povos indígenas na universidade. *Revista Brasileira de Educação*, 24, pp. 1–18.
Kilomba, G. (2010). *Plantation Memories: Episodes of Everyday Racism*. 2nd ed. Münster: Unrast-Verlag.
Krenak, A. (2020). *Ideas to Postpone the End of the World*. Toronto: Anansi International.
Lima, A. C. S. (2007). Educacao Superior para indígenas no Brasil sobre cotas e algo mais. In: *Seminário Formação Jurídica e Povos indígenas Desafios para uma educação superior*. Belém: LACED.
Lima, A. C. S. and Barroso, M. (2018). Ações afirmativas no ensino superior e povos indígenas no Brasil: Uma trajetória de trabalho. *Horizontes Antropológicos*, 24(50), pp. 377–448.
Martins-Baniwa, E. (2012). Educación superior y pueblos indígenas: Avances y desafíos ¿conmemoración o reflexión? *ISEES: Inclusión Social y Equidad en la Educación Superior*, 10, pp. 115–130.
Menezes, G. H. (2005). Conhecimento e poder: Dilemas e contradições. *Revista de Estudos e Pesquisas*, 2(2), pp. 123–144.
Mignolo, W. D. (2000). *Local Histories/Global Designs: Coloniality, Subaltern Knowledges, and Border Thinking*. Princeton: Princeton University Press.
Mignolo, W. D. (2021). *The Politics of Decolonial Investigations*. Durham: Duke University Press.
Nunes, G. (2021). *Fieldwork Conversation*, 15 October. Unpublished interview.
Pérez, A. L. (2007). Escola indígena: Uma reflexão sobre seus fundamentos teóricos, ideológicos e políticos. *Perspectiva*, 25(1), pp. 227–244.
Quijano, A. (2007). Coloniality and Modernity/Rationality. *Cultural Studies*, 21(2–3), pp. 168–178. https://doi.org/10.1080/09502380601164353.
Ramos, A. R. (1998). *Indigenism: Ethnic Politics in Brazil*. Madison, WI: University of Wisconsin Press.

Rockwell, E. and Gomes, A. M. R. (2009). Introduction to the Special Issue: Rethinking Indigenous Education from a Latin American Perspective. *Anthropology & Education Quarterly*, 40(2), pp. 97–109.

Santos, B. D. S. (2007). Para além do pensamento abissal: Das linhas globais a uma ecologia de saberes. *Novos Estudos—CEBRAP*, 79, pp. 71–94. https://doi.org/10.1590/s0101-33002007000300004.

Santos, B. D. S. and Meneses, M. P. (2010). *Epistemologias do Sul*. São Paulo: Editora Cortez.

Smith, L. T. (2008). *Decolonizing Methodologies: Research and Indigenous Peoples*. London: Zed.

Spivak, G. (2010). *Pode o Subalterno Falar?* Belo Horizonte: Editora UFMG.

Walsh, C. (2013). *Pedagogías decoloniales: Prácticas insurgentes de resistir, (re)existir y (re)vivir. Tomo I*. Quito-Ecuador: Ediciones Abya-Yala.

Zahavi, D. (2017). Phenomenology, Empathy, and Mindreading. In: H. L. Maibom, ed., *The Routledge Handbook of Philosophy of Empathy* (pp. 33–43). Routledge/Taylor & Francis Group.

10 "A society only as wealthy as its most deprived"

Rita Izsák-Ndiaye

Despite the progress made in establishing international binding treaties codifying equality in dignity and rights, we continue living in a world where constructed racial hierarchies between people and nations define status, life opportunities, and access to resources, money, time, health, education, support networks, or power. Scarcity for minorities, migrants, and other vulnerable groups with distinct identities comes in many forms, and this book pays testament to its various manifestations. Roma, Mexican migrants, indigenous peoples, rural communities, or international students in a foreign country, despite having very different histories and environments, all find themselves in uncertain scenarios fighting intergenerational injustices, trauma, and deprivation.

Growing up in the 1980s in a small Hungarian town, I knew my family had a modest standard of living, but I never associated it with scarcity. Most kids around me shared the same experiences; we lived in the same concrete-panelled block building, had one pair of good shoes at a time, and our parents queued up to buy bananas if they were available. Only later in life, especially at law school, did I meet others from higher social classes and realise a marked difference in living standards. Interestingly, my major discovery was not that I had less money (which became apparent quickly) but that I needed certain non-material assets that others seemed to have in abundance. For example, others could advance their studies with less effort and more rapidly because they always seemed to have the phone number of a court judge, police chief, or law professor who could answer their research questions and help them deliver better papers. They could also easily secure internships at famous law firms because they had relatives or family friends who had connections and facilitated their access. Additionally, they had more time to study because they never had to work several jobs to pay their school fees and survive in the capital, Budapest, alone, like I did. So, scarcity for me translated into less study time, weaker support networks, or reduced access to opportunities, among others.

This book makes a right and desired shift from material to immaterial perspectives to allow us to explore emotional, socio-psychological, and representational scarcity structures. It also reminds us that people are not only—or

DOI: 10.4324/9781032661780-11

sometimes not at all—the story others tell about them. I have vivid memories of my Romani mother dutifully cleaning our home daily, scrubbing our clothes and shoes until they shone, and committing to extra hours at work so we do not fit into the typical "dirty, lazy Gypsy" narrative and get treated accordingly. She is among the millions of Roma trying to challenge collective negative perceptions. As Antonio Montañés Jiménez writes in his chapter, his Gitano interlocutor and co-author Gory also gently refused to focus on damage-centred approaches and to engage with overarching negative frameworks. This is indeed an objective that we, Roma rights and human rights advocates, have tried to achieve for decades: to remove Roma and other minority communities from a narrow poverty and burden paradigm and portray them as active and important contributors to societies, cultures, and prosperity of nations.

The COVID-19 pandemic affected us profoundly in countless ways. Importantly, it made scarcity saliently present. Globally, the idea of running out of toilet paper, bottled water, or canned food kept millions in agony, although, ironically, shortages were often only observed after widespread stockpiling as the onset of COVID-19 quickly led to extreme buying in the United States, with up to an 845 per cent increase in household consumption (Schumacher and Micheli, 2024). However, material scarcity was only one aspect of pandemic-induced scarcities. As Faith Mkwananzi, Patience Mukwambo, Winter Seshoka and Nomzingisi Notenga wrote, South African universities' responses to COVID-19 also created a specific kind of scarcity that affected students' well-being where because of emerging conditions of material scarcity, an equally harmful emotional scarcity ensued for international students.

Many women faced scarcity and a vacuum of support networks during the pandemic. A UN study looking at the impact of the pandemic on minority communities found that a disproportionate number of essential workers were migrants and minorities, and that closures of schools and day-care centres meant that minority women often faced disproportionate childcare responsibilities (OHCHR, 2020). The pandemic also drew attention to caregivers and triggered research on care and support provisions. A UN resolution highlighted how unpaid care work creates and perpetuates inequalities, contributes to the perpetuation of the feminisation of poverty, and hinders gender equality, especially for women and girls in vulnerable situations, such as migrant women, rural women, indigenous women, women of African descent, refugee women, and others (OHCHR, 2020). Lacking financial resources, support networks, relevant information, access to services, language skills, or transportation, women from these communities often find themselves in precarious situations when they become unpaid caregivers of children, elderly, sick, or disabled persons, all of which often further their isolation. Research in Brazil found that Black women are more likely to be engaged in low-paid or unpaid care work and are less likely to have help outside of the family than white women. Lack of care support results in work overload and social isolation, which have negative health impacts and erode their quality of life

(MRG, 2023). Women who struggle to provide for their children and families often need to rely on external assistance, as shown in Ana P. Gutiérrez Garza's chapter about Mexican migrants. Mexican migrants in Tulsa, Oklahoma, escaped from poverty and scarcity in Mexico to find an abundance of resources offered by philanthropic organisations that oversee helping people experiencing poverty. However, as she points out, it is imperative to reveal the complex ethical-moral terrains in which such programs and policies are played out and assess how they are at odds with historically and culturally produced ethics of the raced poor by understanding their agency, rationalities, and moral orders of the factors that keep them poor.

Indeed, the dominant colonial, white, ethnocentric Western lens over distinct minority and migrant communities and/or over the Global South pushes dangerous narratives, creating notions of superiority and inferiority, both at national and global levels. In several country contexts, bias and racism led to social stratification, maintaining structures and systems of inter-generational exclusion and marginalisation, pushing certain population groups to the periphery of societies, subjecting them to a permanent scarcity of resources, opportunities, and power. Tragically, States are often reluctant to change the status quo, as majority communities may benefit from the perceived lower status of groups who may be discriminated against based on work and descent and provide much-needed cheap or free labour. Hate speech against minority and migrant communities often remains unpunished, which fuels tensions and is used to justify violent acts. In many countries, three-quarters or more of the victims of online hate speech are members of minority groups, and women belonging to these groups are disproportionately targeted (OHCHR, 2021).

Through the case examples presented in this book, we understand better how States can contribute to keeping communities in inferior positions and, hence, subject to various types of permanent scarcities. As Kyriaki Topidi explained in her chapter, under the weight of scarcity the Nigerian State has provided compensation to local communities in the Niger Delta region. However, dozens of ethnic groups continued to live in extreme poverty. As she pointed out, ongoing generational conflict and poverty are deeply rooted in colonialism and the failure of the Nigerian government to compel oil multinationals to engage in environmental protection. Similarly, Arpan Roy highlighted how the long-term consequences of systems and structures of dispossession in the Middle East became inscribed in the Romani consciousness, with each generation reproducing material conditions of scarcity.

Racism, racial discrimination, and the absence of inclusivity are the fate of people at the national level but at a global level, too, subjugating millions to diminished development opportunities. The 2030 Agenda for Sustainable Development and its 17 specific goals (SDGs), adopted by UN Member States in 2015, is an urgent call for action to end poverty and other deprivations, together with strategies that improve health and education, reduce inequality, and spur economic growth while tackling climate change. However, progress is slow and was significantly halted by the global COVID-19 pandemic, a historical episode in which an additional 119–124 million people were pushed back into poverty in 2020. Progress on more than 50 per cent of targets of the SDGs is weak and insufficient, and on 30 per cent of them, progress has stalled or reversed. These include key targets of poverty, hunger, and climate change (SDG, 2023). The latest Multidimensional Poverty Index of 2024 found that across 112 countries and 6.3 billion people, 1.1 billion (18.3 per cent) live in acute multidimensional poverty, considering their access to food, water, sanitation, cooking fuel, education, and other indicators (GMPI, 2024). More than 83 per cent of the world's multidimensionally poor people live in sub-Saharan Africa and South Asia. It is not by accident that countries in the Global South face the biggest challenges in achieving the SDGs. A 2022 report by the UN Special Rapporteur on contemporary forms of racism, racial discrimination, xenophobia, and related intolerance highlighted that the 2030 Agenda has great potential to advance the principles of racial equality and non-discrimination. However, it is "characterised by a shallow commitment to racial justice and equality and fails adequately to address the systemic racism and xenophobia that remain barriers to the attainment of the Sustainable Development Goals". She pointed out that the global development framework and institutional setup preserves colonial injustice, perpetuates the domination of powerful nations over peoples and territories that were subject to historical colonial extraction, and preserves structural racial discrimination within nations (OHCHR, 2022a). Civil society and academic reports also have expressed criticism. Although the SDG framework called for transformative development, it seems to be a continuation of business as usual, as it "remained weak in addressing structural obstacles and fails to explicitly take into account structural inequalities and power distributions between or within countries" (Fisher and Fukuda-Parr, 2019). As a matter of fact, the SDGs, targets, and indicators remain "disturbingly silent about the eradication of systemic racism and racial and ethnic discrimination which constitute global barriers to human development and the fulfilment of human rights throughout the lifespan" (SPSSI, 2020). A global consultation on structural racism and the aid system by Peace Direct and its partners concluded that current practices and attitudes, such as the "White saviour" ideology, reinforce colonial dynamics and beliefs. They found that structural racism benefits organisations in the Global North and those from the Global South who know how to play the system. Programmes and research designs are rooted in Western values and knowledge systems, meaning that many programmes inadvertently create a standard based on the West that communities in the Global South are required to meet (Peace Direct, 2021).

In recent years, a growing number of countries of the Global South came forward with demands to address historical injustices and reform Bretton Woods establishments. In their "10 Point Plan for Reparatory Justice", the Caribbean Community (CARICOM), a collective of 21 countries, reminded that European governments were owners and traders of enslaved Africans who instructed genocidal actions upon indigenous communities and created the legal, financial and fiscal policies necessary for the enslavement of Africans. However, as CARICOM stressed, European governments refused to acknowledge such crimes or to compensate victims and their descendants and imposed racial apartheid and designed policies to perpetuate suffering upon the emancipated and survivors of genocide. Therefore, CARICOM called for a full formal apology for slavery, a repatriation program for those who wish to return, an Indigenous Peoples Development Program, the creation of cultural institutions, the eradication of illiteracy, and debt cancellation, among others. The 2023 World Bank Group and International Monetary Fund (IMF) annual meetings took place in Marrakech, Morocco, marking 50 years since they were last held in Africa. It became clear to the gathered leaders, economists, and representatives that the Bretton Woods institutions—the IMF and the World Bank—must undergo structural changes to remain relevant and legitimate in a geopolitically charged environment. It was concluded that recent IMF reviews of quotas and the World Bank's capital increases were insufficient in adapting to economic and geopolitical shifts. Challenges of representation seem to be further underpinned by "geopolitical considerations, entrenched path-dependencies, and a tug-of-war between the desire to maintain historical precedence and the urgency to democratise institutional representation" (Nordquist and Christoph, 2024). Calls were made for a democratised governance structure, emphasising the need to reevaluate quota allocations and diversify leadership roles (Nordquist and Christoph, 2024).

Fair representation, inclusive decision-making, and local ownership can only be achieved if institutions are ready to do the necessary soul-searching and understand the existing racial bias that shapes their operation and approaches. According to the Organisation for Economic Co-operation and Development, several countries have carried out reviews on racism in the development sector, in some cases making direct links with power structures and paternalism that are the legacies of colonialism and taking steps to redress the balance (OECD, 2023). Similarly, a UK Parliament report concluded that racism manifests in decisions around whose expertise is valued across the global aid sector (International Development Committee, 2022). Due to a belief that these institutions represent the gold standard, local partners must often adapt to their way of working. Racist attitudes also play out in dominant narratives stating that local organisations are "high risk" and need "capacity building". The same report found that "the manner in which the cuts to UK aid took place, with little or no consultation of downstream partners, or the communities where they are implemented has sent a harmful message that the UK does not care about the people affected, many of which are Black, Indigenous and People of Colour". This trend is discussed in the chapter written by Camila Ferreira Marinelli, who makes a direct connection between the invisibility of indigenous knowledge and coloniality and the phenomenon of epistemic violence as a structural prerogative. Indeed, epistemic violence causes Western knowledge to be perceived as more accurate and valuable than other systems of knowledge, which are treated as inferior and unreliable. It is most unfortunate that these value choices disregard the positive differences in value systems originating from the existence of pluralistic approaches to the generation of knowledge. As Silvia Bagni suggested in her chapter, in a capitalistic society, people live in abundance of material goods, but in scarcity of social, cultural, and spiritual relationships, and a shift in ideological values and cosmologies would be compulsory to affect the global society.

This book draws a connection between minorities, scarcity, and conflicts. Research found that nearly 40 percent of poor people (455 million) live in countries experiencing war, fragility, and/or low peacefulness (GMPI, 2024). In 2023, there were more ongoing conflicts than ever since the Second World War. According to the UN Special Rapporteur on minority issues, the root causes of most violent conflicts are linked to violations of the human rights of minorities (OHCHR, 2022b). Scenarios leading to violence may be complex, involving several intertwined factors, such as unequal competition for resources, poverty, good governance deficits, impunity, and polarisation of ethnic and religious characteristics. In his chapter, Joshua Castellino makes a vital case to argue that the climate emergency, in conjunction with political systems unable to tackle growing inequality, has generated emerging scarcities and fierce competition for resources. Such conflict, Castellino argues, is fragmenting societies along ethnic, religious, racialised, linguistic, and indigenous fault lines.

One relatively quick fix to fill the scarcity gaps for minorities and migrants may be, put simply, to ensure meaningful representation. A world in which they sit at decision-making tables of governments, municipalities, police departments, courts, school boards, hospitals, banks, businesses, or media companies would be better prepared to ensure the representation of their interests and their access to resources and serve them long-awaited justice. We will also need to strive for a human rights economy where the socio-economic inclusion of minorities is not an afterthought but a raison d'être of the economy (OHCHR, 2022b). However, as long as structural, institutional, and systemic exclusion exists catering to the most powerful, deliberately disregarding or silencing those at the margins of society, material and immaterial resource scarcity will resurface and remain a reality for millions. Following what Roberta Medda-Windischer and Federica Maino proposed in their chapter, fostering a sense of common belonging, unity, and respect for diversity is a central challenge in modern societies because seeking to accommodate minority claims implies the need to look for a balance between unity and separation, cohesion, and respect for diversity. Albeit challenging, it is certainly not an impossible task. Unity in diversity would indeed benefit all of us collectively. As Maya Angelou once wrote: "If it is true that a chain is only as strong as its weakest link, isn't it also true a society is only as healthy as its sickest citizen and only as wealthy as its most deprived?" (Angelou, 1997).

References

Angelou, M. (1997) *Even the Stars Look Lonesome*. New York: Random House.

Fisher, A., and Fukuda-Parr, S. (2019) "Introduction—Data, Knowledge, Politics and Localising the SDGs", *Journal of Human Development and Capabilities*, vol. 20(4), pages 375–385.

Global Multidimensional Poverty Index (GMPI) (2024) *Poverty Amid Conflict*. Global GMPI Report 15. United Nations Development Programme (UNDP) and Oxford Poverty and Human Development Initiative (OPHI). Available at https://ophi.org.uk/Publications/GMPI15–2024 (Accessed: 15 December 2024).

International Development Committee (2022) *Racism in the Aid Sector*. House of Commons Committee Report, UK Parliament. Available at https://publications.parliament.uk/pa/cm5803/cmselect/cmintdev/150/report.html (Accessed: 15 December 2024).

Minority Rights Group (MRG) (2023). *The Situation of Black People with Disabilities in Brazil*. Reports and Briefings, Minority Rights, March. Available at https://minorityrights.org/resources/the-situation-of-black-people-with-disabilities-in-brazil/(Accessed: 15 December 2024).

Nordquist, S., and Christoph, J. (2024) *Governance Reform of the Bretton Woods Institutions*. Washington, DC: Atlantic Council.

Office of the United Nations High Commissioner for Human Rights (OHCHR) (2020) *COVID-19 and Minority Rights: Overview and Promising Practices*, 4 June. OHCHR. Available at https://www.ohchr.org/sites/default/files/Documents/Issues/Minorities/OHCHRGuidance_COVID19_MinoritiesRights.pdf (Accessed: 15 December 2024).

Office of the United Nations High Commissioner for Human Rights (OHCHR) (2021) *Report: Online Hate Increasing Against Minorities, Says Expert*, 23 March. OHCHR. Available at https://www.ohchr.org/en/stories/2021/03/report-online-hate-increasing-against-minorities-says-expert (Accessed: 15 December 2024).

Office of the United Nations High Commissioner for Human Rights (OHCHR) (2022a) *Special Rapporteur on Contemporary Forms of Racism, Racial Discrimination, Xenophobia and Related Intolerance, Tendayi Achiume A/HRC/50/60*, 17 June. Available at https://www.ohchr.org/en/documents/thematic-reports/ahrc5060-2030-agenda-sustainable-development-sustainable-development (Accessed: 15 December 2024).

Office of the United Nations High Commissioner for Human Rights (OHCHR) (2022b) *Minorities and Their Rights Matter in Conflict Prevention—UN Expert*, 22 March. OHCHR. Available at https://www.ohchr.org/en/press-releases/2022/03/minorities-and-their-rights-matter-conflict-prevention-unexpert#:~:text=GENEVA%20(22%20March%202022)%20%E2%80%93,efforts%20at%20the%20United%20Nations (Accessed: 15 December 2024).

Organisation for Economic Co-operation and Development (OECD) (2023) *Development Co-Operation Report 2023: Debating the Aid System*. Report, OECD. Available at https://www.oecd.org/en/publications/development-co-operation-report-2023_f6edc3c2-en.html (Accessed: 15 December 2024).

Peace Direct (2021) *Time to Decolonise Aid—Insights and Lessons from a Global Consultation*. London: Peace Direct. Available at https://www.peacedirect.org/time-to-decolonise-aid/ (Accessed: 15 December 2024).

Schumacher A., and Micheli, L. (2024) "Anticipated Scarcity and Stockpiling During the COVID-19 Pandemic: The Role of Perceived Threat, Childhood SES and Materialism", *PLoS One*, 19(3), page 25.

Society for the Psychological Study of Social Issues (SPSSI) (2020) *Beyond the Human Rights Rhetoric on "Leaving No One Behind: Integrating the Elimination of Systemic Racism, and Racial and Ethnic Discrimination, into the Implementation of the SDGs.* Statement in Commemoration of the 75th Anniversary of the United Nations, UN Headquarters. New York. Available at https://www.spssi.org/index.cfm?fuseaction=Page.ViewPage&PageID=2609 (Accessed: 15 December 2024).

Sustainable Development Goals (2023). *The Sustainable Development Goals Report 2023: Special edition, Towards a Rescue Plan for People and Planet.* United Nations. Available at https://unstats.un.org/sdgs/report/2023/ (Accessed: 15 December 2024).

Index

affective dimensions of scarcity 21, 126, 158
anthropology of scarcity 1, 90; case studies in Italy and South Africa 107, 126
approaches to scarcity 1, 21; economic and demographic models 1, 21; relational and legal theories 90, 107, 126
Arab minorities 147
austerity politics 7, 11; *see also* neoliberalism

biodiversity and scarcity 147
biopolitics and scarcity 147; Romani experience in the Middle East 147
Brazilian Indigenous scholars 158; *see also* Indigenous peoples

capitalism 5–6, 12, 14, 66, 91, 102, 147; accumulation 10, 24, 31, 80, 82; consumption 4–5, 17, 103, 176; hyperaccumulation 4; *see also* neoliberalism
civil society 10, 109, 178
colonialism 24, 148, 161–163, 171, 177, 179; colonial structures 16
conflict and scarcity 1, 21, 74, 147, 175; *see also* social conflict
cultural perspectives on scarcity 90, 147

democracies under scarcity 74; institutional tensions 74
demographic approaches to scarcity 1, 21
dilemmas for minority responses 74, 126

emotion 1, 3, 128, 162, 166, 170, 172
emotional scarcity 6, 126; isolation, stress, and displacement 21, 126
empathy 97, 101, 172; *see also* scarcity of empathy
environmental scarcity 30
epistemic violence 158; colonial and academic practices 158
ethics of scarcity 90, 147
ethno-cultural minorities 21, 36, 55

federalism and minority rights 90
feminist perspectives 96–98
Foster, G. 6, 18
Foucault 27, 151

gender 25–26; gendered neoliberal subjectivities 38–39; motherhood 14, 50
governance 9–10, 13–14, 17, 22–24, 27, 31–33, 74, 77–79, 82, 88, 179–180; polycentric governance 32, 35; state exploitation 6; state failure 6

Homer-Dixon, Thomas F. 6, 18, 23, 28, 34
human rights 9–10, 33, 57, 75, 82, 84, 85, 87, 116, 178, 180

Identity: cultural identity 58, 69; ethnic identity 159, 163, 167; group identity 114; identity politics 14, 83, 144
Indigenous peoples 91, 101–102, 158; cosmovision 90, 92, 97, 99, 101; Indigenous knowledge 80, 92, 94, 158–159, 161–162, 165, 168–170, 179

Knight, D. 7, 19, 127, 129, 141, 144

law 27, 63, 80, 84, 90, 155, 163–164, 167, 175; immigration law 43–44; international law and minorities 8–9, 74–75, 77
literature on scarcity 1, 6, 13, 16, 23, 26, 31, 91, 102, 147

majoritarianism and nationalism 74
Malthus, T. R. 4, 19, 27, 34, 35
Mehta, L. 2, 7, 18, 25, 27, 28, 35, 128, 131
memory 1, 3, 14, 55, 58, 60, 69; life narratives 55, 57, 59, 60, 69, 70; social memory 58
migration 16, 23, 36–37, 40, 42–45, 64; American dream 13, 36–37, 40; migrants 11, 16, 36–46, 48, 51–54, 64–66, 76, 116, 127, 158, 175–177, 180; undocumented migrants 36, 38, 41, 44–45, 153
minority rights 8–10, 75–76

nationalism 10, 74, 76, 82, 84; and othering 74
neoliberalism 56; austerity politics 7, 11; *see also* capitalism

Pueblo Gitano 58

refugee 16, 62, 116, 152, 155, 176
Ricardo, D. 4, 19
Robbins, L. 4, 20, 39, 54
Ross, A. 7, 20, 56, 73
rural scarcity solutions 107

scarcity: as lived experience 28, 40; constructed 2, 5, 23–24, 27–29, 32, 56, 83, 151; material 15, 60, 64, 129, 160, 176; as multidimensional 1, 3, 17, 21, 26; relative 1, 7, 56; symbolic 13; *see also* emotional scarcity
Schwartz, R. 3, 20
Scoones, I. 2, 5–7, 20, 56, 73
Sen, A. 5, 20, 25, 35, 128, 131, 145
social exclusion 23, 25–26, 32, 136, 140
Stewart, M. 7, 19, 58, 73

violence 16, 36, 42, 55, 63, 69, 85, 98, 151; structural 158, 176; *see also* epistemic violence
vulnerabilities 107; in rural communities 114, 117

Williams, R. 6, 18, 73, 149, 157

For Product Safety Concerns and Information please contact our EU representative GPSR@taylorandfrancis.com Taylor & Francis Verlag GmbH, Kaufingerstraße 24, 80331 München, Germany